SOCIAL
SECTOR
COMMUNICATION
IN INDIA

SOCIAL
SECTOR
COMMUNICATION
IN INDIA

CONCEPTS,
PRACTICES,
AND
CASE STUDIES

JAISHRI JETHWANEY

SAGE www.sagepublishing.com
Los Angeles | London | New Delhi | Singapore | Washington DC | Melbourne

First published in 2016 by

 SAGE Publications India Pvt Ltd
B1/I-1 Mohan Cooperative Industrial Area
Mathura Road, New Delhi 110044, India
www.sagepub.in

SAGE Publications Inc
2455 Teller Road
Thousand Oaks, California 91320, USA

SAGE Publications Ltd
1 Oliver's Yard, 55 City Road
London EC1Y 1SP, United Kingdom

SAGE Publications Asia-Pacific Pte Ltd
3 Church Street
#10-04 Samsung Hub
Singapore 049483

Published by Vivek Mehra for SAGE Publications India Pvt Ltd, typeset in Times New Roman 10.5/12.5 pts by by Zaza Eunice, Hosur, Tamil Nadu and printed at Chaman Enterprises, New Delhi.

Library of Congress Cataloging-in-Publication Data

Names: Jethwaney, Jaishri, author.
Title: Social sector communication in India : concepts, practices, and case studies / Jaishri Jethwaney.
Description: New Delhi ; Thousand Oaks : SAGE, 2016. | Includes bibliographical references and index.
Identifiers: LCCN 2015041355 (print) | LCCN 2015044752 (ebook) | ISBN 9789351508144 (hardback) | ISBN 9789351508137 (epub) | ISBN 9789351508151 (ebook) | ISBN 9789351508151 (eBook) | ISBN 9789351508137 (ePub)
Subjects: LCSH: Social planning–India. | Communication in social action–India. | Communication in community development–India. | Social action–India. | Community development–India. | Social service–India.
Classification: LCC HN687 .J47 2016 (print) | LCC HN687 (ebook) | DDC 306.0954–dc23 LC record available at http://lccn.loc.gov/2015041355

ISBN: 978-93-515-0814-4 (HB)

The SAGE Team: Shambhu Sahu, Sanghamitra Patowary, and Vinitha Nair

*To those tens of thousands of grassroots
social workers who work relentlessly to
bring about the change*

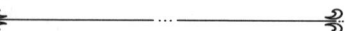

Contents

List of Abbreviations

ACSM	Advocacy, communication, and social mobilization
ADRA	Adventist Development and Relief Agency
AHF	AIDS Health care Foundation
AID	Alternative for India Development
APEC	Asia-Pacific Economic Cooperation
ARDA	African Radio Drama Association
ASR	Asian Sustainability Ranking
BCC	Bharti Computer Centers
BDOs	Block development officers
BLAC	Bharti Library and Activity Centers
BPL	Below poverty line
CBGA	Centre for Budget and Governance Accountability
CBOs	Community-based organizations
CGWA	Central Groundwater Authority
CMC	Community mobilizing coordinators
COL	Commonwealth of Learning
CPI	Corruption Perceptions Index
CSE	Centre for Science and Environment
CSOs	Civil society organizations
CSR	Corporate social responsibility
CSS	Centrally sponsored schemes
DCGI	Drug Controller General of India
DDS	Deccan Development Society
DINCS	Double income, no children
DMC	Disaster Management Committee
DPAP	Drought Prone Areas Programme
DPE	Department of Public Enterprises
DTH	Direct to Home
DU	Drug users
EDI	Entrepreneurship Development Institute of India
EPF	Employees' Provident Fund

EU	European Union
FAO	Food and Agriculture Organization
GAIN	Global Alliance for Improved Nutrition
GDP	Gross Domestic Product
GOI	Government of India
GRI	Global Reporting Initiative
HDI	Human Development Index
HLFPPT	Hindustan Latex Family Planning Promotion Trust
HUL	Hindustan Unilever
IB	Intelligence Bureau
ICMR	Indian Council of Medical Research
ICT	Information and Communication Technology
IGO	Intergovernmental organization
IHDS	Indian Human Development Survey
ILO	International Labor Organization
IMRB	Indian Marketing Research Bureau
IPEN	INCLEN Program Evaluation Network
IPPF	International Planned Parenthood Federation
ISO	International Standardization Organization
IT	Information Technology
IUCN	International Union for the Conservation of Nature
IVR	Interactive voice response
KAP	Knowledge, attitude, and practices
KMVS	Kutch Mahila Vikas Sangathan
KWs	Knowledge workers
MGNREGA	Mahatma Gandhi National Rural Employment Guarantee Act
MISA	Maintenance of Internal Security Act
MKSS	Mazdoor Kisan Shakti Sangathan
MSM	Men having sex with men
MoEF	Ministry of Environment and Forests
NACO	National AIDS Control Organisation
NCAER	National Council of Applied Economic Research
NCEUS	National Commission for Enterprises in the Unorganized Sector
NGO	Nongovernmental organization
NIRT	National Iranian Radio and Television
NITI	National Institution for Transforming India
NPI	Nonprofit institute

NPVS	National Policy on the Voluntary Sector
NRHM	National Rural Health Mission
OECD	Organisation for Economic Co-operation and Development
OPL	Operation Lighthouse
ORG	Organization Research Bureau
OWSA	OneWorld South Asia
PE	Peer educators
PKVY	The Paramparagat Krishi Vikas Yojana
PLI	Peer-led intervention
PMJDY	Pradhan Mantri Dhan Jan Yojana
PMKSY	Pradhan Mantri Krishi Sinchayee Yojana
PPP	Pulse Polio Programme
PRI	Principles for Responsible Investment
PRIA	Participatory Research in Asia
PSA	Public service ad
PSE	Public Sector Enterprise
PSI	Population Service International
PTA	Parent–teacher association
REACH	Radio Education for Afghan Children
RNTCP	Revised National Tuberculosis Control Programme
SM	Social marketing
SPYM	Society for Promotion of Youth and Masses
SSA	Sub Service Area
SSC	Staff Selection Commission
TA	Target audience
TB	Tuberculosis
TCL	Tata Chemical Limited
TISS	Tata Institute of Social Sciences
UNCHR	United Nations Commission of Human Rights
UNDP	United Nations Development Program
UNFPA	United Nations Fund for Population Activities
UNIDO	United Nations Industrial Development Organization
UPA	United Progressive Alliance
UPSC	Union Public Service Commission
VKCs	Village Knowledge Centres
VO	Voluntary organization
WDI	World Development Indicators

Preface

India has a burgeoning social sector, both from the perspective of public expenditure on various schemes aimed at reaching out to the teeming impoverished millions and a humongous involvement of nongovernmental organizations (NGOs) at the grassroots level. India can boast of having about 3.3 million NGOs and voluntary organizations (VOs) that make it one VO/NGO for every 400 people. Despite that, India has consistently been performing extremely poor on various development indicators when compared with other developing nations, including some Sub-Saharan countries.

The social sector is now attracting not only communication experts, but also young college graduates from schools of social work, communication and media, and even management.

This book aims to provide an understanding of the various tools and strategies required in social sector communication, especially from the NGOs' and program implementers' perspective. With corporate social responsibility (CSR) becoming mandatory for public sector enterprises (PSEs) and the Companies Act 2013 expecting the private sector to contribute to the social sector, it is only natural that a large trained workforce would be required in the social sector, including social communication.

The social sector communication is multipronged and multidisciplinary in approach. If on one hand communication is crucial to reach out to people to inform and sensitize them about their rights and the various schemes meant for them, communication on the other hand is also imperative for mobilizing the people. Often, most social issues need behavior change among the targeted public for which behavior change communication is required.

An important endeavor of social sector communication is to influence policy to bring about the desired change and at the same time ensure commitment on the part of the policy-makers and program implementers. To achieve that, the social sector communicator would need an avid understanding of the tools of advocacy aimed at opinion makers, media, and public at large. Similarly, for the corporate sector–NGO interface, an understanding of each other's functioning and expectations is required for achieving synergy in projects undertaken under CSR.

Many empirical studies suggest that media can be a catalyst for change. Media is often referred to as the fourth estate in a democracy, the other three being the executive, legislature, and judiciary. Therefore, from the social communicator's perspective, it is important to study and scrutinize media content to see what and how much coverage is given to the developmental sector and which agendas are being set and pursued. It will help the social communicator to know how the neoliberal policies adopted by India in the 1990s have impacted the life of the poor and what have been media's concomitant reflections on this. All this will equip the social communicator to work on media advocacy to help achieve program goals.

The book has seven chapters, beginning with an overview of the social sector in India, followed by social marketing, CSR, advocacy, communication and social mobilization, and grassroots communication. Chapter 6 takes the reader through a few case studies delineating the process of social campaigns from concept to launch. The last chapter provides readers with hands-on skills on writing various kinds of documents, such as concept notes, annual reports, field visits providing prototypes. It then takes readers through writing skills used in media, including online writing, such as blogs, and the functions of an interactive newsroom.

In a nutshell, readers would be able to understand and comprehend the conceptual framework of social sector communication and learn the use of basic tools and strategies in social sector communication.

1

Overview of Social Sector in India

Introduction

The definition of what comprises the social sector varies from country to country and even within a country. It is often referred to as the third sector, public and private being the other two. Some analysts define it by what it encompasses. Many believe that the social sector, to be truly called so, must address health and education.

The Asian Development Bank has segmented various sectors under two major classifications, namely, the public and private as given in in the table as follows.[1]

Public Sector	Private Sector
National government (including legislatures, ministries, and departments)	Commercial enterprises
Provincial/state government	Private hospitals, universities, and schools
District/municipal administration	NGOs
Local government institutions, public health and educational institutions	Families and parent communities
International agencies	Advocacy groups (including labor unions, gender groups, etc.)

Source: Asian Development Bank.

The emergence of the social sector, as believed by some scholars, is the result of a market economy in which those who are unable to effectively compete for resources often require outside assistance for survival. Such assistance comes from a variety of sources that include the state, charitable organizations, individuals, the private sector, or a combination of more than one factor. Social welfare primarily aims at providing material, psychological, and social support to people having difficulty providing for them.

In much of the developing world, where a lot many people struggle to eke out a living for themselves, the responsibility on the social sector to redistribute resources is phenomenal. No efforts seem sufficient to bridge the gap between a few privileged and the teeming millions underprivileged masses. Madhav Gadgil in an opinion piece quoted Nobel laureate Joseph Stiglitz, who once said, "Development should enhance the totality of nation's four-fold capital stocks: that of material goods; natural capital such as soil, water, forests, and fish; human capital including health, education, and employment; and social capital, comprising mutual trust and harmony," but India's "current imbalanced pattern of economic development certainly does not enhance the totality of these stocks," rued Gadgil.[2]

India has had a rich tradition in social sector spending since a long time. The country has been home to many major religions of the world, which have all along propagated social service and looking after the poor and needy people. According to an estimate, 40 percent of households in India participate in one or another form of charity. However, ironically, the poor have been contributing more than the rich at the individual level.

India has an enviable legacy of many social reformers who have contributed immensely in addressing various social issues. Some of the well-known Indians include Swami Vivekananda, Raja Ram Mohan Roy, Dayanand Saraswati, Bal Gangadhar Tilak, Jyotiba Phule, Ishwar Chandra Vidyasagar, Mahadev Govind Ranade, Gopal Krishna Gokhale, Vinoba Bhave, Mother Teresa, Sunder Lal Bahuguna, etc. These reformers fought against various issues such as child marriage, sati pratha (burning of widows on the pyre of the dead husband) and untouchability, and fought for the emancipation and education of women, and environment protection, among other issues.

The first recipient of the coveted Ramon Magsaysay Award in 1958 for community leadership, Vinoba Bhave, a Gandhian, will be remembered for his "out-of-the-box" social reform movement called Bhoodan (donating land) Movement. He started his land donation movement at Pochampally of Nalgonda district in Telangana. He took donated land from landowners and gave it away to the poor and landless for cultivation. Later, after 1954, he changed the strategy by asking for donations of whole villages in a program which he called Gramdan. He got more than 1,000 villages by way of donation. Out of these, he obtained 175 donated villages in Tamil Nadu alone. His land reform movement was spread in a number of states including Andhra Pradesh, Tamil Nadu, and Orissa. Bhave was conferred the Bharat Ratna in 1983. The movement, however, failed to take off beyond its initial success.

Size of Social Sector in India

The size of the social sector is humongous, given the size of the population and the large number of impoverished people residing both in rural and urban areas. India has a large social sector spending, mostly through the public exchequer of the central and state governments.

In retrospect, India inherited a truncated economy aggravated by a divided nation at the time of its independence in 1947. This was followed by two wars in the 1960s, one each with the neighboring countries of China and Pakistan, another in 1971 for the liberation of Bangladesh, and yet another in 1999 at Kargil in Jammu and Kashmir, coupled with insurgency in many bordering states, various natural disasters, dependence on rain in large measure for agriculture, and poor health and education infrastructure. The problem has only got compounded further with an astronomical growth in population. The Nehruvian model opted for a socialistic pattern with the government's say in almost all sectors of the economy. Thus, a huge social sector was created with public funds, with little or no contribution from the private sector.

In the liberalized economy of the 1990s, one saw a surge in the private sector entry in health and education sectors, but that in no way meant that benefits were accrued to those who were on the fringes. It only added to creating an unequal world for the poor. Just to cite a couple of examples, educational institutions in the field of higher learning such as medicine and engineering auction seats, thus filling the coffers of the proprietors who are often politicians or have the backing of politicians. Similarly, in the health sector, prime land has gone to corporate hospitals for a song, who could not care less for the poor in their vicinity, despite an understanding that such hospitals would admit a certain percentage of patients free of cost. It may be on paper but if a large number of people do not know about this, they obviously cannot avail of the facilities.

Sixty-eight years is not a long period in the making of a nation, but India has proved that it can do wonders in various fields, such as science, technology, IT, power generation, and infrastructure development; then why can it not be replicated in the social sector, given the resources allocated to it, is a moot point.

The last few decades have witnessed a spurt in the contribution toward the social sector from the corporate sector, United Nations' agencies, and philanthropists—both from India and overseas—but it has still a long way to go. One has also seen the growth of a strong civil society backed by the NGO sector working at the grassroots level. The 2013 Companies Act has made contributions toward social spending mandatory for public-funded companies. The private sector is also expected to contribute toward its social responsibility. The chapter on CSR will discuss the various aspects in detail.

Successive governments in India, both at the central and state levels, have launched various welfare schemes during their tenure, but despite that the number of impoverished people has not decreased.

Despite the much publicized Mahatma Gandhi National Rural Employment Guarantee Act (MGNREGA) that guaranteed 100 days of employment in a year to at least one member per rural family, the National Rural Health Mission (NRHM) and various other schemes for the very poor and minorities, among others, including the Food Security Bill in 2013, which meant an expenditure of over 1,000 billion in subsidizing food grains for over 70 percent of the population, the Congress party in India suffered its worst electoral defeat during the 16th Parliamentary Elections held in April–May 2014.

The incumbent government expressing its disgust with the Planning Commission has now created NITI Aayog in its place. NITI is an acronym for National Institution for Transforming India. It is supposed to be the policy think tank for the government and aims at involving the state governments to have their say in the economic planning and governance of the country. NITI Aayog had its first meeting in February 2015. Quoting from the e-book released by the government, Live Mint noted:

NITI Aayog will function in close cooperation, consultation, and coordination with the ministries of the central and state governments. While it will make recommendations to the central and state governments, the responsibility for taking and implementing decisions will rest with them.[3]

What India Spends on Social Welfare

When one compares the spending on social welfare, India performs poorly even vis-à-vis the poorest nations of the world.

Among the developed countries, Sweden, Germany, and the UK spend over 20 percent of their gross domestic product (GDP) on social welfare, while USA and Japan spend over 15 percent. These countries spend most of the amount to ensure unemployment allowance, health care, and pension.

According to 2014 World Development Indicators (WDI) data, public spending on health and education is just 4.7 percent of the GDP in India, compared with 7 percent in Sub-Saharan Africa, 7.2 percent in East Asia, 8.5 percent in Latin America, and 13.3 percent in Organisation for Economic Co-operation and Development (OECD) countries. Even the corresponding figure for "least developed countries," 6.4 percent, is much higher than India's.[4]

Media writer M.R. Venktesh comments that India languishes at the bottom half of the Human Development Index (HDI), wedged among underdeveloped countries such as Namibia, Sao-Tome, Principe, and Solomon Islands. "The countries endowed with less natural resources and lower caliber human capital have performed better due perhaps to responsive and effective governance," laments Venktesh.[5]

India has the highest number of undernourished people in the world. As per the state of food insecurity in the World Report, India continues to be home to nearly a quarter of the world's hungry although the world has 216 million fewer undernourished people compared to 25 years ago. The report rues that India's record is poorer than her neighbors, such as Bangladesh, Nepal, and China, which have been able to halve the proportion of their hungry people in the same period.[6] To quote Brij Patnaik, principal advisor to the Supreme Court commissioners on Right to Food case, "The situation in India is likely to worsen due to severe cutbacks in the Union budget on key programs on child nutrition and mid-day meal scheme." Only 11 states have implemented the National Food Security Act.[7]

There has been a lot of confusion on the figures relating to the number of people living "below poverty line" in India. In a shocking revelation, the rural development committee on below poverty line (BPL) survey, chaired by Supreme Court-appointed Food Commissioner N.C. Saxena, has sought to revise the Planning Commission's figure of 28 percent to 50 percent of people that are said to be living below the poverty line. This, it said, was based on the data on the United Progressive Alliance (UPA) government's social sector schemes, both existing and proposed ones, such as the enhanced pension scheme. Analysts argue that the drastic difference in the figures of the Planning Commission have surfaced because of the difference in defining poverty. This has happened because of the varying definitions of poverty floated by the government, independent sources, and committees. For instance, the Planning Commission defined poverty on the basis of per capita spending of below ₹356 a month in rural India and ₹539 in urban India. The Saxena Panel on the other hand defines poverty when the per capita spending in rural India is less than ₹700 per month against ₹1,000 per month in urban India.[8]

The *Business Standard* in one of its editorials entitled "Poverty of Thought" commented on various poverty figures supplied by different organizations and experts. Calling it à la carte menu of poverty estimates to choose from, it referred to Arjun Sengupta's estimates a few years ago that put a staggering 77 percent of Indians under the poverty line who lived on a per capita consumption of ₹20 a day. Beside Saxena's figure of 50 percent and the Planning commission's estimate of 28 percent, the World Bank, commented the editorial, had yet another definition of poverty that is based on the international poverty line of $1.25 per day of income (adjusted for each country's purchasing power parity). This would work out to 42 percent people in India living below the poverty line. To quote from the editorial: "When different numbers float around, people will choose to go by the number that fits their theory, personal predilections or political position."[9]

India is said to have the poorest social security net in the world. This despite some 90+ welfare schemes including various funds encompassing women, elderly, and disabled, scholarships for Scheduled Castes/Scheduled Tribes, rural employment, national rural health, and dozens others. Corruption, nepotism, bureaucratization, and wastage of resources are ascribed as some of the reasons the poor are not able to access even the meagerly available funds.

In an insightful article, "Employment Outcomes along the Rural-Urban Gradation" in *Economic and Political Weekly (EPW)*, Urmila Chatterjee et al. have observed that for a long time poverty reduction in India was aligned to rural areas and agriculture but since the 1990s, the rural transformation to the nonfarm sector has assumed a greater role. The authors feel that despiite "a remarkable gain on the poverty front, India's transformation has been rather disappointing on job creation."[10]

MGNREGA has its share of critics, but a new study reveals that it has contributed to almost a third of the poverty reduction in India between 2004 and 2005, and 2011 and 2012. The study conducted jointly by the National Council of Applied Economic Research (NCAER) and the University of Maryland says that about 14 million people would have become poor but for the program, which gave 100 days wage employment every year to one member per rural household. The study was a part of the Indian Human Development Survey (IHDS). An insightful finding of the survey conducted with a sample of 26,000 was that 13 percent of rural men and 10 percent of rural women work under MGNREGA.

The NITI Aayog in consultation with states is planning to prune centrally sponsored schemes (CSS). As per media reports, the NITI Aayog's meeting with chief ministers in June 2015 concluded about the unworkability of the various CSS. The responsibility and accountability of states has increased with the recommendations of the 14th Finance Commission that gave unprecedented share of tax revenues to states, thus enabling them to use the resources to suit the respective needs of the social sector spending.[11]

Jean Dreze, renowned development economist, in an insightful article in a newspaper titled "On the Mythology of Social Policy" has commented that India is among the "world's champions of social under spending." He cautions that without "enlightened social policies, growth mania is unlikely to deliver more under the new government than it did under the previous one."[12]

NDA Budget Allocations (2015–2016) on Social Sector Spending

The Modi Government came to power in May 2014 and presented its first budget in July 2014 which according to analysts seemed like an extension of the UPA's interim budget. Several big bang schemes, which promised to boost agricultural productivity, were announced in it such as Pradhan Mantri Krishi Sinchayee Yojana (PMKSY), Paramparagat Krishi Vikas Yojana (PKVY), creation of Price Stabilization Fund, development of a Common National Market for Agricultural Commodities through e-platforms, etc. However, a huge cut in social sector spending in the 2015–2016 budget has surprised many. The infographic (as follows) provides a bird's eye view of the difference in allocation in its two budgets. The government's perspective, however, has been that with the increase in central allocations for the states, following the recommendations of the Finance Commission, these shortfalls can be met.

THE BIG SQUEEZE

PERHAPS AIMING AT OUT-SOURCING WELFARE MEASURES TO THE STATES, THE UNION BUDGET SLASHED ALLOCATION TO MINISTRIES THAT ARE PART OF THE SOCIAL SECTOR. A LOOK

₹4,39,192.25 crore

OVERALL DROP IN ALLOCATION TO SOCIAL SECTOR MINISTRIES IN THE BUDGET		
MINISTRY/ DEPARTMENT/ PLAN	2014–15 (in Cr)	2015–16 (in Cr)
Panchayati Raj	₹3,400.69	₹94.75
Agriculture	₹19,852	₹17,004
Women and Child Development	₹18,588.39	₹10,382.40
Drinking Water and Sanitation	₹12,107	₹6,243.87
Water Resources	₹6,009	₹4,232
Scheduled Caste Sub Plan	₹43,208	₹30,000
Tribal Sub Plan	₹26,714	₹19,000
Land Resources Dept	₹3,759	₹1,637
Swachh Bharat Abhiyan	₹12,100	₹6,236
Mid-day meal scheme	₹11,770	₹9,236

Source: The Indian Express; March 2, 2015.

Frontline, in its cover story of April 15, 2015, commented that from the analysis of the budgets 2014–2015 and 2015–2016 and the various policy measures of the NDA government,

[I]t appears that there is no immediate plan to raise the income of small and marginal farmers that touched a new low. The long-term plans are symbolic in nature and may result in increased productivity but without translating into farmer income, which it can even affect adversely sometimes. The worrying factor is that the Central government shifted financial responsibility to the State government for continuing schemes that have a proven track record of helping farmers.[13]

In a nut shell, the Center's assistance to the states for social sector schemes came down from a budgeted ₹3.56 lakh crores in FY15 to ₹2.20 lakh crores in FY16. The *Business Standard* effectively commented:

> While the National Democratic Alliance (NDA) government gave ₹1.42 lakh crore additionally to the states from the divisible tax pool, it cut back ₹1.16 lakh under central government schemes. This is presuming the schemes' funding in 2015–16 would have been maintained at least at this year's budgeted levels.[14]

The government stopped funding for eight schemes, including the setting up of 6,000 model schools, the National Mission on Food Processing, and the Backward Regions Grant Fund. These schemes entailed a budgetary support of nearly ₹10,000 crores in the year 2015. The Center has also asked the states to bear a larger share of spending in 24 schemes, including the government's flagship Swachh Bharat Abhiyan. The funding for the scheme to expand coverage of sewage systems in rural and urban areas has been cut from ₹4,135 crores, budgeted for 2014–2015, to ₹3,500 crores.

One cut that was not expected, as it went against NDA's own proposal, was on health. In its draft National Health Policy, it had recommended an expenditure from 1.2 percent of GDP to 2.5 percent, but when it came to actual transfer of funds to states, it came down from ₹24,203 crores to ₹18,000 crores. Analysts believe that the MGNREGA will also meet the same fate unless additional funds are made available. The Center approved a labor budget at the beginning of this financial year at ₹60,000 crores: a projection of demand for the jobs by the poor. It, however, allocated only ₹33,364 crores in the budget. In its election manifesto, the Bharatiya Janata Party (BJP) had promised increased allocation to education, that is, 6 percent of the GDP; however, it is less than 3 percent including food subsidies.

Similarly, for 2015–2016, the total outlay for agriculture has come down by 10.4 percent, that is, to ₹28,050 crores from ₹31,322 crores, in 2014–2015. The allocation for crop husbandry has been reduced to ₹39,868 crores from ₹41,681 crores, while for animal husbandry it is down to ₹330 crores from ₹599 crores. The allocation for major and medium irrigation has been reduced to ₹572 crores from ₹1,121 crores, while for minor irrigation it is down to ₹306 crores from ₹468 crores. Critics believe that Budget 2015 extended this tokenism and for the first time shifted the responsibility of agricultural development to the state governments. This followed the increased tax devolution recommended by the 14th Finance Commission. The irony, however, felt by analysts, is that most states do not have any clear policy on how to strengthen and advance agriculture.[15]

The financial inclusion of the poor through Pradhan Mantri Dhan Jan Yojana (PMDJY) and the three social security schemes—the Pradhan Mantri Suraksha Bima Yojana, Pradhan Mantri Jeevan Jyoti Yojana, and Atal Pension Yojana—that seek to provide accidental death and disability risk cover, life insurance, and contributory pension, the government argues, is a major step toward increasing social security.

The following graphic in the *Business Standard* gives a bird's eye view of the central assistance to states, social sector projection, and share of social sector expenditure as percentage of the GDP.

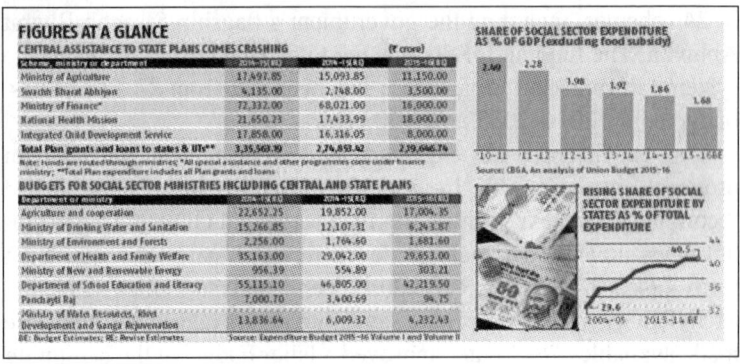

Source: Business Standard; March 11, 2015.

The much-publicized PMDJY, announced by Prime Minister Modi in his first speech on Independence Day on August 15, 2014, has also been seen as populist. It is believed that 1.5 crore bank accounts were opened under this scheme on the first day between August 23 and August 27, 2014. Popularized as the largest financial inclusion scheme in the world, it was also lauded by the Guineas Book of World Records. In less than a year's time, more than 17 crore people opened their accounts in banks under the PMDJY.

As per a government press release, all six lakh villages across the entire country were mapped according to the service area of each bank to have at least one fixed-point banking outlet catering to 1,000 to 1,500 households, called sub service area (SSA). The SSAs were expected to be covered through a combination of banking outlets, that is, branch banking and branch-less banking. *Branch banking* means traditional brick and mortar branches. *Branchless banking* comprises fixed-point business correspondent agents, who act as representatives of a bank and were required to provide basic banking services.[16] A huge media blitzkrieg was launched exhorting people to open their zero balance accounts which carried an overdraft facility of ₹5,000 and an accidental insurance cover of a maximum of ₹100,000 and ₹30,000 medical insurance for those who enrolled before January 26, 2015. The amount was supposed to go down subsequently.[17]

Critics feel that it was a populist measure in hoodwinking gullible people. *Live Mint* talking to many experts from the banking sector commented that an effort was made to please voters that was bound to create unnecessary work burden on the public sector banks. To quote:

> The Mahatma Gandhi National Rural Employment Guarantee Scheme (MGNREGS), a make-work scheme that was the pet project of Congress president Sonia Gandhi, was considered by many in the Indian Right as the epitome of wasteful populism. Indeed, there could be very little said in defence of any such government programme that promises to "empower" the poor by doling out unearned benefits. But now with a "right-wing" prime minister in office, the erstwhile critics in the Right have gone mute even as Narendra Modi launched a big bang welfare programme last week.[18]

According to experts, temptations presented by the Prime Minister, such as zero balance, free insurance, and overdraft facility, would result in duplication. If one were to see the fine lines, not all would be eligible for insurance benefit.

Noted economic journalist Swaminathan Aiyer said:

> This will mean ₹75,000 crore for 150 million accounts, if these are not repaid, banks will lose ₹75,000 crore at a time when the PJ Nayak Committee says they need to raise an additional ₹5.8 lakh crore just to meet the new Basel norms for capital adequacy.[19]

Analyzing the pro-poor schemes, Arun Kumar wrote in *Mainstream*,

> Schemes, like Jan Dhan Yojana and pension for the poor, have been announced with much fanfare as examples of inclusive policies. But there is a danger of these turning out to be mere show. The government claims that about 15 crore accounts have been opened under the Jan Dhan Yojana,

but the moot point is: how many of them have any savings in them or are active or genuinely belong to the poor?[20]

Setting at rest the scepticism, Prime Minister Modi in his second address to the nation from the ramparts of the Red Fort on August 15, 2015, said that the there was a deposit of `20,000 crores by 15 crore people who could open a zero balance account under the PMDJY.[21]

What Ails Social Sector in India

Corruption, nepotism, and nonseriousness on the part of the implementers have generally been the bane of the social sector in developing countries, and India is no exception. The disposition often is "welfare" and not "rights" of the receivers. Because it is seen as a welfare measure, anything done by the government is considered as an act of altruism, a top–bottom approach, a matter of obligation, and generosity. More recently, many organizations, especially from among the donor organizations in the international sector have been perusing the rights approach that aims at keeping the person in the center, who has the right to a decent life. The recipient is not seen as a beneficiary but a rights holder.

The social sector is believed to be a big business, both in the developed and developing countries. It is estimated that in USA alone, there are more that 1.5 million nonprofit organizations and social outfits that have contributed combined revenues of $700 million and control assets valued at $2 trillion. In India, as said earlier, most of the funding in the social sector comes from the public exchequer. The supply chain in terms of handling the money and providing the services has various actors, both from the governmental agencies, private bodies, and NGO/civil society operators. It is often a business opportunity for them. With a general lack of accountability and passivity on the part of the "demand" side, that is, those at the receiving end, who often are poor, sick, unlettered, disempowered, and inarticulate, it generally is a free ride on the "supply" side who are ambitious, greedy, cunning, and smart.

Harvard Professor Jane Wei-Skillern feels that despite the strides made in the social sector, the traditional approaches are falling short, especially as the intensity and complexity of social problems has grown tremendously. She recommends that new approaches and paradigms are needed to get over the problems of poverty, health, and education that do not seem to go away anytime soon. Her book *Entrepreneurship in Social Sector*, along with E. James, B. Austin Herman and H. Stevenson addresses questions such as these.[22]

Corruption and Inefficiency in Social Sector

There have been many allegations on how inefficiently the social sector is run in India, especially by the states. There are many rating agencies that keep a constant watch on polity and governance. It is not good news for India as it has been constantly scoring poorly on many counts. Here are some glimpses:

According to a research study conducted by VV Giri National Labour Institute (which happens to be a government funded institute), there is rampant corruption in the much touted MGNREGA, the rural employment scheme. The research team found out that in certain cases the people worked for one day, but were asked to sign for 33 days. The wages for 32 days were siphoned off by the concerned officers and contractors.[23]

There have been many instances in India when the relief officers have embezzled money and resources pledged for victims of disasters, without being accountable to the system. To top it all, narrow politics and sectarianism also play the part in setting or changing priorities in the social sector. Continuity of schemes more often suffers when a new government takes over after the election process.

In a report by Transparency International, its anti-corruption resource center reflected that despite India emerging as the 6th largest economy in the world, its growth has been uneven across social and economic groups with a large number of India's population living in abject poverty.

India was ranked 94 by Transparency International's 2012 Corruption Perceptions Index (CPI). The official website of Central Vigilance Commission states that 91 percent of the bribes were demanded by government officials and 77 percent of the bribes demanded were for avoiding harm rather than to gain any advantage. Of these, 51 percent were for timely delivery of services to which the individual was already entitled. Some of the examples include clearing goods from customs or getting a phone connection.

According to the UN's HDI, India ranks 136, that is, just two ranks above Laos and Cambodia. Even Morocco and Ghana outperformed it at 130 and 135, respectively, in the year 2012. Freedom in the World Report 2014 indicated in the context of India:

> Political corruption has a negative effect on government efficiency and economic performance. India was ranked 94 out of 177 countries and territories surveyed in Transparency International's 2013 Corruption Perceptions Index. Though politicians and civil servants are regularly caught accepting bribes or engaging in other corrupt behavior, a great deal of corruption goes unnoticed and unpunished.[24]

Global Integrity Organization explains that forms of corruption even include when there is "lack of transparency in governance, rules and procedures are complicated and the bureaucracy enjoys broad discretionary powers." It commented that nepotism is embedded in the civil service, and journalists have been harassed for reporting on corruption.[25]

Some of the sectors vulnerable to corruption include public procurement, licenses, and public utilities. According to a World Bank insight, 15 percent of the contract value is generally taken as a bribe to obtain any contract. Despite all that, there is a glimmer of hope as India is said to have a vigorous and vibrant society and one of the freest media in South Asia. Both have played an important role in placing corruption on the national agenda. However, most civil society organizations, according to Bertelsmann Foundation Report 2008, are "poorly institutionalized, politically fragmented, and rather weak."[26]

P. Sainath, one of the better-known development writers in the media, in his book *Everybody Loves a Good Drought* comments,

> Drought is beyond question, among the more serious problems this country faces. Drought relief, almost equally beyond question, is rural India's biggest growth industry. Often there is little relation between the two. Relief can go to regions that get lots of rainfall ... those most in need seldom benefit from it.

The poor, he writes, very well know about it that is the reason they call drought relief as the "third crop," only they may not be the ones who harvested it! In other words, the money thus received is siphoned off, rarely benefiting the poor.[27] Citing examples of various states that come under the Drought Prone Areas Programme (DPAP), Sainath writes that once an area comes under the DPAP purview it attracts huge amounts of money under various schemes, such as the employment assurance scheme, anti-desertification projects, drinking water missions, and a host of other schemes. The powerful landowners, thus, try their best to get their land declared under the DPAP. Why else would Maharashtra, where 73 percent of sugar cane is produced, come under DPAP, when it is a scientific fact that sugar cane is the "most water-intensive crop" one can get?[28]

The workers in the unorganized sector in India are not on the wish list of any government. According to the National Commission for Enterprises in the Unorganized Sector (NCEUS), there are 470 million or 92 percent of the workforce in the sector, out of which 77 percent work on a paltry amount. Critics have pulled up successive governments for not including the vast unorganized sector that lives on the fringes. A *Times of India* story "Where Is My Social Security Mr Prime Minister?" quoted Guy Standing who said something very wise:

> We have found in Africa that when you provide low-income people with a little money without conditions, they mostly spend in the best interests of their families and communities. They do not need to be told or led to do what state bureaucrats tell them what they should do.

In the context of India, this is what he had to say, "If India is really to escape from its caste-driven and Raj-affected past, it must loosen up."[29]

The study conducted by the Centre for Budget and Governance Accountability (CBGA) has found in general low capacity of some states to increase spending on plan schemes and poor quality of spending/fund utilization in the plan schemes across various states in the implementation of social welfare projects.[30]

Role of Nongovernmental Organizations and Voluntary Organizations in Social Sector in India

There are various kinds of voluntary organizations (VOs) engaged in voluntary work at various levels that include the international, national, and grassroots level. Experts classify these organizations in various genres. Let us look at the typology:

INGO: International NGOs work at least in more than two countries. One World, Plan International, Action Aid, Department for International Development (DFID), and Oxfam are some examples of international NGOs (INGOs).

BINGO: Business-oriented INGOs, such as the International Labor Organization and audit and control organizations, fall in this category.

ENGCO: Environmental NGOs (ENGCOs) work specifically in the direction of environment protection, which in fact has become quite broad based. World Wildlife Fund (WWF) and Greenpeace are some of the prominent ENGCOs that work in almost all the continents.

GINGO: Some analysts prefer naming some NGOs as genuine NGOs (GINGOs), hence the nomenclature. Amnesty International that works cent percent on membership funding qualifies in this category.

GONGO: Government-operated NGOs (GONGOs) that sustain purely on government funding such as the International Committee of Red Cross.

QUANGO: Quasi-autonomous NGOs (QUANGOs) that also allow membership to states and draw funds from them includes examples such as International Organization for Standardization (ISO) and International Union for the Conservation of Nature (IUCN).

Networks: Networks of NGOs from various policy fields join together to form a network. Ben Landmines, for example, has 1,400 NGOs across 90 countries or Voluntary association of NGOs in India (VANI) has a membership of over 1,000 NGOs. Such networks have been able to exert great influence on policy-makers.[31]

According to a government study, there are 3.3 million NGOs or nonprofit institutes (NPIs) in the country which makes for one NGO per 400 Indians. NGOs can be registered under various Acts, such as the Societies' Act, 1860, Indian Trust Act, 1882, Public Trust Act, 1950, Indian Companies Act, 1956 (Section 25), Religious Endowment Act, 1863, The Charitable and Religious Trust Act, 1920, the Mussalman Wakf Act, 1923, the Wakf Act, 1954, and Public Wakfs (Extension of Limitation Act) Act, 1959, etc.

The largest number of NGOs, as per the Study are registered in Maharashtra (4.8 lakhs), followed by Andhra Pradesh (4.6 lakhs), Uttar Pradesh (4.3 lakhs), Kerala (3.3 lakhs), Karnataka (1.9 lakhs), Gujarat (1.7 lakhs), West Bengal (1.7 lakhs), Tamil Nadu (1.4 lakhs), Orissa (1.3 lakhs), and Rajasthan (1 lakhs). More than 80 percent of registrations come from these 10 states. NGOs, or NPIs, raise anywhere between ₹40,000 crores and ₹80,000 crores in funding annually, as noted by the study.[32]

As per Participatory Research in Asia (PRIA), India has over 10.2 million VOs engaged in the social sector, most of them rural and small, and many unregistered. At least one-fourth have religious identity, 21 percent community/social services, and 20 percent educational services. The sector employs 2.7 million people full-time or equivalent. According to one estimate, the voluntary sector has a turnover of ₹20,000 crores per annum, overseas funding accounting for merely 7.5 percent. At least 20,000 professionals are believed to be engaged in the voluntary sector. Although the voluntary sector has an uneven presence in various states, according to PRIA, there are at least five good organizations per district.[33]

Many NGOs may be nonexistent, and there seems to be no mechanism to find out about their existence and activities. However, since 2010, the NGOs are required to register themselves and renew their registration every five years.

Rajesh Tandon of PRIA feels that in the absence of any centralized databank or nationally coordinated system of information, accurate data on the voluntary sector is not possible in India. However, looking at the registration under the Society and Trust Acts in the country, some two million VOs have been registered that may also include Mahila Mandals, youth clubs, private schools, charitable hospitals, and some government organizations, such as Council for Advancement of People's Action and Rural Technology. It was estimated that 60 percent of these VOs were concentrated in four states, namely, West Bengal, Andhra Pradesh, Maharashtra, and Uttar Pradesh. It is believed that the VOs broadly contribute in the following three areas:

1. *Innovations:* Through risk taking and experimenting with new ways of promoting more sustainable growth and people-oriented development, the VOs have used models that later were emulated both by state and central government agencies with success.

2. *Empowerment:* Through promotion and empowerment of socio-economically marginalized and exploited section of the society, especially women, dalits, tribals, slum dwellers, and rural poor, the VOs have brought their issues in the public domain. This did result in tensions and conflict situations in our traditional society governed by power relationships and social conditioning, but an important milestone in social transformation has been brought by the VOs.

3. *Research and advocacy:* Through advocacy and research by VOs, many dormant issues have come out of the closet and become agendas of public discourse and nation policy, especially relating to women, dalits, environment protection, human rights, education, etc.

These have had various implications that include creating an enabling environment to regulate legal identity of VOs on a uniform basis; funds from foreign donors hitherto have been distributed to VOs besides sundry organizations, such as hospitals, religious trusts, etc. which need to be regulated. VO activists in many states have been victims of harassment from local people and social institutions due to their stand on certain issues that question age-old traditions and practices that need to be addressed.

Based on the recommendations of various participants, the Planning Commission articulated the following for circulation:

1. Quick redressal of VO grievances through joint collaborative machinery at the state level with planning department as the nodal department.
2. Income tax authorities to take time-bound decision on applications from VOs for IT exemption.
3. To extend the term program and project support to VOs of long standing in the form of program support rather than institutional support.
4. Transparency in funding policy procedures, systems of monitoring, and evaluation of projects.
5. VOs to adopt appropriate standards of accountability of procedures and guidelines.
6. Information on various schemes to the readily and freely made available to VO.

7. Acknowledgement of proposals from the VOs.
8. A decentralized system of sanctioning of projects.
9. Flexibility of working without interference from state and district committees.
10. VO to be seen as partners in development and not contractors.
11. Established VOs to be treated on fast-track basis for clearance of projects.
12. Special assessment and speedy clearance for disaster and emergency relief activities.

Now that NITI Aayog has replaced Planning Commission, the National Policy on the Voluntary Sector (NPVS) prepared and circulated by the Planning Commission in May 2007 is expected to be revisited and redrafted by the new body. The annexure to the chapter carries the NPVS for reference.

The all India conference on the role of the voluntary sector in the national development held in 2002 by the Government of India (GOI) brought together on the same platform a large representation of the government in most cases represented by chief ministers and ministers and various central ministries and leading experts from the NGO sector. The then Prime Minister Atal Behari Vajpayee compared nation building to a chariot that he said was driven by five horses, that included the central government, the state governments, panchayati raj institutes, the private sector, the voluntary sector, and community-based organizations (VS and CBOs).[34]

Thousands of NGOs have seen their licenses being cancelled for failing to submit their accounts as per the legal requirement after the coming of the National Democratic Alliance (NDA) government in May 2014. Similarly some INGOs and donors such as Greenpeace and Ford Foundation have been put under scanner. Based on the supposed input from the Intelligence Bureau (IB), the NDA government is seeking more transparency in financial transactions in the NGO sector, especially when it comes to funding from INGOs and funding agencies. There seems to be a growing perception in the government that the funds received through foreign funding could have been used for disrupting some developmental projects by vested interests.

Some analysts believe that after the initial dust settles down, it could lead to better NGO governance in the future. After all propriety and integrity in governance, be it political or social, is what one is looking for.

Media and Developmental Sector

There is a general belief that development is a story badly told, both from the perspective of the program implementers and media writers. With the proliferation of media, an increasing competition among them and the coming of new media formats, one has seen an increase in stories on development and sustainability taken up both by mainstream media writers and bloggers. With a large NGO sector, stories on the work undertaken by them and the challenges faced, besides the beneficiary perspectives, also finds reflection especially in the social media sphere.

Prithi Nambiar based on her empirical research has argued that because of media pluralism in India there have been a few mainstream publications that have kept the issues of development and sustainability on the front burner. She specially refers to *The Hindu* and the *Frontline* which in her view "buck the trend by doing exceptional work in constructing and framing environmental and sustainability issues in ways that enrich the public discourse and play a protective and watchdog function in the public sphere."[35]

Magsaysay Award winning journalist P. Sainath, an inspiration for young journalists, has traversed thousands of miles in the countryside to bring the issue of rural poverty in the public domain. His writing in the media, especially from Maharashtra and Andhra Pradesh, brought to focus stories of despair and anguish of the farmers and the failure of various government schemes involving thousands of crores of rupees which have not brought any succour in the their lives. The digital media reflects that students in the developing countries are now being exposed to development discourse based on the work of the likes of P. Sainath in India.[36]

Analyzing the developmental news, Kalpana Sharma reflects on the successful rally of farmers by Mahinder Singh Tiket in 1988 that virtually brought the capital city of Delhi to a halt, bringing more than 0.2 billion (2 lakh) farmers to register their voice. He surfaced after more than two decades on the cover of *Down To Earth* voicing the same concerns. The author regrets that the mainstream media seemed to have forgotten to write about issues concerning the agrarian crises. The words, rabi, kharif, rain-fed, rural indebtedness, land holdings, and the like, she lamented, were hard to find in newspapers. However, whenever a farmer committed suicide, it surely made news, albeit without looking at the big picture.

There is a lot of sense in what the journalist has written. Over 10,000 farmers from western Uttar Pradesh came to Delhi backed by politicians from various political parties bringing the central part of the city to a virtual halt on November 19, 2009. The timing was strategized to coincide with the first day of the winter session of Parliament. A mainstream newspaper carried four stories on the issue, including a front page story. It included 10 pictures, but when one read all the stories, these were only event-driven dispatches, a criticism generally leveled against media when covering development news. Nowhere was any in-depth analysis of the genesis of the problem and what it meant for the common man, except that their lives were disturbed by the rally. The headline of its front page story was "Kisan Jam" (literally nothing wrong, but the reference in all probability was to a fruit jam by the same name—the height of creative writing!).

Farmers made news when they took on the might of the state power during Nandigram and Singur agitations against the Tata's Nano car plant. Sharma argues that it is not only covering the stories their placement in the media made the difference, which the media gatekeepers have to bear in mind.[37]

Doordarshan that took the message of Green Revolution to the farmers through its initial satellite communication in the late 1960s for years with its Krishi Darshan program continues with the program, albeit without the earlier enthusiasm and content. The 24 × 7 DD Kisan Channel was launched by Prime Minister Modi, on May 26, 2015, on the occasion of the completion of one year in office of the BJP government. DD Kisan aims at providing "information about best agricultural practices and related content."[38] It hopefully will look at the agrarian issues more closely.

It was however a pleasant sight to see a full page devoted by the *Indian Express* to a story with the caption: "A Living Legend: Swaminathan @90" on August 13, 2015, taking the readers through the Green Revolution that "changed India 50 years back- and the man who made it possible." The infographic revealed that India indeed had traversed a long journey from producing 10.40 mt wheat in 1965–1966 to 95.85 mt in 2013–2014 and rice from 30.59 mt in the same period to 106 mt, respectively. The story carried a black and white picture of young Swaminathan with Norman Borlaug, the persons behind the Green Revolution in India. Columnist Harish Damodaran took the readers through what the nonagenarian M.S. Swaminathan had to say about the challenges and how these were overcome.[39]

Of late, the entertainment television media has taken up certain issues concerning the social sector. Many such soap operas start with a promise, but given the race for eyeballs and television rating points, fall in the trap and make a mess of the theme. Some cases in point are *Balika Vadhu, Bairi Piya,* and *Na Aana is Desh Lado* that took up the issues of child marriage, exploitation of the farming community, and female feticide, respectively, but went on to become ordinary soaps with family squabbles and intrigues, with no connect to the original theme.

Is It the Corporate versus the NGOs?

Is the corporate sector's CSR at variance with the NGOs sector's development agenda? Some scholars have spoken of the near demise of the NGO sector with the corporate sector jumping into the social sector as a strategy that may only make a good business sense for them. CSR, feel some, may kill the spirit of the voluntary sector. In many CSR cases, it has been seen that the actual work is passed on to NGOs for implementation, thus making NGOs an appendage to the corporate organizations.

Coke going in for rain harvesting, Bharti Airtel opening schools, Infosys augmenting rural libraries, Bharat Petroleum working against drug abuse, Apollo Tyres sensitizing truckers on HIV and AIDS, Tata's contributing to environment and host of other areas, and Microsoft pledging millions of dollars in health and education in poor countries, are some of the examples to suggest that the CSR sector will only grow further. As per media reports, over 70 NGOs met in Bangalore in 2007 to deliberate on the role of NGOs in CSR times. Coordinator for Delhi Forum of NGOs, M.V. Vijyan commented that more and more NGOs were turning to become the implementing agencies of various CSR schemes of the corporate sector. This he said might not be a healthy trend as earlier; NGOs per se were activists and political in nature. With corporate organizations funding them, they have "deactivated" the once vibrant voluntary sector. This is an issue that needs more probing.

Ashok Chaudhary of National Forum for Forest Workers and Forest People feels that big money is not required for working on issues.

Groups who take up causes, in his view, do not really need money for that as they would survive through the change they wished to bring about. The need of the hour, he commented, was to classify NGOs into two broad categories, namely, watchdogs and charities.[40]

Peter Drucker, considered the guru of management, in an article in the *Harvard Business Review* has said that America's NGOs could be management leaders in two areas, namely, strategy and effectiveness of their boards. He feels that NGOs such as the Red Cross and the Girl Scouts practice what most management only preached. The voluntary sector, he reasoned, was more money conscious but did not base their strategy on money nor did they make money the center of their planning, unlike the corporate organizations. To quote Drucker, "starting with the mission and its requirements may be the first lesson business can learn from successful non-profits, because it focuses the organization on action. It defines the specific strategies needed to attain the crucial goals. It creates a disciplined organization."[41]

Communication Challenges in Social Sector

Despite hundreds of welfare schemes, a robust voluntary sector, and the awakening of corporate consciousness, how much is enough may be a difficult question to answer; but it indeed is a matter of fact that a large majority of those who are supposed to reap the benefits are blissfully unaware of the schemes.

It seems wishy-washy and irresolute that millions of rupees are spent both by the central and state governments on publicizing the schemes for the poor, but more often in mainstream English newspapers that have literally no reach and access among the people who are supposed to be informed! The India Shining campaign by the NDA government and the many phases of the Bharat Nirman campaign of the UPA bear testimony to this. Why do successive governments do it? One of the reasons possibly is that the government of the day wishes to keep the middle class in the cities and the elite media informed of its achievements. They will not ordinarily question because the former are not directly concerned, but get a "feel good" factor for the government they elected, and the latter, the media, earn revenue through advertisements. Probably no newspaper or news channel has ever questioned any government's claim on its "achievements" projected in their umpteen ads with pictures of their political leaders. With the Supreme Court's ruling of May 13, 2015, at least the pictures of the politicians on advertisements, with the exception of the prime minister, will become illegal. To quote *The Hindu*: "In a historic judgment holding that taxpayers' money cannot be spent to build 'personality cults' of political leaders, the Supreme Court on Wednesday restrained ruling parties from publishing photographs of political leaders or prominent persons in government-funded advertisements."[42]

Reaching out to the right holders does not mean spending colossal amounts in expensive mass media. The chapter "Grassroots Communication for Development" would discuss media other than mass media for achieving development communication goals.

In the chapters "Social Marketing" and "Advocacy, Communication, and Social Mobilization," we shall closely look at the tools, strategies, and their application in the social sector projects.

In summation, the social sector, despite the hiccups, has a bright future in India. With an overzealous media, judicial activism, an active social media space, and the Right to Information Act in place, governments, corporate sector, and the voluntary sector will be constantly watched, judged, questioned, and their accountability demanded.

The social sector in India hopefully will become more vibrant and creative in bringing about innovative solutions with a view to improve the lot of millions who live on the fringes.

Annexure

National Policy on the Voluntary Sector
Voluntary Action Cell
Planning Commission
Government of India
May 2007
Government of India Planning Commission (Voluntary Action Cell)
National Policy on the Voluntary Sector: 2007

1. Preamble
   1.1 This policy is a commitment to encourage, enable, and empower an independent, creative, and effective voluntary sector, with diversity in form and function, so that it can contribute to the social, cultural, and economic advancement of the people of India.
   1.2 The voluntary sector has contributed significantly to finding innovative solutions to poverty, deprivation, discrimination, and exclusion, through means such as awareness raising, social mobilization, service delivery, training, research, and advocacy. The voluntary sector has been serving as an effective non-political link between the people and the Government. This policy recognizes the important role that the voluntary sector has to play in various areas and affirms the growing need for collaboration with the voluntary sector by the Government, as well as by the private sector, at the local, provincial, and national levels.
2. Scope of the Policy
   2.1 In the policy, VOs mean to include organizations engaged in public service, based on ethical, cultural, social, economic, political, religious, spiritual, philanthropic or scientific & technological considerations. VOs include formal as well as informal groups, such as:
   Community-based organizations (CBOs); nongovernmental development organizations (NGDOs); charitable organizations; support organizations; networks or federations of such organizations; as well as professional membership associations.
   2.2 To be covered under the Policy, VOs should broadly have the following characteristics:
   a) They are private, that is, separate from the government
   b) They do not return profits generated to their owners or directors
   c) They are self-governing, that is, not controlled by the government

d) They are registered organizations or informal groups, with defined aims and objectives.

3. Objectives of the Policy

  3.1 The specific objectives of the policy are listed below:

    3.1.1 To create an enabling environment for VOs that stimulates their enterprise and effectiveness, and safeguards their autonomy;

    3.1.2 To enable VOs to legitimately mobilize necessary financial resources from India and abroad;

    3.1.3 To identify systems by which the government may work together with VOs, on the basis of the principles of mutual trust and respect, and with shared responsibility; and,

    3.1.4 To encourage VOs to adopt transparent and accountable systems of governance and management.

  The following paragraphs describe how these objectives are to be achieved.

4. Establishing an Enabling Environment for the Voluntary Sector

  4.1 The independence of VOs allows them to explore alternative paradigms of development to challenge social, economic, and political forces that may work against public interest and to find new ways to combat poverty, deprivation, and other social problems. It is therefore crucial that all laws, policies, rules, and regulations relating to VOs categorically safeguard their autonomy, while simultaneously ensuring their accountability.

  4.2 VOs may be registered as societies, as charitable trusts, or as non-profit companies under central or state laws. Some states have adopted the Societies Registration Act (1860), with amendments, while others have independent laws. Similarly, laws relating to charitable trusts vary across states. Over time, many of these laws and their corresponding rules have become complex and restrictive, thus leading to delays, harassment, and corruption. As the nodal agency for interface between the government and the voluntary sector, the Planning Commission will encourage state governments to review prevailing laws and rules and simplify, liberalize, and rationalize them as far as possible. In order to facilitate registration of non-profit companies, the government will examine measures to simplify procedures under section 25 of the Companies Act (1956), including those for license, registration, and remuneration to member-employees.

4.3 The government will also examine the feasibility of enacting a simple and liberal central law that will serve as an alternative all-India statute for registering VOs, particularly those that wish to operate in different parts of the country and even abroad. Such a law would co-exist with prevailing central and state laws, allowing a VO the option of registering under one or more laws, depending on the nature and sphere of its activities.

4.4 There has been much public debate on the voluntary sector, particularly its governance, accountability, and transparency. It is widely believed that the voluntary sector must address these issues through suitable self-regulation. The government will encourage the evolution of, and subsequently accord recognition to, an independent, national level, self-regulatory agency for the voluntary sector.

4.5 At the same time, there is a need to bolster public confidence in the voluntary sector by opening it up to greater public scrutiny. The government will encourage central and state level agencies to introduce norms for filing basic documents in respect of VOs, which have been receiving funding by government agencies and placing them in the public domain (with easy access through the internet) in order to inculcate a spirit of public oversight.

4.6 Public donation is an important source of funds for the voluntary sector and one that can and must increase substantially. Tax incentives play a positive role in this process. Stocks and shares have become a significant form of wealth in the country today. In order to encourage transfer of shares and stock options to VOs, the government will consider suitable tax rebates for this form of donation. The government will also simplify and streamline the system for granting income tax exemption status to charitable projects under the Income Tax Act. At the same time, the government will consider tightening administrative and penal procedures to ensure that these incentives are not misused by paper charities for private financial gain.

4.7 International funding of VOs plays a small, but significant part in supporting such organizations and their work in the country. An organization seeking foreign funding must be registered under the Foreign Contribution (Regulation) Act. This law prescribes stringent screening norms that often restrict the ability of VOs to avail foreign funds. When approved, there are problems like funds must be held in a single bank account, thus presenting enormous difficulties to VOs working at different locations. The government will review the FCRA and simplify its provisions that apply to VOs, from time to time, in consultation with the joint consultative group to be set up by the concerned ministry (as suggested under Para 5.4).

4.8 The central government has framed guidelines for bilateral agencies to give direct assistance to VOs for projects of social and economic importance. It controls access to such funds and their utilization, both through the FCRA and through regulation by the Department of Economic Affairs. This system needs to be simplified in consultation with the joint consultative group to be set up by the concerned ministry (as suggested under Para 5.4).

4.9 The government will encourage all relevant central and state government agencies to introduce pre-service and in-service training modules on constructive relations with the voluntary sector. Such agencies should introduce time bound procedures for dealing with the VOs. These would cover registration, income tax clearances, financial assistance, etc. There would be formal systems for registering complaints and for redressing grievances of VOs.

5. Partnership in Development

5.1 The voluntary sector can play an important role in the development process, particularly through community participation. VOs can offer alternative perspectives; committed expertise; an understanding of the local opportunities and constraints; and perhaps most importantly, the capacity to conduct a meaningful dialogue with communities, particularly those that are disadvantaged. It is therefore essential that the government and the voluntary sector work together. Where feasible, such partnership may also include other entities such as panchayati raj institutions, municipalities, academic institutions, and private sector organizations.

5.2 Partnership between government and VOs implies identifying shared goals and defining complementary roles. It must be based on the basic principles of mutual trust and respect, with shared responsibility and authority. These principles must be explicit in the terms and conditions of the partnership. They must also be evident in the formal and informal systems of collaboration.

5.3 This policy recognizes three instruments of partnership, namely, (i) consultation, through a formal process of interaction at the center state, and district levels; (ii) strategic collaboration to tackle complex interventions where sustained social mobilization is critical over the long term; and (iii) project funding through standard schemes. The government will ensure that these three instruments of partnership are given due attention in Annual Plans prepared by ministries and states. The action that will be taken in respect of each of the three instruments is discussed in the following paragraphs.

5.4 The government will encourage setting up of Joint Consultative Groups/Forums or Joint Machineries of government and voluntary sector representatives, by relevant central departments and state governments. It will also encourage district administrations, district planning bodies, district rural development agencies, zilla parishads, and local governments to do so. These groups will be permanent forums with the explicit mandate to share ideas, views and information, and to identify opportunities and mechanisms of working together. The government will introduce suitable mechanisms for involving a wide cross-section of the voluntary sector in these groups/forums.

5.4.1 The expertise of the voluntary sector will also be utilized, by including experts from VOs in the committees, task forces, and advisory panels constituted by the government from time to time to help address important issues.

5.5 The country faces a number of complex problems that require adaptive, multi-sectoral solutions where sustained social mobilization is particularly important. These include poverty alleviation, skill promotion, entrepreneurship development, empowerment of women, population stabilization, combating HIV/AIDS, managing water resources, elementary education, and forest management, to name a few. Such areas urgently require strategic collaboration between the government and VOs, through national level programs that are long-term in duration, and utilize multiple strategies, methodologies, and activities to achieve their objectives. The government will identify national collaborative programs to be implemented in partnership with VOs. Each national collaborative program will involve a finite set of reputed, medium or large VOs with a proven track record, and the ability to work on a reasonably large scale. The government will ensure that such national collaborative programs are given due importance in plan documents.

5.6 The third instrument of partnership between the government and the voluntary sector is project funding. A large number of government agencies operate schemes for financial assistance to VOs. These schemes usually deal with activities such as surveys, research, workshops, documentation, awareness raising, training, creation, and running of public welfare facilities, and so on. Project grants are a useful means for the government to promote its activities without its direct involvement. They are also a valuable source of support to small and medium VOs. Nevertheless, there are legitimate concerns regarding the effectiveness of grant-in-aid schemes. Out-dated design of funding schemes, arbitrary procedures, selection of unsuitable VOs, poor quality of implementation, and misuse of funds are some of the reasons for the possible defeat of the objectives of such funding. Concerned government agencies would be encouraged to ensure proper accountability and monitoring of public funds distributed to VOs.

5.6.1 Some central agencies have achieved good results by decentralizing the process of project funding. Rather than administering various schemes directly, they appoint regional or state-level intermediary organizations to do so on their behalf. This allows for closer interaction for better selection and monitoring of VOs. Intermediaries could include umbrella VOs, professional or academic institutes, state government agencies, or multi-stakeholder standing committees. The Government will review the experience of such decentralized funding and make suitable recommendations to central agencies.

5.6.2 There is reason to believe that accreditation of VOs will lead to better funding decisions and make the funding processes more transparent. Further, accreditation may provide incentives for better governance, management, and performance of VOs. No reliable accreditation system is in place at present. The government will encourage various agencies, including those in the voluntary sector, to develop alternative accreditation methodologies. It will allow time for such methodologies to be debated and gain acceptability in the voluntary sector, before considering their application to government funding of VOs.

6. Strengthening the Voluntary Sector

6.1 The Indian society has a well-established tradition of philanthropy. While a regime of tax concessions facilitates donations to charitable organizations, there is considerable untapped potential to channelize private wealth for public service. The government will support and encourage existing, as well new, independent philanthropic institutions, and private foundations to provide financial assistance to deserving VOs. It will also promote a dialogue among public and private grant makers so that they may take advantage of the best practices in grant making and fundraising strategies.

6.2 Accountability to all stakeholders and transparency in functioning are key issues in good governance. The voluntary sector is expected to set its own benchmarks in these areas. Since VOs vary in their objectives and activities, it would be impractical to expect uniform norms for accountability and transparency. The government will encourage support organizations, and VO networks and federations to facilitate discussion and consensus building on these issues. It will also encourage such agencies to advise and assist VOs to adopt norms that they find acceptable and useful. The government will recognize excellence in governance among VOs by publicizing best practices.

6.3 Training is a crucial requirement for people working in the voluntary sector. However, this is often neglected on account of limited availability of good quality training courses that are reasonably priced. The government will support and encourage organizations that train aspirants to enter the voluntary sector, as well as those already working in the sector. It will make available physical facilities currently available with its training institutes as a measure of such support.

6.4 Innovation in institutional, technical, and social approaches to development problems is an essential ingredient of voluntary action. The government will encourage and recognize innovative and pioneering work.

6.5 Databases of VOs working in different fields and at different levels are useful for communication within the voluntary sector, as well as between the voluntary sector and the public and private sector. The government will commission suitable agencies to prepare and update such databases.

6.6 Information on government policies and programs is often difficult for VOs to access. The websites of various government agencies will be re-designed to provide links to key documents and databases, including those related to project funding schemes.

6.7 The government will encourage involvement of volunteers in public services, such as, at family welfare centers, primary health centers, hospitals, schools, vocational training centers, sanitation campaigns, etc.

This National Policy on the Voluntary Sector, 2007, is the beginning of a process to evolve a new working relationship between the government and the voluntary sector, without affecting the autonomy and identity of VOs.

Notes and References

1. Yidan Wang, ed., *Public-Private Partnerships in Social Sector Issues and Country Experiences in Asia and the Pacific* (Tokyo: ADBI Publishing, 1999), 3.
2. Madhav Gadgil, "Pluck Not the Surangi: Cong, BJP? No, Our Anti-nature, Anti-people Policies Are Bi-partisan," *Outlook*, LV, No. 36 (August 10, 2015): 52.
3. http://www.livemint.com/Politics/za35wOH7FfSKH8CfGQsbCI/Government-outlines-objectives-of-NITI-Aayog.html (accessed on December 26, 2015).
4. http://data.worldbank.org/data-catalog/world-development-indicators/wdi-2014 (accessed on December 26, 2015).
5. www.hindibuisnessline.com, February 2007.
6. Satyan Bera," India Misses Global Hunger Reduction Targets: Report," *Mint* (May 28, 2015): 1 and 3.
7. Bera, "India Misses Global Hunger Reduction Targets: Report," 1 and 3.
8. *Times Now* and *CNN-IBN*, Prime time news bulletins (9.00 pm), July 1, 2009.
9. *Business Standard*, "Poverty of Thought," July 2, 2009.

10. Urmila Chaterjee, Rinku Murgai, and Martin Rama, "Employment Outcomes along the Rural-Urban Gradation," *Economic & Political Weekly* L, no. 26–27 (June 27, 2015): 5–10.

11. *Mint*, "Unshackling Centrally Sponsored Schemes," *Mint* (July 1, 2015): 30.

12. Jean Dreze, "On the Mythology of Social Policy," *The Hindu*, July 8, 2014.

13. Sudhir Kumar Panwar, "In True Colours," cover story, *Frontline*, 32, No. 7 (April 17, 2015): 20–23.

14. http://www.business-standard.com/article/economy-policy/how-the-budget-short-changed-states-social-security-schemes-115031101450_1.html (accessed on December 27, 2015).

15. Panwar, "In True Colors."

16. http://pib.nic.in/newsite/erelease.aspx?relid=109113 (accessed on December 27, 2015).

17. http://indianexpress.com/article/india/india-others/pm-narendra-modi-launches-jan-dhan-yojana-to-focus-on-ending-finacial-untouchability/ (accessed on December 27, 2015).

18. http://www.livemint.com/Opinion/9huedGeHxU770Gq7vvi13M/Jan-Dhan-Yojana-populism-gone-berserk.html (accessed on December 15, 2015).

19. http://www.moneycontrol.com/news/economy/critics-attack-wasteful-ineffective-pm-jan-dhan-yojana_1169557.html?utm_source=ref_article (accessed on December 15, 2015).

20. Sukhamoy Chakravarty, http://www.mainstreamweekly.net/article5710.html (accessed on December 15, 2015).

21. Doordarshan and other news channels in a direct live telecast on August 15, 2015.

22. http://hbswk.hbs.edu/item/putting-entrepreneurship-in-the-social-sector (accessed on February 12, 2016).

23. "Study Finds Massive Corruption in Govt's Flagship NREGA," May 23, 2010, http://www.rediff.com/news/report/study-finds-massive-corruption-in-govts-flagship-nrega/20100523.htm (accessed on December 9, 2015).

24. https://freedomhouse.org/report/freedom-world/2014/india#.VV73wCaJjIU (accessed on December 13, 2015).

25. https://www.globalintegrity.org/ (accessed on November 14, 2015).

26. http://www.bti-project.org/uploads/tx_itao_download/BTI_2008_India.pdf (accessed on February 12, 2016).

27. P. Sainath, *Everybody Loves a Good Drought* (New Delhi: Penguin Books, 1996), 316–17.

28. Sainath, *Everybody Loves a Good Drought,* 319.

29. Subhodh Varma, "Where Is My Social Security Prime Minister?" *TOI*, June 28, 2009 quoted from Guy Standing. "Globalisation: The Eight Crises of Social Protection," *The Indian Journal of Labour Economics* 45, No. 1 (2002): 17–46.

30. subrat@cbgaindia.org http://www.downtoearth.org.in/content/plan-spending-social-sectors-and-paradox-budgetary-policies (accessed on November 23, 2015).

31. http://www.ngo.in/types-of-ngos.html (accessed on February 17, 2016).

32. Archana Shukla, "First Official Estimate—An NGO for every 400 Indians," *The Indian Express*, July 7, 2010. See http://archive.indianexpress.com/news/first-official-estimate-an-ngo-for-every-400-people-in-india/643302/ (accessed on December 4, 2015).

33. Source: Voluntary sector in India, Scale, Impact and Potential presented by PRIA (Participatory Research in Asia) to the Planning Commission of India on September 5, 2005.

34. Ashish Kumar Sen, "Heat on NGOs Triggers Chill on US Campuses," *Mint* (June 12, 2015): 22.

35. Prithi Nambiar, *Media Construction of Environment Sustainability in India* (New Delhi: SAGE, 2014), 234.

36. Journalism of P. Sainath, lecture by Robert Jensen: https://www.youtube.com/watch?v=Intp4IUphPo (accessed on November 30, 2015).

37. www.india-seminar.com (accessed on November 30, 2015).

38. http://www.firstpost.com/india/modi-launches-dd-kisan-channel-pushes-for-farmers-growth-2263812.html (accessed on November 17, 2015).

39. Harish Damodaran, "Swaminathan@90," *The Indian Express*, August 13, 2015, 23.

40. www.rediff.com, September 12, 2007.

41. Peter Drucker, quoted by Dibeyendu Ganguly. Ibid.

42. http://www.thehindu.com/news/national/sc-no-to-politicians-photos-on-government-ads/article7200970.ece (accessed on November 30, 2015).

2

Social Marketing

Introduction

As commodities are marketed with a desired consumer response in view, can patriotism, brotherhood, and myriad social issues be marketed with the precision of marketing principles and strategies? Weibe probably had the same question on his mind when he said way back in 1952: "Why can't you sell brotherhood like you sell soaps?"[1] The idea behind this perhaps was that social campaigns were often lackluster without a proper branding or positioning around social issues, unlike brand campaigns which used all marketing and communications principles to ensure that they got the desired response from the target audience (TA). Almost two decades later, in 1971, Philip Kotler and Gerald Zaltman coauthored an article in *The Journal of Marketing* using for the first time the term "social marketing" in the title: *Social Marketing: An Approach to Social Change*. The authors said that social marketing (SM) was a promising framework for planning and implementing social change, but at the same time it was "poorly understood and viewed by behavioral scientists." Kotler and Zaltman at that point of time suspected,

> [T]he application of commercial ideas and methods to promote social goals will be seen by many as another example of business's lack of taste and self-restraint. Yet the application of logic of marketing of social goals is a natural development and on the whole a promising one. The idea will not disappear by ignoring it or rallying against it.[2]

What is Social Marketing?

Philip Kotler, interestingly, has expanded on his conceptual framework around social marketing (SM) a number of times spanning over four decades. In 1971, SM was defined as "the design, implementation and control of programmes calculated to influence the acceptability of social ideas and involving considerations of product planning, pricing, communication and market resources."[3] Later, in 1975, Kotler expanded on the definition: "Social marketing utilizes market segmentation, consumer research, concept development communications, facilitation, incentives and the exchange theory to maximize target group response."[4]

In 2006, Kotler, along with Lee and Rothschild, defined SM as a "process that applies marketing principles and techniques to create, communicate and deliver value in order to influence target audience behaviors that benefit society (public health, safety, the environment, and communities) as well as the target audience."[5]

When we analyze all the definitions, it is clear that the core remains the same, that is, the confines of commercial marketing can be befittingly used to market social products to achieve desired results.

According to A.R. Andreasen, "Social marketing is the application of commercial marketing technologies to the analysis, planning, execution and evaluation of programmes designed to influence the voluntary behavior of a target audience to improve their personal welfare and that of their society."[6]

SM as a concept, according to Kotler and Zaltman, has over a period of time acquired two dimensions, namely, the social responsibility of business mainly in response to consumer advocacy movements and pressures of government regulations and the applicability of marketing philosophy and principles to the introduction and dissemination of ideas and issues of social significance.[7]

The need for social change campaigns arise because of the belief among some people and organizations that they can direct, shape, and control change. The 20th century with the advent of technology and mass media was able to bring the world to a common platform. The two bloody World Wars and the many wars thereafter, the sufferings of the common man, the rise in population vis-à-vis the resources, an unequal world where more than one-third population lives below the poverty line, deaths, diseases, ignorance, among other perils have set governments, civil society organizations, academics, and scholars thinking on finding a solution to these myriad issues that plague societies and nations at large. Many social reformers have done it before, albeit without probably knowingly using brand communication techniques, but when we look at the campaigns closely, especially the community mobilization and positioning of advocacy campaigns to bring about social change, those did have the remnants of modern day SM precincts. Some of the cases in point include the crusade against apartheid, slavery, *Sati Pratha* (the custom of burning widows on the pyre of their dead husbands), widow remarriage, among many others. Early reformers such as Martin Luther, Nelson Mandela, Mahatma Gandhi, Dayanand Saraswati, Vinobha Bhave, Ram Mohan Roy, etc. worked relentlessly to achieve the desired results to a great measure.

The terminology "social marketing" has gained currency in the last couple of decades and one finds its use both in the government and voluntary sectors.

For instance, in the National Strategy on Social Marketing, prepared by the Ministry of Health and Family Welfare, GOI, one finds the following objectives of SM:

1. To promote the acceptability and adoption of socially beneficial, voluntary health behavior.
2. To improve access to, and availability of a wide range of quality health information, products, and services with a public health benefit, for the rural, underserved, low-income, and vulnerable populations.
3. To provide more affordable health care products and services, with more equitable distribution so as to reach the low-income groups.
4. To sustain increases in total contraceptive use, especially spacing methods, among all segments of the population.
5. To adequately research the segmented market for contraceptives and other products and services for basic and essential health care, as well as consumer preferences in respect of product attributes.

6. To decentralize the SM program in the field and to mainstream the coalition envisaged in the National Population Policy, 2000, for private (NGO)–public partnership maybe through a consortium that has the potential to catapult the SM program into a national movement to improve availability, access, and affordability of basic health care products.

7. To simultaneously ensure the strengthening of logistics at state levels to enable an uninterrupted flow of products and services.

8. The National Strategy for SM seeks to ensure that essential health services reach low-income groups and the "economically active" poor people, through an "appropriate public–private mix of financing and provisioning so that they do not pay exorbitant sums for quality health care."[8]

In the voluntary sector, there are many examples to cite where SM has been adopted as a strategy to fulfill program goals. For example, the Global Alliance for Improved Nutrition (GAIN), an INGO in partnership with the Federation of Flour Millers, has been able to make hundreds of large flour millers voluntarily fortify flour to address the problem of micronutrient malnutrition in India, especially in some of the vulnerable states. The millers call it SM in public interest.

SM versus Commercial Marketing

Let us first look at the definition of marketing followed by how commercial marketing is different from SM.

The American Marketing Association released a new definition of marketing in 2008, delineating a broader role for the discipline: "Marketing is the activity, set of institutions, and processes for creating, communicating, delivering, and exchanging offerings that have value for customers, clients, partners, and society at large."[9]

Philip Kotler defines marketing as:

[T]he science and art of exploring, creating, and delivering value to satisfy the needs of a target market at a profit. Marketing identifies unfulfilled needs and desires of people. It defines measures and quantifies the size of the identified market and the profit potential. It pinpoints which segments the company is capable of serving best and it designs and promotes the appropriate products and services.[10]

Kotler talks of the four Ps which are the essence of marketing, namely, product, price, promotion, and place. The four Ps of commercial marketing are believed to work in SM also with the objective of achieving the desired social change. A product in marketing can be both tangible such as a soap bar or an aerated drink, or intangible such as service in a hotel or an act of kindness; for accessing the product, there is a certain price in tangible terms to be paid. As there may be many similar products and services, the marketers promote their products to inform and enthuse potential buyers to prefer their products and services by talking about the competitive edge. The product or service is available at a certain place, in other words the product is distributed at places where the potential buyers can be located. The buyer must know about it to access it. Like these four Ps, the social marketers also use the same fundamentals to reach out to those whose behavior they wish to change. While commercial marketing is aimed at persuading the TA to buy a certain product, the SM aims at behavioral change. In commercial marketing, the benefit accrues to the marketer's organization, but in SM the beneficiary is the person whose behavior is to be changed. This is what makes SM distinctly different from commercial marketing.

Let us look at how the four Ps would work in a SM scenario:

Product: Product in SM can be both tangible and intangible (condoms to breast feeding, planting trees to caring for the old, or loving one's country).

Price: Price refers to what consumers must do to obtain a social product. The cost may be tangible when one has to buy something or invest in time which may mean sacrificing the working hours or intangible like risking embarrassment or disapproval of people one cares for.

Place: Place describes the way the product reaches the consumer. For a tangible product, it refers to the distribution system. For an intangible product, say in health, the place may be a community gathering, a doctor's clinic, a mass media vehicle, etc.

Promotion: Promotion consists of the integrated use of advertising, public relations, advocacy, personal selling, and entertainment vehicles.

Additional Ps for SM

Many scholars have talked about additional Ps for SM. Some of these include the following:

Publics: Publics refer to both external and internal groups involved in the program. External groups are the primary and secondary TA. Internal public comprise the program officials, etc.

Partnership: Social and health issues are often complex and need interdisciplinary effort and networking.

Policy: SM program can do well in motivating individual behavior change, but it is difficult to sustain unless the environment supports it (for example, child marriage, Sati, etc.).

Purse string: Most organizations that develop SM programs operate through funds provided by sources as foundations, governments, or from corporate donors and philanthropists. Hence, organizing funds is an integral part of SM.

Behavior change depends on various factors, such as personal experience, a sudden change in life or environment, legal requirement, technological shift, etc. Kotler et al. point out that people change their attitude or behavior due to one or more of the following factors:

1. Legal (for example, ban on smoking in public)
2. Technological (for instance the communication techniques have changed with the coming of computers/Internet, etc.)
3. Economic (economy doing better, money getting devalued, stock market crash, etc.)
4. Informational (empowerment through knowledge, persuasive communication which generally results in changed behavior)

Process of SM

SM primarily aims at behavioral change of people, a process which is both complex and tedious. Communication plays an important part in the process. In the following paragraphs, we shall take a look at the various steps.

Problem Definition

Before an SM organization begins work, the issue termed as product needs to be identified, so that it can be marketed to a designated audience. For example, the issue could be helping the truckers to adopt safe sexual behavior. This would require not only change from the current behavior but also convincing them about safety precautions through condoms. The problem is often defined through primary research and secondary data on the subject.

Customer Analysis

The next step would be to explore TA's behavior, the reasons for their existing behavior, and what could be the trigger that would help change the behavior. Often program implementers conduct knowledge, attitude, and practices (KAP) studies to arrive at insights. This would help in working out the communication strategy and plan.

Goal Setting

Once the social product is identified, it is imperative to make quantifiable goals which can be assessed. The goals would be in terms of reach of the social product to a certain number of potential adopters. To illustrate, if there are X number of truckers in the country spread in various parts of the country, the social marketer would take a decision based on the resources available to reach out either all or the most vulnerable groups on priority within the total population of truckers.

Market Segmentation

Who are the potential adopters, which are the most critical in terms of program goals, and where are they located need to be worked the same way the market is segmented for a commercial product.

Developing Marketing Strategies

Strategy is the "how" of a program. In other words, what could be done in terms of tactics that would make the program/product familiar and acceptable to the desired TA? To illustrate, the strategy in terms of location for truck drivers can be to reach out to them on highway eateries or petrol stations where they generally stop by.

Where Can We Use SM as a Strategy?

SM techniques have been used for bringing about attitudinal or behavioral changes among a designated TA in many social and political areas, especially health, education, civil liberties, etc. Given below are the major areas of SM use:

Social: Health, disability, sanitation and hygiene, social conditioning, empowerment, issues relating to gender, female feticide, HIV and AIDS, drug abuse, environment, pollution, global warming, etc.

Political: Civil liberties, human rights, Right to Information.

Educational: Reforms, universal access to education, adult education, etc.

Understanding Social Product

A social product on offer, according to Kotler and Roberto, comes with various expectations, such as:

1. It satisfies the need that no other product is satisfying;
2. The social product satisfies a need that other social products are addressing, but the one on offer satisfies it better;
3. The social product on offer cannot satisfy a need that target adopters currently perceive or have but nevertheless addresses a real underlying need of the people.

When we analyze the three types referred to (1) would be the easiest to penetrate and (3) the most difficult.[11]

There are social products that a marketer needs to sell once or repeatedly. For example, it could be one shot of immunization for life or use of family planning product regularly or going for breast cancer test once in a year. Each category would require handling the issue differently. Sometimes, the target adopters may not be sure, if things would change for good, if they yield to a changed behavior. Marketers handling the obesity issue among children and adults have a tough job of gaining credibility as obesity keeps returning when the target adopters do not follow the diet regimen or in the case of drug users where going back to drugs is very common. In case of such campaigns, drawing positive response is challenging, if not impossible.

For some social products, there may be a latent demand that the social marketers have to find out so that it can be made available. When Inspector General Kiran Bedi was in charge of Tihar Jail in Delhi, she introduced the distribution of condoms in the male wards earning the ire of many including her peers and politicians. Her decision was based on the fact that many men did indulge in sex with men and ran the risk of acquiring HIV/AIDS.

In many university campuses in the West, it is not uncommon to find condom vending machines, but every time there is talk about this in India, it is criticized for promoting promiscuity among the youth. For instance, when an emergency anti-pregnancy pill was advertised by a pharmaceutical company in the mainstream media, the television spots reflected a married woman taking the pill because the couple was not careful in using family planning device the previous night. The pill could be taken by women within 72 hours to avoid pregnancy. Interestingly, a number of media reports suggested that there was a great demand for the pill from young unmarried girls: an insight that could have been tapped by the social marketers addressing teenage pregnancy issue.

However, it created a lot of controversy. Sharon Fernandes reported that the Drug Controller General of India (DCGI) shared that a committee would be set up to examine whether *Unwanted 72* and *i-pill*, two morning-after contraceptive pills, now sold over the counter, should be reclassified as "prescription drugs." This came after the DCGI sent a letter to the two manufacturers pulling them up for running TV ads which was "misrepresenting abortion" and pushing the pills as a way to the "tension-free" after-sex scenario. The catch was if it was made a prescription drug then it could not be advertised as per the Indian laws.[12]

Contesting this, Amar Lulla, Joint Managing Director, Cipla, one of the manufacturers when asked about the DCGI's complaint that the ads pushed "tension-free sex," said that the pill was a woman's way to choose and prevent the trauma of an abortion. "We will accept the guidelines but the government should also participate in educating people. The government is on record that emergency contraceptives should be publicized," said Lulla.[13]

A spokesman from Mankind Pharma, as reported by the media, said, "We have shown a married couple. The product is such that we cannot not talk about sex. The use of the word 'tension-free,' is relevant especially for a woman who is unsure of whether she is pregnant she goes through a traumatic phase." He added: "We will do whatever the government asks us. If they provide guidelines, we will follow those for the advertisements."[14]

In other cases, there may be one or more social products to fulfill the need, but for some reason despite the demand, the product may not get picked up. Therefore, the social marketers have to create the necessary imagery and hype to suit the emotional and life style needs of particular target groups. Population Service International (PSI) campaign in Swaziland used emotion to urge for HIV testing. The "Love test," as a campaign, was branded to target couples, urging them to reflect their love for each other and test together. The initiative was widely covered by the media that resulted in a multiplier impact. Introduced in April 2009, the number of couples who came for testing more than tripled. The overall testing increased by 400 percent over the previous year.

There could be cases for "unwholesome" demand as defined by Kotler and Roberto. This is when the target adopters advocate socially harmful ideas, such as racism, drug abuse, excessive drinking, violence, etc. These issues are "marketed" as macho and glamorous. The social marketer would have to be careful in providing substitute products, both tangible and intangible ones, that may promise the same "high" to those the program is aiming at.[15]

There are times when a social marketer has to deal with a dual demand, namely, the change of behavior followed by a tangible product to help reinforce the changed behavior. To illustrate, the social marketer may have to convince target adopters for planned parenthood. Once they yield, then the necessary product/s have to be made available to facilitate change. Or to quote another example, if a TA has been convinced of using toilets against defecating in the open, it is only necessary that toilets have to be there.

"Sathiya," is an SM and pharma partnership campaign designed to meet the reproductive health needs of young couples in urban India. It was spearheaded by an NGO with USAID support with the aim to enable young couples to make an informed choice on when to start childbearing and how many children to have. A number of contraceptive-producing companies were involved that offered a "basket" that included condoms, emergency contraceptives, and standard day method "cycle beads." About 300 chemists and trained doctors underwent a training program on adolescent health and counseling skills. The program was backed by a media campaign that included print, outdoor, cinema slides, community theatre, and over the counter (OTC) publicity at health facilities and chemist shops. A "Sathiya" helpline was put in place that received about 12,000 calls in the first six months.[16]

Sometimes when a social product is targeted to the entire group successfully, the demand may go down or completely vanish. For a long-term change of behavior, it is important for the social marketer to continue reinforcing the demand. To illustrate, in the late 1970s, some of the Australian states were running shortage of electric power. An engaging social campaign resulted in so much reduction in the consumption of power that it left a lot of surplus power with the company. As power cannot be stored, the company ran the risk of loss. That was when another campaign had to be released to specifically exhort the target adopters to reduce consumption only by a certain percentage.[17]

Building SM into a Program

As discussed earlier, SM involves the whole chain of processes to achieve the desired goal. In the following paragraphs, let us look at the various imperatives in detail to understand the process of SM.

Understanding Social Product: Giving It a Tangible Form

Unlike a commercial product, it is not always easy to define a social product. For instance, how does one define national integration or patriotism? What words and imagery can possibly be used to give it a tangible base? The Indian government after Independence in 1947 has invariably used national integration as a social issue campaign. "Awaz do, hum ek hein" and "Unity in Diversity" have often been the baselines. The mention of rivers and mountains denote the geographic connotation and religion is manifested through visual imagery of faces and accessories to avoid any mistaking in identification. There is always a Sikh (with turban and beard), Muslim (beard and cap), Hindu (tilak on the forehead), and Christian (Western attire) in such campaigns. It does establish stereotype but is simple to follow.

Let us take another example of the same issue that was very subtly tackled. During Rajiv Gandhi's premiership, after the assassination of Indira Gandhi, a five-minute film *Mile sur mera tumhara* (when my song blends with yours) represented all the communities, languages, and geographic locations. Famous singers, actors, and other celebrities representing various languages and regions were used to create an orchestral symphony that truly defines India. The public service ad is more than 25 years old, but still evokes the same emotional response from viewers every time one is exposed to it.[18]

In a short documentary film on national integration communication, the film reflected on what went into the making of the public service ad (PSA). Bharatbala, the moving spirit behind the film narrated how the one line "Mile sur mera tumhara" was adapted in various Indian languages and sung by both well-known singers and actors, besides ordinary folks.

Later, after the Babri Masjid demolition on December 6, 1992 and the riots that followed in the country, filmmaker Subhash Ghai came out with a PSA "Sun sun sun mere mune" endorsed by the younger generation celebrities including Govinda, Aamir Khan, Jackie Shroff, etc. It spoke about "Dosti ki baat ho" (let us talk of friendship). But the treatment and melody could not match the "Mile sur" PSA.

On the 50th freedom anniversary of India in 2007, Bharatbala came out with the "Vande Matram" PSA along with the Oscar-winning musician A.R. Rehman. The team traveled more than 1.5 lakh kilometers to capture the essence of India.

Another PSA, around the same time, had some of the famous Indian playback and classical singers singing the national anthem in slow speed. They included Mangeshkar sisters, Kumar Gandharv, Pandit Jasraj, Jagjit Singh, among others. Each one rendered a line. The film was shot in black and white (B/W), except when it ended with the tricolor, the Indian flag.[19]

A PSA on nonviolence made by the same filmmakers included many Nobel laureates, such as Nelson Mandela and Dalai Lama who were influenced by the Gandhian philosophy of nonviolence.

Celebrities from art, culture, film, and sports have wholeheartedly supported and endorsed the national integration theme in India.

Profiling and Segmenting the Target Audience

Once a social product is defined, the next step is to position it vis-à-vis the designated target adopters. They can be segmented varyingly, for example, by geographic regions, urban and rural, by demographics such as age, sex, education, or income. The target population can also be segmented by family size, family life cycle such as young, old, family with children, one-income families, two-income families, double income, no children (DINCS); occupation (professional, business, salaried, retired, unemployed, house wives, students, etc.). The segmentation can also be based on religion or caste.

The audience profiling should also be based on psychographics based on their life styles and attitudes. The typology can also be on behavior types.

An example of audience segmentation for a hygiene and sanitation campaign in rural India

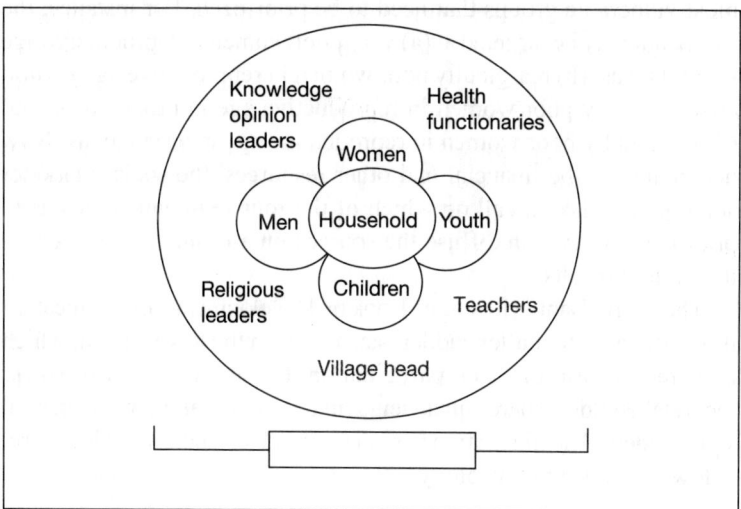

Source: Author.

An example of target segmentation against prenatal sex determination in rural India

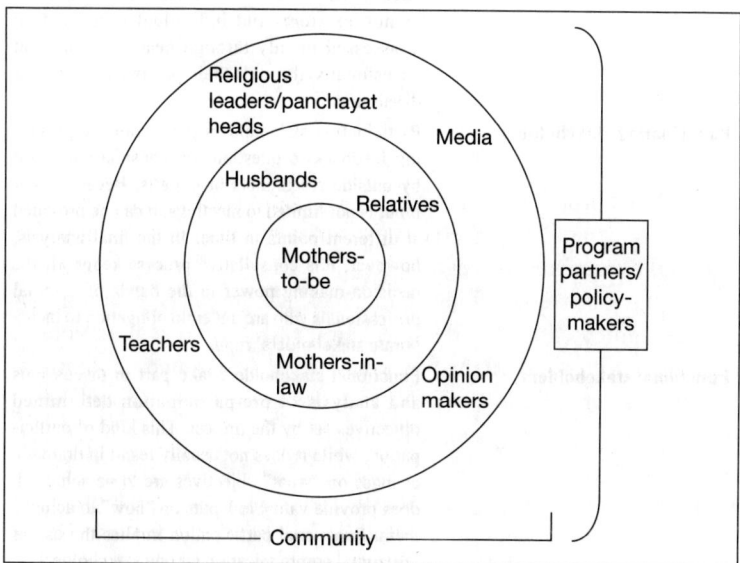

Source: Author.

Once the target audiences have been segmented, the social marketer would have to decide on who are the most critical and the most vulnerable groups that need to be prioritized. For instance, the campaign may be targeted at (a) very poor women in reproductive age in rural areas, (b) marginally poor women in reproductive age in rural areas, (c) very poor women in reproductive age in urban areas, and (d) marginally poor women in reproductive age in urban areas. Now depending on the financial and other resources, the social marketer shall have to take a call on which of the four segments he needs to prioritize, rather than diffuse the sources on all four without getting the desired results.

The World Bank's Resource Book on Development Communication illustrates a participation ladder, starting from the lowest form, which is merely a form of token participation, to the highest form, where local stakeholders share equal weight in decision-making with external stakeholders. The illustration has been reproduced below.[20] The matrix below illustrates the typology.

Typology of participation in development initiatives

Passive participation	Passive stakeholders participate by being informed about what participation is going to happen or has already happened. People's feedback is minimal or non-existent, and individual participation is assessed mainly through head-counting and occasionally through their participation in the discussion.
Participating stakeholders	Participation stakeholders participate by providing feedback to questions by consultation posed by outside researchers or experts. Because their input is not limited to meetings, it can be provided at different points in time. In the final analysis, however, this consultative process keeps all the decision-making power in the hands of external professionals who are under no obligation to incorporate stakeholders' input.
Functional stakeholders	Functional stakeholders take part in discussions and analysis of pre-participation determined objectives set by the project. This kind of participation, while it does not usually result in dramatic changes on "what" objectives are to be achieved, does provide valuable inputs on "how" to achieve them. Functional participation implies the use of horizontal communication among stakeholders.

Empowered stakeholders	Empowered stakeholders are willing and able to be part of the participation process and participate in joint analysis, which leads to joint decision-making about what should be achieved and how. While the role of outsiders is that of equal partners in the initiative, local stakeholders are equal partners with a decisive say in decisions concerning their lives.

Source: http://siteresources.worldbank.org/EXTDEVCOMMENG/Resources/
DevelopmentCommSourcebook.pdf (accessed on December 10, 2015).

Evart Roger's Diffusion of Innovation Thesis

Evart Roger's Diffusion of Innovation thesis in the context of social message outlines that when an innovation (for example, new idea, approach, strategy) is communicated through various channels over a period of time among members of a social system, the characteristics as perceived by members of a social system determine its rate of adoption. Whether the message is accepted (or the behavior adopted) depends upon the following factors:

1. When the target group perceives it as beneficial;
2. Sees it as being in accordance with their needs and values;
3. Finds it easy or difficult to understand or adopt;
4. Can consider trial behavior;
5. Feel that the results of the trial or acceptance are viewed positively by their peers.[21]

Branding of Social Product

A brand, it is believed, is in the mind space of consumers. It provides both rational and emotional connect. An interesting yet simple name and attractive packaging of a tangible product supported by media buzz can help build a strong brand. Brand names are put to various tests to find out what image conjures up in the mind of person. Recall tests are conducted to gauge the memorability of the social brand. Marketers also conduct preference tests to know potential adopters' preference for a certain name over other names.

The family planning program in India had a tangible social product, the condom named Nirodh which means "control." Despite being top-of-the-mind brand in recall, it was not able to create a positive and user-friendly image, though it went on to become a generic name for condoms. Later, social marketers especially from the civil society organizations, based on research, introduced various brand names that played on the fun and pleasure quotient such as Bliss, Milan, Masti, Pick me, Mauj, Sangam, Ustad, Ahsaas, etc.

Distribution of Social Product

Making the social product available to the target audience is imperative to the success of a SM program. Keeping in view the resources, it is not uncommon that the social marketer would plan to reach out to the most vulnerable section on priority. To quote Kotler, "The point of production is the social change campaign and the points of consumption are the target adopters. Managing a distribution channel involves managing a network of intermediaries."[22]

> **Supply Chain → Distributor→ Target Adopter**

Who should manage the distribution: the SM organization itself or the intermediaries? The answer lies in how large is the universe of distribution and the availability of expertise and resources. As referred above, the GOI has been using the services of many private players in the distribution of health and family planning products for more than 40 years. Any SM program must create the same reliability factor as commercial marketing does. Any weak link in the supply chain would fail the effort, besides the risk of the loss of credibility. To illustrate, if the children are being taken for immunization on a publicized day, it is important that all arrangement, both human and material, are in sync. The polio vaccines must be available, and the health functionary also needs to be there. For a social product of intangible nature, such as a service, it is similarly important that functionaries in the chain need to fulfill their obligations that are expected of them. In a research study conducted to gauge the gap between health facilities and the experience of the patients in various hospitals created for industrial workers through their and employers' contribution in 2006, some very interesting insights emerged.

The workers, in general, felt that health functionaries by and large, especially in Delhi and Patna were apathetic (the survey was conducted in three places, namely, Delhi, Kolkata, and Patna). The doctors would not touch them, even if the diagnosis demanded (for example, checking the pulse or touching the patient). The reason ascribed by some workers was that this was so because they were perceived as unclean and lacking hygiene standards. The doctors, however, denied such allegations.

There was a general perception that the doctors did not give them the right prescription. When asked how they would know the prescription was not right, the quick answer was that for every ailment they were given the same analgesic tablet! They also argued that why was it so that when they went to a private doctor they were cured, but when the government doctor attended to them, they rarely did (a commonsensical answer).

One interesting insight among the right holders, however, was apparent when some of them said that the hospitals were established and doctors were paid salaries through their contribution, so they better worked towards their welfare.[23]

In any SM program, bringing the issue in the public domain and creating a buzz around the brand is necessary. Mass media plays the role of an important link in the supply chain, being the distributor of information. Thousands of crores of rupees have been spent on public information campaigns from the time the Pulse Polio Programme (PPP) was launched in India. India has been declared polio free since 2014.

The Union Minister of State for Labour Bandaru Dattatreya conceded in May 2015 as reported by media that over ₹27,000 crores was lying with the Employees' Provident Fund (EPF) operator with no claimants in site. This is a classic case of government not reaching out to stakeholders with information to claim their hard-earned contributions to the EPF, which in the first place was created for their welfare. The supposed claimants are workers from the unorganized sector who may not even know that from their wages some amount was deducted along with employers' contribution to the EPF fund. Even if they know, they may not know how to claim it. Being in temporary employment, they may have changed many jobs. The government needs to streamline the process for providing social security to the people who need it the most. One of the ways could be by making the employers and the

EPF operator responsible for disbursal. It may be challenging but it is certainly not difficult to reach out to such people or their kin after the mandatory time span required for facilitating disbursal is complete.

Besides the mass media, interpersonal communication through various means and volunteers also plays an important role in the supply chain. In fact, many believe that no SM program can succeed without the spirit of voluntarism.

Price/Cost of Adoption

Every tangible product comes at a price. Similarly, a tangible social product will also be procured at a cost, but it needs to be ensured that the price is not beyond the reach of the person the program implementer is trying to reach out to. For instance, for a social product such as an anti-pregnancy pill, a condom, or an ORH packet, there would be a cost of production. So the decision will have to be taken on the price that it would be made available at. Will it be distributed for free or at subsidized rates? These are some of the important factors the social marketer has to keep in view. There is no denying that the higher the price, the more difficult task it would it be for the potential adopter to purchase it.

In free tangible products also, the target adopter does pay a price for adopting it, a fact often overlooked by program implementers. Let us illustrate the case of a mother, a daily wage earner who is convinced about taking her child for immunization drops until the child reaches the age of five. The number of days she takes her child would also be the number of days she loses her wage, which would be a substantial price to be paid by her from her perspective. So in a way, she also pays a price for the social product.

In other cases, the price of a product is enhanced so that the target adopter finds it hard to access. Cigarettes and alcohol fall in this category. In this case, it is generally the government that increases the taxes. Companies producing cigarettes continue to make profits; they often have huge clout in the government so they go on unabashedly advertising through the surrogate route. The increased price may create holes in the pockets of buyers but without really affecting the companies or the governments, who earn more and more through enhanced excise duties.

The other tangible price that the adopters often pay is the emotional connect with a certain behavior or product. The adoption would likely happen, if the price to be paid is lesser than the gain that would accrue from adopting. Analysts term these as "psychic costs."

Information campaigns do often create a demand for that social product, but the cost both in tangible terms and intangible terms becomes the deciding factor on how the adopter would react to the product.

Weibe speaks of five things from the point of view of those whose behavior has to change.

Force: The intensity of a person's motivation towards a goal that is based on the predisposition before the message is received and the stimulation level of the message.

Direction: Knowledge/information of how and where to respond positively to a campaign's objectives. In other words, the presence of a means of carrying out the objectives.

Mechanism: Through which motivation is translated into action.

Adequacy and compatibility: The effectiveness of the agency in performing the task.

Distance: What will it take in terms of cost and energy to change an attitude or behavior in relation to the expected reward?[24]

According to UNAIDS, "Making quality products and services affordable and available is just one part of the social marketing equation, encouraging their use represents the other. Market research and a strong communications component are essential to the success of a social marketing program."[25]

Social Change Campaigns

There are umpteen examples of social change campaigns found in the relics of history spanning many centuries. One finds a reference of campaigns to free slaves in ancient Greece and Rome. The atrocities and the long struggle of Blacks in the USA, the sacrifice of Martin Luther, the crusade against apartheid in Africa and the role of Nelson Mandela are some of the not-too-old examples.

In our part of the world, the untiring zeal and tirade by social reformer Raja Ram Mohan Roy against the Sati Pratha, the remarriage of widows, the crusade against untouchability by Mahatma Gandhi, and the Bhoodan movement by Vinoba Bhave are a few examples of the social change brought about in the Indian society. Mass media was hardly used in any of the above-mentioned campaigns. The change was facilitated to a great extent by social reformers through interpersonal communication tools and the backup received from the political system that enforced laws so that there was no going back to the barbarian ways. Sati Pratha ended because of the synergy between the social and the political will. Lord William Benttinck helped pass the law when the time to bring about change was just ripe.

A number of social change campaigns that are presently active in India include crusade against female feticide, HIV and AIDS, domestic violence, sexual harassment at workplace, drug abuse, anti-smoking, drunken driving, environment protection, cruelty against animals, global warming, education, other health-related issues, etc. During the past couple of years one has seen the entry of the corporate sector and media in adopting certain issues for wider dissemination. The Tata group with its "Jago Re" campaign and *The Times of India*'s "Teach India" and "Lead India" have resulted in sensitizing the public in general and the youth in particular on the need to participate in the social and political life of the country. Some of these campaigns have been included in Chapter 3, "Corporate Social Responsibility."

In SM, unlike commercial marketing, it is not a brand switch or reinforcement; here the marketer is aiming at fighting some long established habit for which the price to be paid is not necessarily in terms of money but sacrificing a pleasure or withstanding social pressure. For example, if cessation of smoking is the objective, the person who yields may have to fight peer pressure and indignation. This can be seen as a price to be paid. Deeply held views generally have low rate of success. In the Indian context, child marriage, preferences for a male child, female feticide, are issues that do not attract much success despite various laws in place. Notwithstanding large-scale programs on family planning, the family planning methods are used by less than 10 percent of people in the reproductive age group. For a nation that is overwhelmingly young, this poses a serious barrier to the success of any population-control program, unless there is serious change in the policy and program in this direction.

In the following paragraphs, we shall take for discussion some social campaigns from India and elsewhere.

Overseas Campaigns: Random

Connecting with Migrant Population

Never abandon. Never give up, a short B/W film was released in partnership with the International Labor Organization (ILO) and Mega-Information Media aimed at reducing stigma and promoting condom use among China's internal migrant workers. The film stars Zhang Xiao, a migrant worker living with HIV, and was the first attempt by anyone in the country to speak publicly about his HIV status. The campaign has been spearheaded with the collaboration of 19 large construction, mining, and transport companies from China's towns most impacted by HIV. The film is expected to reach 40 million workers. The migrant laborers in China are believed to share a strong social bond based on their common provincial origin. Besides the film, the campaign also included radio spots and peer education programs at the work place. All the key messages are delivered in their native voice.

Reaching Out to Those on the Fringes

Men having sex with men (MSM) in Africa are said to run an enormously high HIV risk factor that is believed to outstrip the general population in nearly every African country. The MSM population by and large lives in closets, posing a great challenge for those who wish to reach out to them. PST/TOGO's HIV project for MSM first started with prevention messages through peer education and referrals for HIV testing and counseling. This established trust levels between the target public and the NGO, PSI. Tapping the subgroups within the MSM groups was the next step. Due to cultural factors, many MSM persons, to be accepted by society, do marry and have children. Reaching out to this group who live a "double life" has indeed been a challenge for the NGO.[26]

Reaching out to Farmers Through Community Radio

Small farmers in Nigeria facing rapidly changing climate conditions pose critical challenges to their livelihood. In an effort to respond to this problem the African Radio Drama Association (ARDA), a production and training center, developed in the local language a 26-episode radio show to address the issue. Each issue had a mix of drama and expert knowledge from agricultural extension officers or an experienced local farmer. This helps combat the harsh conditions in the region. The listeners were encouraged to phone in or send text messages to get expert replies on their specific issues.

Responsible Drinking

In the UK, a £100 million campaign in the recent past was launched to encourage responsible drinking. The aim behind the campaign was to aim at reducing public acceptance of drunkenness and shift attitudes in order to reduce excessive consumption for 18–34-year-olds. Former British Prime Minister Gordon Brown met Britain's top alcohol company senior brass to harness their marketing capabilities to drive change in social norm and cultural attitude towards alcohol in the UK. Analysts put it as the highest ever ad spends on responsible drinking campaign. The drive was supported by 45 companies over a period of five years. The tagline "Why let good times go bad?" was seen in various media encompassing outdoors, signs, drink mats, and point-of-purchase (POP) display.[27]

Indian Campaigns: Random

Family Planning Campaign in India

The Indian government has over a period of five decades invested a lot of public money in massive advertising and awareness campaigns. The family planning campaign in India for many decades had the abstract "red triangle" against a yellow background and black lettering. Up to the late 1980s, the campaign spoke of "Do ya teen bus," highlighting an average family size of five members including two or three children. By the 1990s, the message was changed to "Hum do, hamare do," emphasizing the two-child norm. When the campaign earned the dubious reputation following forced sterilization during the Emergency period of 1975–1977, there was a general indignation for any campaign that conveyed family planning message. Politician Lalu Prasad Yadav who has nine children had no hesitation in saying at public forums that one of the reasons for a large family for him was defiance to the political system. His argument was that the government cannot decide on the number of children one would have. In fact, he named his eldest child MISA, who was born during the Emergency (MISA is the acronym for Maintenance of Internal Security Act).

Despite a general apathy with the campaign, the imagery and color scheme came to be associated with the family planning campaign in no uncertain terms. In an interesting evaluation study of the government's various social campaigns in 1992, it was found that when this color combination was used for other themes such as national integration, people reckoned it to family planning campaign without reading the copy in the outdoor media.[28]

James G. Chadney writes that for a campaign to succeed, political will is an imperative. Before Mrs Indira Gandhi became the prime minister in 1965, no systematic effort was made to curb population. Some funds were made available to states to handle family planning and health sector. It was at the initiative of Mrs Gandhi that a Department of Family Planning Services was created at the center. The mandate of the department was to ensure subsidized sale of condoms and encourage sterilization. Gandhi, comments Chadney, failed to continue providing dynamic leadership post Emergency in India during which there were allegations of forced sterilizations under the stewardship of her son Sanjay Gandhi, who incidentally did not hold any official position but represented the Congress party. Her debacle in 1977 General Elections and her resurgence after a couple of years put the family planning program on the back-burner.[29]

The issue in fact has become so contentious that no one wishes to mess up with it. Ironically, it has not been addressed by any government or political party seriously. The way population is multiplying in the country, very soon India would beat its neighbor China in being the most populated country in the world. China incidentally now has a one-child norm.

The then Union Health Minister Gulam Nabi Azad during a function in July 2009 to felicitate couples who married late exhorted people to marry after 30 years of age as the country, he said, was unable to meet the demands of growing population. Despite the legal age of marriage in India being 18 years for girls and 21 years for boys, it was an open secret that 70 percent girls in India are married off at an age as low as 13 years. India has only 2.5 percent of global land but 17 percent of the world population. Analysts comment that India despite the problem in the face has not formulated any comprehensive policy for controlling population in the past three decades, owing to vote politics and social structures.[30]

The GOI has listed the following milestones in its SM Program related to family planning during the past four decades.

1968: SM was launched to distribute contraceptives through six leading consumer goods/oil companies with three lakh outlets, with territories allotted to each. The organizations included Lipton, Brooke Bond, Union Carbide, Hindustan Lever, Indian Tobacco Company, and Tata Oil Mills. Initially, only unlubricated condoms under the name Nirodh were launched.

1977: Introduction of the Trade Bonus Scheme for retailers on purchase of condoms to encourage sale.

1983: Introduction of promotional incentive on sale of condoms to SMOs instead of trade bonus on condoms.

1984: Lubricated Nirodh added on seeing consumer preference and was named Deluxe Nirodh.

1987: A thinner variety, in multiple colors was added in the name Super Deluxe Nirodh.

1987: Oral pills—The SM program was extended to include oral contraceptive pills with the brand name Mala-D.

Initially, four leading pharmaceutical companies started marketing in the areas allocated to them. These were, Parke Davis Ltd., Hoechst India Ltd., Rallis India Ltd., and Day's Medical Stores (Manufacturing) Ltd.

1988: VOs in SMP included Parivar Sewa Sanstha (Marie Stopes), a VO that joined the program and introduced its brand named Sawan and Bliss under condom and Ecroz under oral pills. Another VO, Population Services International, also joined the program and introduced another brand of condom, Masti.

1991: Most of the companies which had active participation and wide outreach withdrew from the SM program.

1991: Another low-priced government brand of condom to meet the need of the poor sections of the society by the name "New Lubricated Nirodh" was added to the program.

1993–1995: Number of organizations, namely, Hindustan Latex Ltd., DKT, Parivar Kalyan Kendra, FPI, etc. joined the program. Since then, following the cafeteria approach SM organizations' brands were introduced in the program. The major prevalent brands under condoms are Zaroor, Mithun, Sawan, Bliss, Milan, Masti, Pick me, Mauj Sangam, Ustad, and Ahsaas. Under oral pills, the major prevalent brands are Choice, Apsara, Ecroz, Pearl, Suvida, Arpan, and Sugam. Besides, these brands are allowed to be marketed by the SMOs on all-India basis as against the government brands (Deluxe Nirodh, Super Deluxe Nirodh, and New Lubricated Nirodh) which are allowed to be marketed in specified territories only.

1994: Revision of sale promotion incentive on condoms; introduction of sale promotion incentive on SMOs' brands of condoms too.

1995: Introduction of Centchroman, a nonsteroidal weekly oral pill under the brand name "Saheli" through HLL under SM; product and promotional subsidy on the sale of Centchroman was also provided.

1996: Introduction of sale promotion incentive on oral pills.

1999: Working group with all SMOs constituted for evolving the SM program strategy. India, despite the problem in the face, has not formulated any comprehensive policy for controlling population in the past three decades. All the political parties that have been in the saddle don't wish to touch the sensitive issue due to electoral politics.

Safe Sex: An NGO's Effort

A youth festival held in New Delhi in February 2009 for creating awareness about HIV and AIDs used a novel tactic that called upon the visitors to drop their views and ideas on the theme: "Can safe sex be sexy?" A kiosk demonstrated female condoms. Annie Philpott, the marketer of the crusade, is the founder of the British *Pleasure Project,* an international education program that promotes safe sex. Speaking to the media, Philpott said, "The whole debate about safe sex has been conducted around fear, danger, disease and death. It is negative-we forget the pursuit of pleasure." The program in India was the outcome of Philpott's experience in promoting safe sex in Sri Lanka, Senegal, and Zimbabwe.

Many youngsters who visited the event said that they could totally relate to the issue.[31]

Stay Negative

AIDS Healthcare Foundation (AHF) launched its Love Condom public service campaign in July 2009 in Delhi. TV actor Ronit Roy kickstarted the campaign in a five star hotel that partnered with the program. Freehivtest.net guides those who visit it on where and how to get a free test done quickly, conveniently. The site has the visual of a semi-nude man with his upper back tattooed Stay Negative. The image is believed to attract tremendous attention resulting in an increased traffic on the AHF Web site. Multinational fast moving consumer goods (FMCG) company Hindustan Unilever has partnered with AHF in the campaign that is aimed at shifting people's attitude around HIV testing. As reported by the media the campaign has brought in public–private partnership to address access to free condoms in tandem with free distribution of condoms by GOI agencies.[32]

Reaching out to High-risk Population

The Maharashtra SM program spanning 2005–2011 has multiple partners supporting the effort that include Hindustan Latex Family Planning Promotion Trust (HLFPPT), Maharashtra State AIDS Control Society, Mumbai District AIDS Control Society, and the Avert project. The overriding goal of the project is to ensure availability and accessibility of high-quality condoms to high-risk groups and people engaged in high-risk behavior. HLFPPT works closely with the Avert project and also coordinates with the Bill and Melinda Gates Foundation project, besides other SM partners, in expanding the program among high-risk groups to avoid duplication of efforts.[33]

Involving Community to Fight HIV/AIDS

In the southern state of Tamil Nadu that has an estimated population of 60 million, of which some 4 million live in the capital, Chennai, community participation paved the way for extensive condom distribution for safe sex. Incidentally, the first case of AIDS in India was reported in Madras (now Chennai) in 1986. Local surveillance systems had shown that HIV infection has risen significantly; for example, rates among pregnant women tripled between 1995 and 1997 to 1.25 percent. Bold safe-sex campaigns, including intensive condom promotion, in Tamil Nadu have resulted in dramatic increases in condom use in risky sexual encounters.[34]

Case Studies: Overseas and India

Educating about HIV and AIDS: The Balbir Pasha Campaign in Maharashtra—An Indian Success Story

"Will Balbir Pasha get AIDS?"—a campaign by the Population Service International (PSI) with financial back-up from the USAIDS created by Lowe, India, is one of the most memorable behavior change campaign on HIV and AIDS in India. The campaign has won quite a few awards. The campaign was however withdrawn for a while, as many women activist groups thought it was insensitive and sexist in approach. The campaign initially ran from November 2002 to February 2003 as a part of an integrated behavior change HIV/AIDS prevention program called Operation Lighthouse (OPL). The project went on from 2002–2005 among 12 major port communities across India.

The bedrock of the campaign according to the implementers was based on the "social learning theory" of Albert Bandura, which posits that people can learn by observing others' behavior. Keeping that in mind, a fictional character Balbir Pasha was created to serve as an "alter ego." The campaign was integrated with support services, helpline, voluntary counseling, and HIV testing services and on-the-ground interpersonal communications. The implementing agency felt that despite criticism from some quarters "for its cutting-edge frankness" impact studies and other data reflected that the campaign had achieved phenomenal reach. Those exposed to the campaign became more knowledgeable about the syndrome, understanding risk and attitude change.[35]

The first of the theme television ad was set in a bar where two friends were shown chatting under the influence of liquor. "Balbir Pasha ko AIDS hoga kya?" (Did Balbir get AIDS?), one asked out of the blue. The other told him, "Tere jaisa rahenga toh hoenga" (Yes, if he behaved the way he did.). He then explained that if Balbir Pasha visited a sex worker under the influence of alcohol and forgot using a condom, he could be at risk. Again, in the "porter" ad, a laborer asked another guy the same question, who did not think it was a possibility because Balbir Pasha visited a "regular." That is when the first guy informed that just because Pasha was seeing a regular did not mean the woman was not seeing clients other than Pasha. The third commercial addressed the "looks healthy" argument. All the three ads were direct, stark, and left no room for ambiguity.[36]

The Balbir Pasha campaign was based on the following consumer insights:

Key Insights

Data carried out by both NACO and Maharashtra AIDS Control Society amply revealed that despite the fact that men in the general population felt that the clients of commercial sex workers were vulnerable to HIV/AIDS, they failed to recognize themselves at risk. The data also pointed out a strong link between alcohol consumption and high-risk sexual activity. The various studies also indicated that young men harbored negative attitude towards condom use and failure to recognize asymptomatic "healthy looking" people as possible carriers of HIV infection. Keeping the above insights, ("I often use condom, but when I get drunk, I sometimes forget"; "I only have sex with this one person and hence I am safe"; and "If a person looks healthy, he/she must be safe from HIV/AIDS"), the campaign team developed the campaign on these three themes that were pretested on a sample group.[37]

Some of the headlines of press and outdoor advertising were as follows:

1. Stage I: Building Intrigue
   Balbir Pasha ko AIDS hoga Kya (Will Balbir Pasha Get AIDS)? (The teaser campaign was aimed at building curiosity and cutting through the clutter in the chosen media).
2. Stage II: Use of Strategy and Leveraging Key Insights
   - *Theme 1: Balbir pasha sharab ke nashe mein condom pehnana bhul jata hoga* (Balbir Pasha sometimes forgets to use condoms when he is drunk). Here, the obvious question in the minds of people was: "By not wearing condom just one time, it is possible to get AIDS. Will Balbir Pasha Get AIDS?"
   - *Theme 2: Balbir Pasha sirf Manjula ke paas jata hai* (Balbir Pasha only goes to Manjula). The inference here was that others also went to Manjula. Will Balbir Pasha Get AIDS?
   - *Theme 3: Balbir Pasha sirf swasth dikhnewalo se sambandh rakhta hai. Par dekhne se pata nahin chalta kise AIDS hai* (Balbir Pasha has relationships with only healthy-looking people. But you cannot tell by looking who has AIDS). Will Balbir Pasha Get AIDS?

For encouraging people to use helpline: SADHAN 2389 4371, the copy used was "Mujhe Balbir Pasha nahin banana. Kya karoo?" (I don't want to be like Balbir Pasha. What should I do?)

The choice of media was made carefully and strategically.

1. Outdoor communication in red-light area: The campaign achieved high visibility as the bill boards and bus shelters in this area were exposed to those who visited sex workers.
2. Outdoor communication and public transport: More than 4 million people in Mumbai commute in local trains. By placing posters in trains and railway stations, it allowed the program implementer to not only target the desire TA but also create the necessary buzz among people.

3. Cinema halls: Ads and slides were projected during popular Hindi and Marathi cinema thus capturing a captive audience.
4. TV and radio: By placing ads in various programs and many channels, the campaign ensured reach among various socioeconomic segments.
5. Print media: The campaign was featured in prominent language newspapers in Hindi and Marathi.

The campaign was widely covered in the mainstream media that also gave it a wider publicity.

Impact of Balbir Pasha Campaign

In an impact study that included 1,500 interviews focused on awareness, attitude and behavior change, and street intercepts focused on men visiting commercial sex workers, some interesting insights emerged. Some highlights:

- 25 percent recalled Balbir Pasha spontaneously.
- 88 percent found Balbir's story believable.
- 54 percent discussed Balbir Pasha with somebody else.
- 28 percent recalled the name of PSI's confidential *Saadhan* HIV/AIDS helpline.
- 250 percent increase in number of calls to PSI's *Saadhan* HIV/AIDS hotline.
- Over half recalled condom usage as the main message of the campaign.
- Over a third stated that one should not engage in sexual intercourse with nonregular partners without a condom.
- The percentage of those who believed that using condoms all the time reduces HIV/AIDS risk increased from 80 to 86 percent.
- Retail sales of condoms in the red-light district tripled after the launch of the campaign.

Criticism

- Some criticized its frankness—"bringing the bedroom into the living room."

- Some thought it "anti-women" because of the implication that HIV is passed on from women to men.
- Others felt it only focused heterosexual transmission; it did not address the behavior of men having sex with men, intravenous drug use, or prenatal HIV testing.[38]

An SM campaign aims at changing the perception or attitudes of people on something they may have believed or practiced for long. Since it generally has to do with their personal or social behavior, it is difficult if not impossible to break ice as may be possible in commercial marketing.

The question is why people do not change when the change is in their own interest.

Many research studies indicate that mass communication may not necessarily be effective in bringing about change. When the United Nations was set up, despite an aggressive mass media campaign, not many people knew about it for long.[39]

In the developing world the myth was exploded when many research studies reflected that despite the reach of the mass media which exposed them to various campaigns, people when asked about the facilitator of change rarely pointed to mass media. Interpersonal channels, peer influence dominated their reason of behavior change. Evart Rogers points out that the possible reason of this anomaly could lie in the contents of the media messages which seldom carried information on where to obtain it, at what cost, and how to use it.[40]

Hyman and Sheatsley opine that this happens due to the following reasons:

1. There are people who cannot be reached through mass media.
2. If the people are not interested in an issue, they would not access information.
3. There is the likelihood of an individual being receptive if there is a compatibility of information with her/his prior attitudes. If the information is conflicting, they would avoid paying heed to it.
4. People would interpret information according to their beliefs and value systems.[41]

Future of Social Advertising in India

The over ₹55,000 crore advertising industry, many believe, may perk up with development sector ads both from the center and the states. The agencies are readying themselves to pitch for social campaigns as reported by the media. Another trend witnessed has been the advocacy campaigns by the corporate sector. Through such campaigns, the objective invariably is to make its critical stakeholder believe in their social responsibility. In early 2010, one found the mobile phone operator Aircel associating itself with World Wildlife Fund in its *Save the Tiger* Campaign. The campaign has the Aircel brand ambassador cricketer M.S. Dhoni espousing the cause, besides football player Baichung Bhutia and others. The series of ads also had a TVC that showed a two-month-old tiger cub in its habitat looking restless, waiting for its mother. The TVC in Hindi and English voiced over the necessary emotion with the copy: *Sirf do mahine ka; akela, asahay, bhukha, pyasa—na jaane kaab lautegi isski ma—jaane lautegi bhi ya nahin, when one hears the gunshot* (He is just two month old; he is hungry, scared; he is wondering when his mother is coming back. May be she is not). And this is followed by the sound of gun shot in the background. There are only 1411 tigers left in India. Speak up; blog; share concern. Every little bit helps in saving our tiger.

The ad resulted in immense response from the public. Over 1 lakh spoke up on social networking sites, "a movement that looks ready, with nowhere to go."[42]

Some of the key players in social sector advertising include Lowe India, which through its decade-old social communication cell is helping corporate India develop its CSR strategy. Leo Burnett India is scouting for professionals to add muscle to its social advertising wing; "Leo Hope" is positioning itself with a strong NGO focus. Dentsu India too has recently launched "Citizen Dentsu," its new division for social communications. DDB Mudra Communications has launched DDB Remedy to strengthen its SM wing, especially in the health arena.

Ad agencies are going all out to woo Indian corporates, government, and semi-government clients to build their SM campaigns. According to Arvind Sharma, managing director of Leo Burnett India,

Social advertising requires different orientation as compared to commercial advertising. The key challenge for us is to find the right people to handle clients' social marketing campaigns. Thus, we are looking for talented professionals to add value to our offerings. We are looking at a number of projects with relevant NGOs too.

There is a general perception that SM is not a profitable sector. People are there for goodness sake. There may be some truism in this, but according Philip Harve, many have made fortunes out of the SM sector. In his insightful article in the *Social Marketing Quarterly* he has referred to the cases of countries such as Ethiopia, Brazil, Vietnam, and India. SM, he writes, is a business proposition for many especially when it involves a tangible product, say condoms. The marketers, he writes, in many African, Asian, and Latin American countries have made fortunes marketing condoms to communities. Similarly, business organizations such as advertising agencies, market research firms, production companies, and packaging and distribution companies also benefit.[43]

In the Indian context, Harvey comments, a country with a more sophisticated economic model when compared with countries in Africa, Vietnam, Ethiopia, or Brazil a few decades ago, SM provided enormous income to media. The mainstream media carried large ads especially on family planning for years. Doordarshan and All India Radio also spearheaded the campaign for decades. In the rural hinterland, advertising was carried on bill boards, wall paintings, and through interpersonal communication. Advertising agencies were thus great beneficiaries. Similarly, market research firms such as the Organization Research Bureau (ORG) and Indian Marketing Research Bureau (IMRB) made fortunes. Ancillary industries such as transport, printing, and packaging also benefited tremendously from SM.[44]

When Doordarshan had the monopoly, it was not uncommon for social marketers to get subsidized rates to carry out their ads. All has changed with the proliferation of media. The marketers do not get any special rates from hundreds of channels. However, it is also a fact that some of the mainstream channels and the print media do give time and space for social campaigns spearheaded by them. Star Care is one such example.

Notes and References

1. G. D. Weibe, "Merchandising Commodities and Citizenship on Television," *Public Opinion Quarterly* 15, winter (1951–52): 679–689.
2. P. Kotler and G. Zaltman, "Social Marketing: An Approach to Planned Social Change," *Journal of Marketing* 35: 3–12.
3. Kilter and Zaltman, "Social Marketing: An Approach to Planned Social Change," 3–12.
4. P. Kotler, *Marketing for Non-profit Organizations* (Engle Wood Cliffs, NJ: Prentice Hall, 1982), 528.
5. Philip Kotler, Nancy R. Lee, and M.L. Rothschild, "Marketing: An Approach to Social Change" *Journal of Marketing* 35 (July 1971): 3–12.
6. A. R. Andreasen, *Marketing Social Change: Changing Behavior to Promote Health, Social Development and Environment* (Jossey Bass, 1995), quoted in Robert J Donovan's "Role of marketing public health change programs," http://australianreview.net/journal/v10/n1/donovan.pdf (accessed on November 4, 2015).
7. Philip Kotler and Eduardo L. Roberto, *Social Marketing: Strategies for Changing Public Behavior* (London: The Free Press, 1989): 13 and 16.
8. Ibid.
9. http://adage.com/article/btob/american-marketing-association-releases-definition-marketing/270184/ (accessed on December 2, 2015).
10. http://www.kotlermarketing.com/phil_questions.shtml (accessed on November 2, 2015).
11. Kotler and Roberto, *Social Marketing: Strategies for Changing Public Behavior*, 140.
12. Sharon Fernandes, http://archive.indianexpress.com/news/morningafter-pill-prescription-drug--govt-panel-to-examine/525651 (accessed on February 12, 2016).
13. Ibid.
14. Ibid.
15. Kotler and Roberto, *Social Marketing: Strategies for Changing Public Behavior*, 143–144.
16. www.psp-one.com
17. The campaign was shared at the International Training Institute in NSW, when the present author went there to study on a fellowship.
18. A student's research at IIMC revealed that the various kinds of viewers including students, bureaucrats, communication experts, politicians, and common men and women feel a rush of adrenalin and a great sense of pride about India after watching it.
19. The documentary was telecast on Delhi Doordarshan in its special program on December 19 at 7.30. p.m.
20. http://www.scribd.com/doc/268338322/Development-Communication-Source-Book#scribd (accessed on February 14, 2016).
21. E. Rogers, *Diffusion of Innovations* (4th ed.) (New York: Free Press, 1995): 17–20.
22. Kotler, *Marketing for Non-profit Organizations*, 161–162.
23. The present author was the lead consultant for the study that also suggests the public sector organization the communication strategy to tackle the issue, given that the various issues identified were managed before that.
24. Weibe, "Merchandising Commodities and Citizenship on Television," 679–689.
25. Condom Social Marketing: Selected Case Studies—Source: http://www.unaids.org (accessed on December 7, 2015).
26. Ben Clapham, a blogger who manages PSI/TOGO's MSM program.

27. www.medicalnewstoday.com (accessed on November 27, 2015).
28. The study was conducted by the Indian Institute of Mass Communication during the Ardh Kumbh fair in 1992 at the holy of Hardwar that is said to have attracted about 40 lakh devotees. The government had put in place a huge media blitzkrieg to inform the people of its welfare schemes besides economic liberalization that had just begun when the Congress-led government won the elections. Incidentally, the campaign on the economic liberalization was recalled the least.
29. James G. Chadney, "Family Planning: India's Achilles' Heel?" *Journal of Asian & African Studies* 22, Nos. 3–4 (1987): 218–231.
30. www.thenational.ac
31. Rama Lakshmi at Indian Youth Festival on Safe-Sex Practices, "Focus Is on Pleasure Principle," Washington Post Foreign Service, Monday, March 2, 2009 http://www.washingtonpost.com/wp-dyn/content/article/2009/03/01/AR2009030101705.html (accessed on February 15, 2016).
32. www.businesswire.com (accessed on November 23, 2015)
33. www.usaid.gov (accessed on November 23, 2015).
34. http://www.unaids.org (accessed on November 23, 2015).
35. http://www.afaqs.com/news/story/5209_Lowe-makes-Balbir-Pasha-a-conversation-point-on-AIDSandhttp://www.psi.org/wp-content/uploads/drupal/sites/default/files/publication_files/balbir-pasha.pdf (accessed on February 15, 2016).
36. http://www.afaqs.com/news/story/5209_Lowe-makes-Balbir-Pasha-a-conversation-point-on-AIDS (accessed on November 23, 2015).
37. http://www.afaqs.com/news/story/5209_Lowe-makes-Balbir-Pasha-a-conversation-point-on-AIDS and http://www.afaqs.com/news/story/5209_Lowe-makes-Balbir-Pasha-a-conversation-point-on-AIDS (accessed on November 23, 2015).
38. Ibid.
39. Kotler and Roberto, *Social Marketing: Strategies for Changing Public Behavior*, 7.
40. E. M. Rogers, ed., *Communication and Development—Critical Perspectives* (London: SAGE, 1976), 136.
41. Herbert H. Hyman and Paul B. Sheatsley, "Some Reasons Why Information Campaigns Fail," *Public Opinion Quarterly* 11, No. 2 (1947): 412–423 in Kotler and Roberto (1989).
42. Anuradha Verma, "Ads That Sell, But Care," *Times Life*, *The Times of India*, February 21, 2010, 3.
43. Philip D. Harvey, "Making Money Saving Lives: Social Marketing Spurs the Private Sector Overseas." *The Social Marketing Quarterly* VI, No. 4 (December 2000): 17–20.
44. Ibid.

3

Corporate Social Responsibility

Introduction

The new buzz word, Corporate Social Responsibility (CSR), has fast gained currency in boardroom talks, though not necessarily for the right reasons, especially in India, after it became mandatory for the public sector to spend a designated amount from its revenue on CSR, and later the Companies Act 2013 that expects the private sector to spend on the social sector. Although it is not mandatory, corporate honchos, in whispers, are making no bones about what would be the possible future directions in this regard. Although the noncompliance may not be questioned, the companies are expected to give reasons for not spending on the social sector, which the analysts feel makes it de facto mandatory.

Traditionally, the concept of CSR implied what the corporates gave back voluntarily to society as an act of charity, philanthropy, or as being a responsible corporate citizen. The word responsibility meant that the giver must identify the task that it was supposed to be responsible about. In other words, the act of CSR needed to be preceded by a thorough audit of the stakeholder needs that called for social intervention.

Defining CSR

Mallen Baker refers to CSR as "a way companies manage the business process to produce an overall positive impact on society."[1]

Archie Caroll describes CSR as a multilayered concept that can be differentiated into four interrelated aspects, namely, *economic responsibility, legal responsibility, ethical responsibility, and philanthropic responsibility.* At the bottom of the pyramid is the economic responsibility, followed by legal and ethical responsibility. At the top of the pyramid is philanthropic responsibility.[2]

The World Bank has defined CSR as operating a business in a manner that meets or exceeds the ethical, legal, commercial, and public expectations that society has of business. Leadership companies see CSR as more than a collection of discrete practices or occasional gestures, or initiatives motivated by marketing, public relations or other business benefits. Rather, it is viewed as a comprehensive set of policies, practices, and programs that are integrated throughout business operations and decision-making processes that are supported and rewarded by top management.[3]

The World Business Council for Sustainable Development in its publication *Making Good Business Sense* by Lord Holmes and Richard Watts uses the following definition: "Corporate Social Responsibility is the continuing commitment by business to behave ethically and contribute to economic development while improving the quality of life of the workforce and their families as well as of the local community and society at large."[4]

Prime Minister Narendra Modi, in his first Independence Day address to the nation from the ramparts of the historic Red Fort on August 15, 2014, exhorted the corporate sector to invest under their CSR budgets on constructing toilets in schools. To quote him:

> I call upon the corporate sector also to give priority to the provision of toilets in schools with your expenditure under CSR. This target should be finished within one year with the help of state governments and on the next August 15, we should be in a firm position to announce that there is no school in India without separate toilets for boys and girls.[5]

In his second speech on August 15, 2015, he announced that in a year's time 400,000 toilets have been constructed for girls in schools.[6]

In a two-day summit organized by Birla Institute of Management Technology (BIMTECH) in collaboration with *The Economic Times* and other corporate organizations in April 2010, some very out-of-the-box ideas came forth on what really should constitute CSR.

One of the speakers, T.K. Arun, the then editor of *The Economic Times* brought out an interesting dimension to the debate on CSR. To quote him: "Would building schools and hospitals in the neighborhood be charity or CSR? In India's predominately rural landscape, a large enterprise often has to build the urban environment in which alone it can operate, often taking over rural land and displacing the occupants." He further said:

> Thanks to India's competitive polity and the Narmada Bachao Andolan's signal contribution of making project displacement a central political issue, such town-building can prove unsustainable due to popular opposition, as happened in Singur. In such a situation, building schools and hospitals and training youth drawn from the displaced local populace to become workers in the enterprise all cease to be charity, but integral to the working of the project. Actions that are conventionally classified as charity become CSR in India.

CSR is a value-loaded term and may mean different things to different people and organizations. Marketing the cheapest car in the world, the Nano, was seen as an act of social responsibility by the Tata Group. The group chairman believed that this would help the lower income strata to partake the pleasure of a risk-free ride when compared to riding a two wheeler. Before marketing its soaps in rural India, Hindustan Unilever educated the rural folk about the gains of personal hygiene and cleanliness. Its Swasthya Chetna Divas (Health Education Day) was considered by the company a step toward its social responsibility. It is a different matter that the company does earn profit selling its basic brand in soap category— Lifebuoy. The Tata Group announced the launch of Swach (pure) water filter brand in December 2009 to address the issue of clean drinking water in India to combat waterborne diseases. The price of the said water filter is ₹1,000 and the gadget would not need electricity support. There are already a few brands in the category, one from its own flagship company namely the Aquaguard and HUL's brand Pureit.

While announcing Swach, Ratan Tata, the Group Chairman, was quoted by the media as saying, "The social cost of water contamination is already enormous and increases every year. I hope it (Swach) makes a mark in deterring the diseases."[7]

Genesis of CSR

CSR's roots can be traced to all religions that exhort people to share their fortunes with the less privileged ones. It is not uncommon to find many business houses giving charities to various trusts and organizations. Many believe that when in 1790s England witnessed the first large-scale consumer boycott over the issue of slave-harvested sugar which finally forced the importer to have free labor sourcing, the foundation of CSR was laid.

Ida Tarbell's 1904 book, *The History of the Standard Oil Company* (Rockefellers), helped leading to the decision of the Supreme Court of the USA to break up the company on antitrust grounds. Similarly, Upton Sinclair's 1906 book, *The Jungle*, led to the passage of the Pure Food and Drugs Act and the Meat Inspection Act by the US Congress. These can be seen as early attempts to mandate socially responsible corporate behavior.

It is widely believed that in the context of the Indian industrial sector, the Tata Iron and Steel Company (TISCO), set up in 1907 in Jamshedpur, was the precursor of CSR when it initiated community outreach around its plant through initiatives in the areas of income generation, health care, and education. In a period of a century, more than 600 villages have been covered under CSR by TISCO.[8]

The term CSR came in common use in the 1970s. By the 1990s the concept was fully recognized. As per research, in 1977, less than half of the 500 fortune companies mentioned the term CSR in their annual reports, but around 1990, 90 percent companies in the Fortune 500 list reflected CSR and their goals in their annual reports.[9]

In the 1990s, one saw a growing concern about the ways the multinational companies did business, especially when they engaged cheap labor in poor developing countries. The issue came on the international agenda. NGOs were the main protagonists against the violation of human rights by some of the companies.

Besides the United Nations, a number of intergovernmental organizations (IGOs) have started to address the issue; among these, the European Union (EU), the United Nations Industrial Development Organization (UNIDO), the United Nations Development Program (UNDP), the United Nations Commission of Human Rights (UNCHR), and the World Bank are some which are now part of the United Nations

Global Compact. The UN Global Compact developed out of the well-known call upon business made in 1999 at the World Economic Forum by the UN General Secretary Kofi Annan to take action in this area.

An important international initiative was recently taken by the International Standardization Organization (ISO) to develop standards for social responsibility under the name of ISO-2600, covering not only corporations but also all organizations. The UN Global Compact and ISO confirm the increasing importance of CSR internationally, and at the same time, give legitimacy to CSR.[10]

The box below reflects some such conventions and codes.

Various global codes and standards of CSR

Various national and international bodies, from time to time, have evolved codes of conduct for best business practices. Following codes, principles, standards, etc. addresses a broad spectrum of CSR and sustainable development.

1. **Universal Declaration of Human Rights**
   - Adopted by the United Nations, this declaration paved the way for many international human rights standards for all sectors and entities.
2. **UN Global Compact**
   - An international multi-constituent, voluntary initiative based on internationally accepted 10 principles in pursuit of a more sustainable inclusive global economy
   - Provides a framework for invocation, creativity, best practices
   - Assist companies incorporating a greater level of social responsibility in their operations
   - Not a substitute for regulatory structure
   - The 10 principles, to be integrated in own business operations and broader spectrum impacted by their business
   - The 10 principles cover human rights, forced labor, child labor, environmental challenges and responsibility, nondiscrimination, freedom of associations, collective bargaining, corruption, etc.
3. **Global Reporting Initiative (GRI)**
   - Established for developing globally applicable guidelines for reporting on the economic, environmental, and social performance of any business
   - Its Sustainability Reporting Guidelines provide a reporting standard, which enable
   - companies to enhance the quality of their reports
4. **The Global Sullivan Principles**
   - The principles consist of eight single-sentence value statements that address a range of human rights-related issues
   - The principles encourage companies to support economic, social, and political justice wherever they do business

---

(continued)

(continued)

5. **Benchmarks for CSR**
   - Drafted for measuring business performance in response to globalization of economy and growth of transnational corporations
   - It offers 100 principles, outlining philosophies to ensure responsible company actions, 129 criteria, relating to company's commitment to implement improved corporate performance, which develops relevant policies and practice, and 118 benchmarks to assist companies about responsible corporate behavior.

6. **OECD Guidelines for Multinational Enterprises**
   - This Organisation for Economic Co-operation and Development (OECD) guidelines contain recommendations on core labor, environmental standards, human rights, competition, taxation, and science and technology for combating corruption and safeguarding consumer rights.
   - Encourages responsible business practices, strengthens relationship between government and multinational enterprises, enhance contribution of multinational enterprises to sustainable development, and plays a prominent role in fostering good governance in the public and in corporate activity.

7. **Social Accountability 8000**
   - A code-of-conduct verification and factory certification program
   - Specifies requirement for social accountability to enable a company to develop, maintain, and enforce policies and procedures in order to manage those issues which it can influence or control
   - Covers standards and monitoring programs for child labor, forced labor, disciplinary practices, nondiscrimination, wages and benefits, working hours, health and safety, freedom of associations, collective bargaining and management system, etc.
   - Applies regardless of geographic locations, industry sector, or company size
   - The standard is maintained by Social Accountability International

8. **Principles for Responsible Investment (PRI)**
   - A set of global best practice principles for responsible investment
   - Provide a framework for achieving better long-term investment returns and more sustainable markets
   - The six voluntary principles are underpinned by a set of 35 possible actions that institutional investors can take to integrate environmental, social, and corporate governance considerations into their investment activities.

9. **Asia–Pacific Cooperation**
   - Asia–Pacific Economic Cooperation, APEC, is an international organization for economic cooperation among the Pacific Rim countries.
   - The code is an inspirational standard that draws significantly on a variety of internationally recognized codes and standards.
   - The code addresses policy recommendations to APEC country governments.

10. **Role of ILO**
    - ILO seeks the promotion of social justice and internationally recognized human and labor rights and formulates international labor standards.

Source: https://www.pwc.in/assets/pdfs/publications/2013/handbook-on-corporate-social-responsibility-in-india.pdf (accessed on February 15, 2016).

Theoretical Underpinning of CSR

Bryane Michael refers to three schools of practice in CSR, namely, the neoliberal school, the state-led school, and the "third-way" school. Let us look at how these schools look at CSR.

The Neoliberal School: The assumption in this line of thinking posits that the adoption of CSR policies by business is rational and profitable in the long run. CSR here is seen as a larger branding strategy. Engaging CSR programs, marketing them, and auditing them is expected to result in creating respect and equity for such organizations. Therefore, it attracts demand from those market segments that wish to do business with socially sensitized companies. Some empirical studies suggest that people prefer to buy products from the company that they perceive as socially responsible and ethical.[11]

State-centered School: Advocates of this school believe that when there is intervention from the policy-makers, people benefit. International bodies such the World Bank, the UN, and EU have been playing an active role in promoting CSR. Companies, especially those that are large and international, have been seen signing many international protocols so that these are seen as benchmarks by employees and clients.

The Third-way School: Some scholars see the third sector, meaning the civil society organizations (CSOs) and the NGOs as the real motor of CSR. Given the overall presence of NGOs and CSOs in CSR programs of the companies reflects the changing times and expectations.

What to Communicate about CSR

There are at least two schools of thought on what to communicate about CSR to the stakeholders. While one school feels that CSR like philanthropy needs to be undertaken without shouting from the rooftop on what the company has done. This, the protagonists feel would eliminate the commercialization or taking credit for what the companies are supposed to do anyways. The other school believes that doing good and not talking about it will deprive the company of earning good name and may also keep the right holders ignorant about what benefits accrue to them via the CSR activities. There is not much empirical research available on the impact of CSR communication on the brand equity or reputation of an organization. Kim and Ferguson argue that "measuring effective CSR communication should be distinguished from the measurement of effective CSR activities."[12]

In their research study the authors examined the consumer-public's expectations from companies' CSR communication through surveying a representative sample of the general public. One of the insights gathered was that the public wished to know "who is benefiting from the company's CSR more than any other CSR information." The beneficiaries were seen as the most preferred communication sources, whereas CEOs and public relations spokespersons were listed as the least preferred sources. As CSR communication channels, consumer-publics tended to prefer company-controlled media such as company websites, local stores, and promotion events to uncontrolled media channels such as newspapers, news channels, expert blogs, and microblogs.[13]

Interestingly, Kim and Ferguson's research study suggested that television commercials and print advertisements ranked higher than blogs and microblogs of experts and friends; on the other hand, research conducted in 2005 by Schlegelmilch and Pollach and, in 1998, by Webb and Mohr suggested that advertising was not seen as an effective communication channel for CSR communication due to public's skepticism and low credibility.[14]

Deconstructing CSR Publicity: Random Glimpses

There cannot be two views about the fact that companies through their CSR acts aim at gaining public support, especially those that find themselves in the eye of storm due to varying reasons. The Internet is replete with umpteen examples of companies uploading their CSR videos, sustainability reports, and activities undertaken by the foundations created by them for CSR work.

Let us critically look at the CSR content of a few well-known companies.

Coca-Cola: One of the most admired company globally, Coca-Cola, has been mired in controversies from the time of its reentry in India in 1993 on allegations of reducing the water level of states where it has its plants, pesticides in its aerated drinks, to writing promotional messages on age-old rocks. The company's CSR policy revolves around water harvesting and restoring ground water. The videos on the Internet reflect the work it is doing. Coca-Cola also uses magazine advertising on its CSR work through the testimonial route.

The company, in 2008, published its first environment report on operations in India which covered its activities from 2004–2007. The company has set up Coca-Cola Foundation called *Anandana* which works with local communities and NGOs to address the issue of local water problems. To quote from the Anandana website: "Wherever possible, the Anandana Foundation will seek to ensure project execution, maintenance, and sustainability through the active involvement and direct participation of the beneficiary community at the grass-root level."[15] Coca-Cola publishes an annual water report, besides a sustainability report, which is available on the Internet. In short, the company mostly uses digital media to reflect its CSR work.

PepsiCo: Rival PepsiCo's perception issues are not very different from Coca-Cola's. The company has set PepsiCo Foundation, which reflects the CSR work by the company. It claims to have spent USD 11 million between 2008 and 2010 and benefitted 300,000 people in nine Indian states. The communication reflects the scale of CSR coverage. Its Save the Children—a community-based intervention to deliver integrated health and nutrition solutions to children under the age of five years including young mothers—reaches one lakh people in Rajasthan. The PepsiCo Foundation page also shares information about its project More Crop Per Drop which talks of mitigating water scarcity through water harvesting. Its "water.org" works as a "catalyst to introduce micro finance to the water and sanitation sector and provide households water connections and constructs toilets." The benefits reach out to 150,000 people in the three southern states of Tamil Nadu, Karnataka, and Andhra Pradesh, besides Odisha and Maharashtra. Its annual report also available on the Internet has input on its sustainability work. To quote from its annual report: "PepsiCo was named as one of the world's most ethical company by Ethisphere for the eighth consecutive year."[16]

Interestingly, the PepsiCo Foundation site has a continuously running scroll at the bottom of the screen showcasing its product line. The idea behind this, of course, is aimed at creating brand awareness, but whether it is the best thing to do on its supposedly CSR page is a moot point.

Vedanta: Vedanta Resources is a global company into metals and mining, headquartered in London. The company was founded in Mumbai, India, in 2008 by Mr Anil Agarwal. Its product rage includes copper, zinc, aluminium, iron ore, oil and gas, etc. The company has often found itself in myriad controversies and public interest litigations against human rights violations, including from Amnesty International. The Dongaria Kondh tribes in The Niyamgiri Hills of Odisha under the aegis of Niyamgiri Surkasha Samiti have been fighting for their right to survival and have refused to part with their forests and land required for the bauxite mining operations of the company. "There's no emotion, no politics, no prejudice," the environment minister of the erstwhile UPA government Jairam Ramesh said as he announced in August 2010 that Vedanta would not be allowed to mine in the Niyamgiri Hills of the eastern Odisha state. "I have taken this decision purely on a legal approach—laws are being violated."[17] Later, in 2014, more than four months after the Gram Sabhas of tribal villages in Odisha's Niyamgiri Hills rejected multinational company Vedanta's proposal to undertake bauxite mining in the area, the Ministry of Environment and Forests (MoEF) put a final "No" to the project. The agitation has seen various political parties getting embroiled in it. After the MoEF decision, Odisha Steel and Mines Minister R.K. Singh was quoted saying: "It is unfortunate that the UPA government is doing politics at the cost of development. We condemn the Center for rejection of the mining proposal at Niyamgiri hills."[18]

The company on its website, vedantaalmunium.co, says:

Vedanta Limited (VL) is a socially responsible corporate that aspires to transform the lives of people surrounding its plant site. VL firmly believes in making the local people a participant in the growth process of the organisation and works as a facilitator of socio-economic transformation of rural parts of Orissa. In accordance with the firm's social objectives, VL has launched several projects for sustained socio-economic and cultural development of local communities adjoining the plant site. It has launched several projects for sustained socio-economic and cultural development of local communities adjoining the plant site. Mid-day meals for school going children, establishment of Anganwadi centers (pre-schools) and health camps among others have recorded growing success.

In one of its over-a-minute-long film *Creating Happiness* the company has used the story telling device through the life of a little girl Binno and her family whose "dreams are being fulfilled one by one (unke eke ek sapano ko hamn saakar kar rahe heon)." The narrator says Binno is going to school while her parents never went; her brothers have toys and electricity, which their parents never had, etc., thus reinforcing how the company is helping in turning around the lives of children like Binno around the project area. Slickly made, the film looks more promotional and top-down in approach rather than being empathetic or reflecting the right holder's perspective.

The largest Public Sector Enterprise in India, the Oil & Natural Gas Corporation has a webpage ongcindia.com that reflects the company's CSR policy. To quote:

> Our CSR activities are essentially guided by project based approach in line with the guidelines issued by the Department of Public Enterprises and Ministry of Corporate Affairs of the Government of India. The CSR initiatives of ONGC were marked by unrelenting commitment to several large-scale key projects as well as initiation of several new projects identified under the 12 focus areas of ONGC, i.e., Education including vocational courses, Health Care, Entrepreneurship (self-help & livelihood generation) schemes, Infrastructure support near ONGC operational areas, Environment protection, ecological conservation, promotion, Protection of heritage sites, UNESCO heritage monuments etc. Promotion of artisans, craftsman, musicians, artists etc. for preservation of heritage, Art & Culture.

In its video uploaded on You Tube, the two-minute film talks about its project Unnati (progress) in village Beri that supposedly was chosen by it for CSR activities. Professionally produced, the video is directed in documentary style with the narrator giving the commentary without any connect with people from the village about which the story of transformation is being talked about.

As we have seen above through the content analyzes of a few CSR communications, it is evident that the aim of such communications is to generate positive publicity for the company and mostly aimed at the opinion makers. This is an area that needs empirical research, especially for the fact that CSR has become mandatory for public sector undertakings and as said above the private sector is also expected to adopt CSR policies.

Why Do Companies Spend on CSR?

Companies invest in CSR for varying reasons. Some aim at managing their risk, some have their eye on the future recruits, some would like to build brand equity around their products, some do it to circumvent tax, while others do it to position themselves differently from competitors. There are also several others who do it because they believe that it is the right thing to do.

Is CSR pure charity, an act of good citizenship, or an exercise in brand building and gaining positive media mileage? These are some of the contentious issues surrounding CSR. In fact, looking at the scale of CSR, one expert was quoted by media, talking of CSR as an independent business vertical. Some MBA courses in India now offer specialization in CSR.

Who should be in charge of CSR in a company: a professional with social work background or marketing, HR, or PR professional? Analysts believe that it is the positioning of CSR within the organization that would decide what aims the CSR would pursue. The marketing and PR people, they fear, would have business and image goals for CSR. They would use CSR achievements to for brand promotion and creating positive buzz in the media. The HR person would be driven by rules and procedures, sometimes at the cost of the beneficiaries. It will help if people with social work background are put in the CSR department.

There is a growing feeling among scholars that employees need to be involved in CSR work. This works in multiple ways. One, the employees tend to respect the company that they see as socially responsible, hence, more loyalty toward it; two, if they are allowed to be involved in CSR work by way of contributing a part of their earning or devoting time in doing CSR within the company or their favorite NGO/VO, they get a sense of self-worth and feeling of pride in the company that they work for.

CSR Culture Catching Up in India

India has been named among the top 10 Asian countries paying increasing importance to CSR disclosure norms. India was ranked fourth in the list according to social enterprise CSR Asia's Asian Sustainability Ranking (ASR), released in October 2009. The 2010 list of Forbes Asia's "48 Heroes of Philanthropy" included four Indians. The 2009 list also featured four Indians.

As per *The Times of India* and TNS survey conducted in 2008, in which 100 companies were included that encompassed 11 PSEs, 39 private national companies, and 32 private multinational companies, education and health seemed the most popular areas of CSR activities amongst a majority of companies surveyed.

The Tata Group emerged as the topmost company with active CSR initiative at 68 percent, followed by Infosys at a distant 14 percent, ITC at 12 percent, NTPC at 11 percent, Anil Dhirubhai Ambani Reliance (ADAR) at 10 percent, Ambuja at 9 percent, Microsoft at 7 percent, and WIPRO, and NILT at 6 percent each.

The research also threw some interesting insights on the reasons for which CSR activities were undertaken by various companies. Many undertook CSR to improve the public perception of the company, others did it to position the company in a certain manner. Two-fifth respondent companies said they undertook CSR to save on tax and another one-tenth did so because it was mandatory.

Over the years it has been seen that many donor organizations, including the UN, have transferred funds to NGO partners and not to state players in development projects, in the belief that there would be less bureaucracy and efficient functioning of schemes at grassroots level.

In an empirical research undertaken in 2013–2014, researchers Shachi Rai and Sangeeta Bansal found that 34 percent of the top 300 firms in India work through own foundations or trusts in areas broadly encompassing community outreach and rural development, etc. About 19 percent of the firms organized free medical check-up camps in rural areas, blood donation camps, and educational camps for farmers in the rural areas and school children. Around 30 percent of the firms collaborated with non-profit organizations to carry out their CSR activities. For example, some companies such as TVS motors and Godrej funded the NGO Smile Train to conduct cleft lip and palate surgeries.

Similarly, Tata Motors collaborated with a number of industrial training institutes to conduct skill development programs. Some firms collaborated with government schools and supported the mid-day meal programs. Around 5 percent of the firms adopted environmentally sustainable methods of production. These firms belong mostly to the environmentally polluting industries such as paper and pulp. Most of the firms in the paper and pulp industry come out with a bi-annual environmental report on environmental compliance as directed by the Ministry of Environment and Forest. Some 12 percent of the firms made donations to local schools and hospitals. Mostly, banks donated medical equipment and school books to local hospitals and schools, respectively.

The researchers felt that by relying on their own foundations to carry out CSR activities, they are able to monitor the CSR activities better, save on transaction costs, and create goodwill for their company.[19]

Various Phases of CSR in India

In a survey, "Altered Images: The 2001 State of Corporate Responsibility in India Poll," conducted by the Tata Research Institute, the evolution of CSR has followed the following pattern in India:

The Ethical Model (1930–1950): This model promoted the concept of "trusteeship" revived and reinterpreted by Gandhi. Under the notion, businesses were motivated to manage their business entity as a trust held in the interest of the community. The efforts of the Tata Group in the beginning can be said to be inspired by this model.

The Statist Model (1950–1970): Under the aegis of the first Prime Minister Pundit Jawaharlal Nehru the model came into being in the post-Independence era when the government went in for a mixed and socialist kind of economy. The important feature of this model was that the state ownership and legal requirements decided the corporate responsibility.

The Liberal Model (1970–1990): This model was propounded by Milton Friedman. According to this model, CSR is confined to its economic bottomline, which implied that it was sufficient for business to obey the law and generate wealth, which through taxation and private charitable choices can be directed to social ends.

The Stakeholders' Model (1990s–present): The model came into being during the 1990s as a consequence of realization that with growing economic profits, businesses also have certain societal roles to fulfil. The model expects the companies to perform according to "triple bottom line" approach. The businesses are also focusing on accountability and transparency through several mechanisms.

Besides CSR, various similar concepts have emerged, namely social accounting, social development monitoring (SDM), corporate citizenship, and corporate philanthropy.

We shall later discuss about the implications of compulsory CSR spending by the public sector and the Companies Act 2013.

Is CSR a Business Imperative?

A critic often feels that "looking good" from being "really good" is what governs the fundamentals behind CSR initiatives by many companies. There are a number of reasons for companies to include CSR as a part of governance.

Globalization has brought in seamless markets, global resource outlets, especially for production of goods in poor nations where labor is cheap. For instance, advocacy groups in the USA at one time were able to convince many youth to boycott Coca-Cola at the college campuses as it was draining away the ground water in many places, thus creating scarcity of water for the poor in India. Nike was lambasted for allowing children to work in poor countries in its production outlets. Similarly, McDonald's is fighting many legal cases for promoting unhealthy eating habits among children.

The scandals involving corporate behemoths such as Enron, WorldCom, Satyam, etc. have reduced public trust in companies and shaken the confidence in the regulatory bodies, thus lowering expectations that the guilty would be booked. Many companies are now going overboard in making their policies and processes open for public scrutiny. As soon as the Satyam sent shock waves in the IT sector, many such as the Infosys and Wipro top brass, in order to distance themselves from Satyam, started talking about the parameters of corporate governance in their companies. They wished the people believed that the Satyam fraud was an exception and not the rule. It must, however, be said to the credit of the GOI and the regulatory bodies that within three months of unearthing the Satyam Fraud, the guilty were booked and a new bidder was given charge to manage the company.

According to World Bank:

> Business approaches to CSR can largely be understood as a response to a series of external and internal drivers that generate a "business case" for CSR. The drivers include the pursuit of new business opportunities through social and environmental innovation, reputational risk management, campaign pressure from nongovernmental organizations (NGOs) or trade unions, media exposure to the practices of individual companies or sectors, regulation, and litigation. A Building effective driver of CSR is one pillar in approaches to build an optimal enabling environment for CSR or responsible business practices.[20]

Companies Act 2013: Implications for the Corporate Sector

The Ministry of Corporate Affairs notified Section 135 and Schedule VII of the Companies Act 2013 as well as the provisions of the Companies (CSR Policy) Rules, 2014, that came into effect from April 1, 2014.

Under the Act, every company, private limited or public limited, which either has a net worth of ₹500 crore or a turnover of ₹1,000 crore or a net profit of ₹5 crore, needs to spend at least 2 percent of its average net profit for the immediately preceding three financial years on CSR activities. The CSR activities should not be undertaken in the normal course of business and must be with respect to any of the activities mentioned in Schedule VII of the 2013 Act. Contribution to any political party is not considered to be a CSR activity, and only activities in India would be considered for computing CSR expenditure.

The net worth, turnover, and net profits are to be computed in terms of Section 198 of the 2013 Act as per the profit and loss statement prepared by the company in terms of Section 381 (1) (a) and Section 198 of the 2013 Act. While these provisions have not yet been notified, it has been clarified that if net profits are computed under the Companies Act, 1956, they need not be recomputed under the 2013 Act. Profits from any overseas branch of the company, including those branches that are operated as a separate company would not be included in the computation of net profits of a company. Besides, dividends received from other companies in India, which need to comply with the CSR obligations, would not be included in the computation of net profits of a company.

The CSR Rules appear to widen the ambit for compliance obligations to include the holding and subsidiary companies as well as foreign companies whose branches or project offices in India fulfill the specified criteria.

The activities that can be undertaken by a company to fulfil its CSR obligations include eradicating hunger, poverty and malnutrition, promoting preventive healthcare, promoting education and promoting gender equality, setting up homes for women, orphans, and the senior citizens, measures for reducing inequalities faced by socially and economically backward groups, ensuring environmental sustainability and ecological balance, animal welfare, protection of national heritage and art and culture, measures for the benefit of armed forces veterans, war widows, and their dependents, training to promote rural, nationally recognized Paralympics or Olympic sports, contribution to the Prime Minister's national relief fund or any other fund set up by the Central Government for socioeconomic development and relief and welfare of SC, ST, OBCs, minorities, and women, contributions or funds provided to technology incubators located within academic institutions approved by the Central Government, and rural development projects.

However, in determining CSR activities to be undertaken, preference would need to be given to local areas and the areas around which the company operates.

To formulate and monitor the CSR policy of a company, a CSR committee of the board has to be constituted. Section 135 of the 2013 Act requires the CSR committee to consist of at least three directors, including an independent director. However, CSR rules exempt unlisted public companies and private companies that are not required to appoint an independent director from having an independent director as a part of their CSR committee and stipulate that the committee for a private company and a foreign company need have a minimum of only two members.

A company can undertake its CSR activities through a registered trust or society, a company established by its holding, subsidiary or associate company or otherwise, provided that the company has specified the activities to be undertaken, the modalities for utilization of funds as well as the reporting and monitoring mechanism. If the entity through which the CSR activities are being undertaken is not established by the company or its holding, subsidiary or associate company, such entity would need to have an established track record of three years undertaking similar activities.

Companies can also collaborate with each other for jointly undertaking CSR activities, provided that each of the companies is able to individually report on such projects.

A company can build CSR capabilities of its personnel or implementation agencies through institutions with established track records of at least three years, provided that the expenditure for such activities does not exceed 5 percent of the total CSR expenditure of the company in a single financial year.

The CSR rules specify that a company which does not satisfy the specified criteria for a consecutive period of three financial years is not required to comply with the CSR obligations, implying that a company not satisfying any of the specified criteria in a subsequent financial year would still need to undertake CSR activities unless it ceases to satisfy the specified criteria for a continuous period of three years. This could increase the burden on small companies which do not continue to make significant profits.

The report of the board of directors attached to the financial statements of the company would also need to include an annual report on the CSR activities of the company in the format prescribed in the CSR rules setting out inter alia a brief outline of the CSR policy, the composition of the CSR Committee, the average net profit for the last three financial years, and the prescribed CSR expenditure. If the company has been unable to spend the minimum required on its CSR initiatives, the reasons for not doing so are to be specified in the board report.

Where a company has a website, the CSR policy of the company would need to be disclosed on such website.[21]

Public Sector Enterprises and CSR Initiative

The public sector in India was conceived with the aim to bring about socioeconomic transformation after the country achieved Independence from British rule in 1947. The overriding objectives were to boost infrastructure growth, bring innovation in technology, and make India self-reliant. CSR may not have been used as a terminology, but it has always been an in-built ethos of public sector governance that aimed at taking care of communities, especially the neighborhood, where the companies were located. Extending access to hospitals, admitting neighborhood children in their schools, creating crèches for children of the workers, initiating adult education programs, forestation, etc. have been some of the popular programs with a large number of PSEs. It is now mandatory for central PSEs to undertake CSR (since March 2010).

CSR budget for CPEs

Types of CPEs	Expenditure (% of Profit)
Less than ₹100 crore	3–5%
₹100–500 crore	2–3%
₹500 crores and more	0.5–2%

Source: http://www.dpemou.nic.in/MOUFiles/Revised_CSR_Guidelines.pdf (accessed on February 13, 2016).

The 2010 guidelines issued by the Department of Public Enterprises (DPE) posited that the implementation of CSR will be a part of the MOU signed between the respective CPSE and GOI; that the performance of CSR activities would be monitored by the concerned ministry periodically; that CSR budget, expenditure, and performance would be reflected in the annual reports of the CPSEs. It made it mandatory that the CSR projects would be independently evaluated by an independent outside agency. The loss-making CPEs were not required to earmark any specific budget. In a matter of three years the

DPE has come out with fresh guidelines for CSR for PSEs, indicating various areas the PSEs could consider. In the new guidelines, effective from April 1, 2013, while the guidelines have been done away with, a list of backward areas identified by the Planning Commission in various Indian states have been indicated as annexure. Another annexure reflects the UN global compact principles. Yet, another annexure has UN Millennium Development Goals.

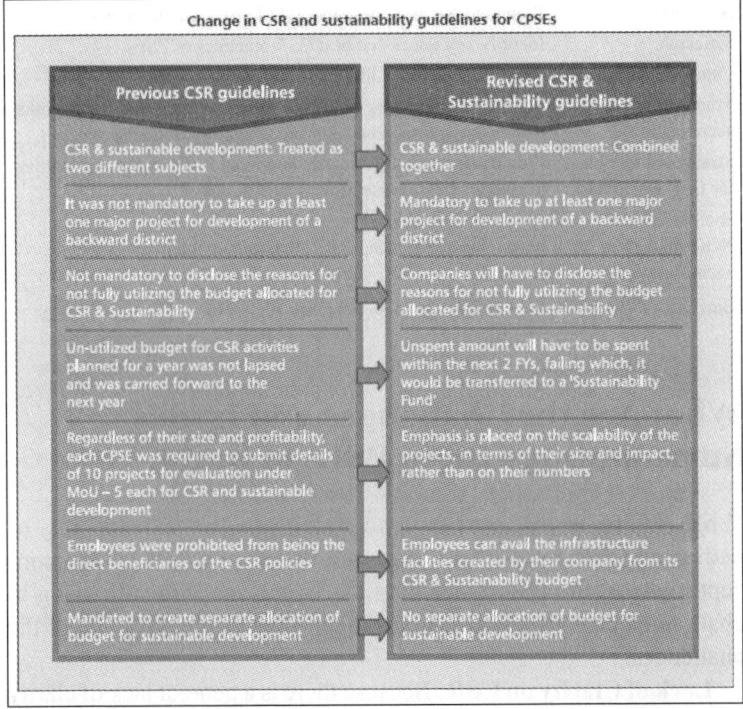

Change in CSR and sustainability guidelines for CPSEs

Previous CSR guidelines	Revised CSR & Sustainability guidelines
CSR & sustainable development: Treated as two different subjects	CSR & sustainable development: Combined together
It was not mandatory to take up at least one major project for development of a backward district	Mandatory to take up at least one major project for development of a backward district
Not mandatory to disclose the reasons for not fully utilizing the budget allocated for CSR & Sustainability	Companies will have to disclose the reasons for not fully utilizing the budget allocated for CSR & Sustainability
Un-utilized budget for CSR activities planned for a year was not lapsed and was carried forward to the next year	Unspent amount will have to be spent within the next 2 FYs, failing which, it would be transferred to a 'Sustainability Fund'
Regardless of their size and profitability, each CPSE was required to submit details of 10 projects for evaluation under MoU – 5 each for CSR and sustainable development	Emphasis is placed on the scalability of the projects, in terms of their size and impact, rather than on their numbers
Employees were prohibited from being the direct beneficiaries of the CSR policies	Employees can avail the infrastructure facilities created by their company from its CSR & Sustainability budget
Mandated to create separate allocation of budget for sustainable development	No separate allocation of budget for sustainable development

Source: http://www.csr.tiss.edu/training-files/lasted-dpe-s-guidelines-on-csr-sustainability-for-cpses-21st-october-2014 (accessed on February 10, 2016).

National CSR Hub

The DPE has set up a hub at the Tata Institute of Social Sciences (TISS) in March 2011 for facilitating CSR activities amongst PSEs.

It is expected that the National CSR hub will "use critical inputs for generation of new approaches that are relevant to business in current social change and development concerns."

Later, the UNICEF organized a consultation with a cross section of large NGOs, UN bodies, and PSEs in three metros, namely Delhi, Mumbai, and Kolkata. The deliberations resulted in deciding the followings tasks for the National CSR Hub:

Roles	Description
Advocacy	Promote CSR activities among PSEs and general public
Research	Identify key issues and best CSR practices of PSEs
Capacity building	Train CSR teams of PSEs and NGOs
Transparency and accountability	Formulate guidelines, standards, tools, systems, and frameworks that ensure transparency and accountability in CSR projects
Strategic direction for CSR expenditure	Provide strategic direction to individual PSEs and group of PSEs to enable effective use of their CSR funds
Facilitator with NGOs and other agencies	Act as an interface between NGOs and PSEs by maintaining a database of NGOs and other potential partners for CSR activities.

Source: http://www.csr.tiss.edu/ (accessed on February 10, 2016).

What Are the Challenges and Issues Surrounding CSR in PSEs in India?

While there is every reason to celebrate the earmarking of dedicated CSR budget to PSEs, due to the newness of the concept, most of the PSEs, including the larger ones are still trying to chalk out a clear-cut road map for themselves. Here are some of the challenges:

Lack of Clarity on CSR: Because there is a general lack of clarity on what should CSR encompass, this gets reflected in taking up projects and linking it with the big picture. Some complain about the challenge of finding good social projects they could invest in.

Unspent CSR Budgets: The budget earmarked for CSR activities generally remains half or partially spent. To quote a news story from *The Economic Times*, "Ten large PSUs, which were together mandated to spend ₹1,313 crore in FY12, managed to disburse less than half that amount." The figure below reflects the gap in the CSR spending of some major PSEs.

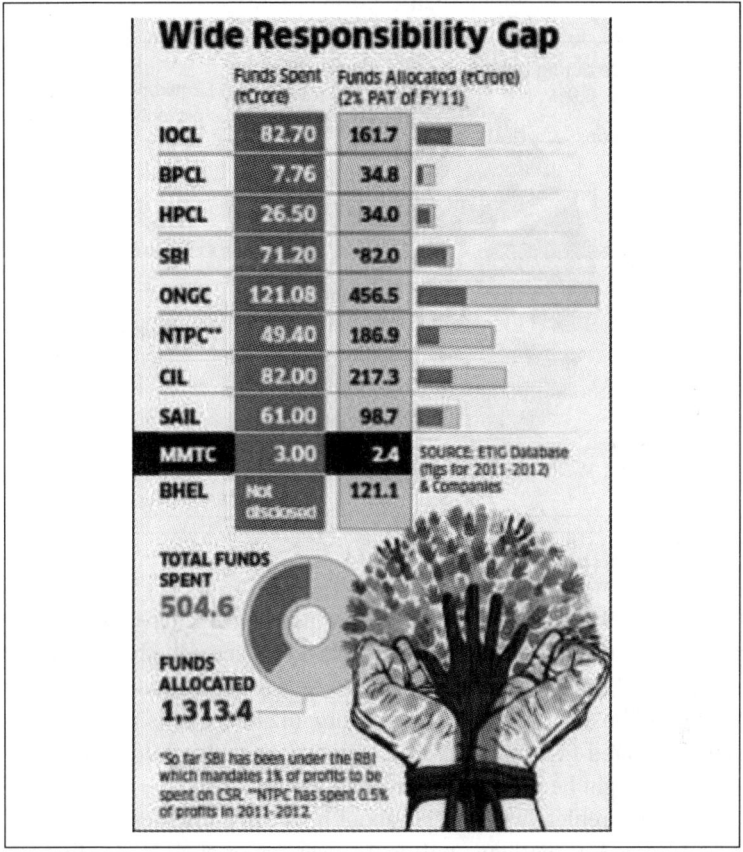

Wide Responsibility Gap

	Funds Spent (₹Crore)	Funds Allocated (₹Crore) (2% PAT of FY11)	
IOCL	82.70	161.7	
BPCL	7.76	34.8	
HPCL	26.50	34.0	
SBI	71.20	*82.0	
ONGC	121.08	456.5	
NTPC**	49.40	186.9	
CIL	82.00	217.3	
SAIL	61.00	98.7	
MMTC	3.00	2.4	
BHEL	Not disclosed	121.1	

SOURCE: ETIG Database (figs for 2011-2012) & Companies

TOTAL FUNDS SPENT
504.6

FUNDS ALLOCATED
1,313.4

*So far SBI has been under the RBI which mandates 1% of profits to be spent on CSR. **NTPC has spent 0.5% of profits in 2011-2012.

Source: *The Economic Times*, January 24, 2013.

Lack of Trained Manpower: In some PSEs, the human resource departments have been handling CSR, while in others it could be marketing or PR. In the PSEs that have dedicated CSR persons heading the activity, it is not uncommon that they have drawn laterally from various verticals such as engineering, finance, etc. while in other cases CSR is an additional responsibility that has been given to the head of a department.

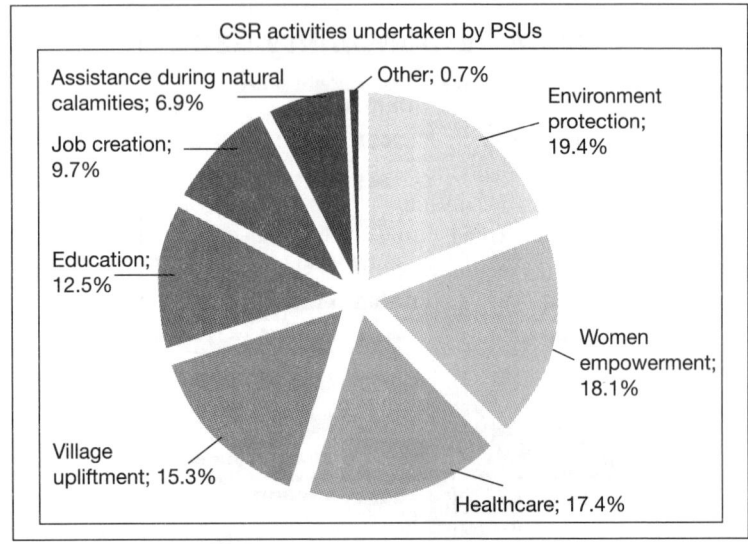

CSR activities undertaken by PSUs

Assistance during natural calamities; 6.9%

Other; 0.7%

Environment protection; 19.4%

Job creation; 9.7%

Education; 12.5%

Women empowerment; 18.1%

Village upliftment; 15.3%

Healthcare; 17.4%

Source: D&B Research.

Finding Suitable NGOs: It is not an easy task to find NGOs who not only have the domain expertise but also direct access to beneficiaries. As the CSR budgets have swollen and NGOs see a good opportunity in doing "business" with corporate organizations, it is important to find dedicated grassroots-level organizations and not any NGO, for whom it might be yet another business opportunity.

Media is replete with stories about how PSEs are pressurized into selecting NGOs that have political patronage or such NGOs that are run by the bureaucrats' wives. These could be sure recipe for ruining honest CSR initiatives.

In a research study conducted by IIMC in 2012, the work done by a government entity was not ascribed by a majority of respondents to the government but to the NGOs who were commissioned to do. The lesson learnt was that NGOs engaged in CSR work need to ensure that the communities must be informed about who was supporting the initiative.

NGOs and Industry CSR: The Implications

With CSR becoming a legal requirement for the public sector organizations in India from 2013 and an expectation from the government that private and global organizations would also undertake CSR activities, the nongovernmental organizations suddenly find themselves in great demand to undertake CSR work on behalf of companies.

It is a matter of fact that some of the well-known NGOs have succeeded in keeping a close vigil on large corporations, thereby bringing their violations in the public domain. Amnesty International, Greenpeace, and other human rights organizations have been able to make some global corporations conscious of their social responsibilities. In the Indian context, the Centre for Science and Environment (CSE) has taken many multinational organizations, such as Pepsi and Coca-Cola, to task over the issue of pesticide content. It is also, however, true that many NGOs are working hand in glove with big corporate organizations in their CSR initiatives. The argument works both ways, that is, by engaging them, the organizations can silence independent voices. The other side of the argument is that by working with corporations, the NGOs can ensure that violations do not occur.

Greenpeace, one of the largest NGOs in the field of environment, has of late been working with industry and government. Its website claims: "We work with industry and government to find solution." The reason behind the repositioning, as argued by analysts, is that when the media constantly dubbed Greenpeace as "too radical" and "too negative," it decided to reinvent itself as an organization that "offered solutions" and worked with industry and government to get desired results in place.

It has fought many a bitter battle, some in the courts of law with a few organizations (for instance with McDonald's, a litigation that went on for years), but when it came to Sydney Olympics 2000, it wrote to some of the official sponsors of Olympics 2000 such as Coca-Cola, McDonald's, General Motors, etc., to earn the name of "Green" in the same way Sydney Olympics 2000 did. It said, "Greenpeace would like to work with you to explore the areas in which you can make an environmental contribution during Sydney 2000 games."[22]

Greenpeace for long has been crusading against the use of polyvinyl chloride (PVC). Nike, which has always been in the eye of storm for environmental and human rights issues for low wages to workers in Third World countries, got a great opportunity to get some accolades from this environmental group. In 1998, Nike announced that it would phase out the use of PVC in its products. Greenpeace's Olympic Report congratulated Nike for "promising to eliminate the use of PVC in its products." The report carried a picture that had Greenpeace presenting a cake in the shape of a green color Nike shoe with the text "Greenpeace is calling on other sportswear manufacturers to follow suit and 'just do it!'" (using Nike's signature line). There is no gainsaying that what Greenpeace did for Nike's reputation, no paid promotion by the company could have done!

The *nuclear power debate* surrounds the issue of whether we could risk the lives of thousands of people due to uranium mining, transportation, storage of waste, and emissions from the nuclear plants. The proponents feel it is a sustainable energy source that avoids air pollution. They also argue that risks of storing waste are small as compared to gains of nuclear power. The latest technology can address the issue adequately.

Sources: http://www.greenpeace.org/india/en/news/Greenpeace-Can-you-spot-the-foreign-hand/ and https://kractivist.wordpress.com/2012/08/08/greenpeace-launches-a-unique-antinuclear-campaign/ (accessed on February 10, 2016).

The Jaitpur and, more recently, the Kudankulam plants have witnessed mass protests, arrests, and debate over the issue. Like-minded advocates and protagonists have entered the fray. Then Prime Minister Manmohan Singh talked about the "foreign hand" in it. Ex-President Kalam visited the site, assuring people of the safety of the plant. The protesters were, however, not interested in listening to him. Greenpeace, an international advocacy organization, has been issuing ads on the subject.

In June, as soon as the NDA government led by Prime Minister Modi took office, the media was full of stories and long debates on news channels on the IB report on the foreign funding of Indian NGOs to disrupt developmental work. Greenpeace, ActionAid, and antinuclear protagonist S.P. Uday Kumar, who also happened to be contesting on the Aam Aadmi Party ticket, was grilled by news channels on the amount he received from foreign sources. As reported by *The Times of India*, the civil society activists named in the leaked intelligence report described the charges against them as a "figment of the IB's imagination," while alleging that the document was deliberately leaked to discredit opposition and set the stage for the government to fast-track environmental clearances without following due process.[23] A number of NGOs have been put under the scanner by the government, which means their funding to various Indian organizations/NGOs would be scrutinized. The names of Greenpeace and Ford Foundation are included in the list of such NGOs.

Some NGOs in India, especially in the area of health, environment, and human rights are very vocal when it comes to questioning the intentions of the powers that be from time to time. Center for Civil Society, an NGO, keeping a close watch on the Bhagidari scheme of the erstwhile Congress Government in Delhi in its report: *ABCDs of Government- Bhagidari: Good Intention, Bad Implementation?*, questioned the real intentions behind Bhagidari, which the NGO felt was more of a publicity stunt than with any real objective. One of the case studies of the Bhagidari event reproduced below says it all about their perception. The report also reflected the opinions of a cross section of representatives of the Resident Welfare Associations (RWAs). The pertinent question that the NGO sought was that in case there was a change of guard at the government level, would the scheme sustain or vanish once the party that has initiated it loses election? That, in fact, is exactly what happened when the Congress was routed in elections in 2014.

Reproduction from the Report ABCDs of Government–Bhagidari: Good Intention, Bad Implementation?

A big banner near Tis Hazari court caught my attention. It had the ubiquitous Bhagidari logo and invited citizens, corporates, NGOs, RWAs, and MTAs to do shramdaan and make our Yamuna clean. This, I thought would be a good opportunity to see Bhagidari in practice. So I went to Garhi Mandu on 4 June to participate in the tree plantation drive. I reached the place at 7 in morning only to find a thin attendance. By 8:30 A.M., the place had a festive look: there were departmental officials, NCC cadets, school kids all wearing "Save Yamuna" caps. Great! I thought. But the euphoria was soon over when I learnt that the crowds had not come voluntarily but were forced to come. The government has directed each department and the concerned agencies to send a fixed number of people at each place. Thus, at Garhi Mandu there were officials from Department Of Food Civil Supplies and Consumer Affairs, Department of Irrigation and Flood Control, Department of Forests and Environment, Cadets from NCC and students from government schools. All of them were busy getting their attendance made and then it was all over. In the name of Yamuna cleaning there were symbolic photo sessions. There was just a single NGO named Social Action Foundation (SAF), but they too seem to have more political reasons to be there as the Chief Minister was supposed to come. The CM graced the place at around 10, got some photographs clicked, and interacted with a few. Then everyone moved to the refreshment table, officials discussed departmental gossips and the event was over by 11 A.M. Thus, another year passed, the government claimed to have done its bit but what about the Yamuna? It remained the same, dirty as ever. All in the name of Bhagidari, a Bhagidari without any public involvement! And the very next day Delhi Government comes out with advertisements in all the leading newspaper thanking the Delhites for their co-operation.

Source: http://cseindia.org/content/about-cse (accessed on February 15, 2016).

Another vocal NGO, CSE, a "public interest research and advocacy organization," which among other things, brings out a publication by the name *Down to Earth*. It conducts surveys and research on various issues. The CSE had reflected the issue of pesticide content in the colas, generating a lot of heat in various quarters. The CSE has been spearheading advocacy on Yamuna cleanliness for a long time. Among other advocacy tools, the CSE brought out a book *Sewage Canal: How to Clean Yamuna* and a documentary on the subject titled *Faecal Attraction: Political Economy of Defecation*. A huge event was organized on April 18, 2007, in Delhi to launch both, the book and the film. The event was attended by virtually everyone who is a who of the environment sector, besides the then cabinet minister in charge of water resources at the center and the Delhi chief minister. The book was released by Professor Saifuddin Soz and Mrs Sheila Dikshit, the then minister and chief minister, respectively. The event sure received a lot of mileage and hype around the issue. Media buzz was created through a preview of the book. This was yet another case of NGOs engaging in strategic PR to garner publicity for themselves too. Interestingly, the NGO did not have any doable alternate plan or concrete suggestion for cleaning the Yamuna. When the then chief minister was invited to the dais, she assured the NGO to come out with a plan, and it would be followed. Even after a lot of rhetoric from both sides, one has not seen the Yamuna getting cleaned because no one seems to be touching the basic reasons of pollution of the river.

A visit to a sewage plant reflects how an average person contributes to the river pollution without his ever realizing it. The dumping of industrial effluents and wastage without fear of law by industries, the culture and tradition of Hindus, who on the one hand worship the river, but on the other mindlessly throw religious-ritual waste. It is not uncommon also to find dead animals and corpses of children floating in the river. Ask the people in charge, they would tell in confidence that it is a distant dream for them to clean Yamuna anytime in the near future. It can only happen, they tell you, if politics is weeded out of it and the task is left to technical people, but with a huge punitive clause against those who contribute to its pollution.

The population of Delhi is four times than its infrastructure can cater to. There are hundreds of unauthorized colonies without the facility of sewage lines. There are thousands of migrants who land up in Delhi without any hope of shelter and basic civic amenities. To make things worse, every political party promises regularization of unauthorized colonies. As soon as a colony is authorized the civic bodies are required to provide water supply and lay sewage lines, a job that takes a long time to get accomplished, due to issues of fund availability and red tape.

In a research study of CSR practices by Dutch companies doing business in India, several MNCs criticized the role of NGOs in India in their dialogue with companies. The most heard complaint was that many NGOs were single-issue oriented which implied that they did not always focus on those CSR aspects which may have the largest impact on society. NGOs sometimes seem to be more concerned with media attention and were not always constructive in their cooperation. One stakeholder mentioned that some representatives of local communities were only after their own gain and tried to take advantage of the willingness of companies to engage with local community. Companies, the study suggested, should therefore seek to use institutional mechanisms to ensure community participation.[24]

In another research paper on the role of NGOs in CSR in Spain that involved a thorough analysis of various stakeholders' perceptions and of NGOs' self-perceptions, it was found that the perceptions of the role of NGOs was recognized in four categories, namely, recognition of NGOs as drivers of CSR; concerns about their legitimacy; difficulties in the mutual understanding between NGOs and trade unions; the self-confidence of NGOs as important players in CSR. Some interesting insights emerged that broadly included the following:

There were discrepancies between the perception of others and the self-perceptions of NGOs, which explained why their role was often controversial. The research reflected that secondary stakeholders, such as NGOs, were indeed the key players in CSR, but their role was still regarded as controversial and their legitimacy contested. Deep-seated misunderstandings and mistrust among various stakeholder groups (particularly between NGOs and trade unions) was a possible hurdle to the integration of social and environmental concerns in business activity and corporate governance in Spain.[25]

Morton Winston writes:

> [Within the NGO world] there is a basic divide on tactics for dealing with corporations: Engagers try to draw corporations into dialogue in order to persuade them by means of ethical and prudential arguments to adopt voluntary codes of conduct, while confronters believe that corporations will act only when their financial interests are threatened, and therefore take a more adversarial stance toward them. The latter approach is more in line with traditional labor union strategies and tactics, and in fact is often motivated by a desire to maintain solidarity with union partners. Confrontational NGOs tend to employ moral stigmatization, or "naming and shaming," as their primary tactic, while NGOs that favor engagement offer dialogue and limited forms of cooperation with willing MNCs.[26]

While the issue of NGOs doing the CSR for companies is still being debated, news comes that looking at the scope and role of CSR many PR consultancies have joined the bandwagon of handling CSR for their clients. Identifying CSR as "new business dimension," Ogilvy PR, a worldwide PR firm claims to have extended the "scope and meaning" of CSR to include employees, regulators, and the larger social community, as reflected in media reports. In the same article Vivek Sengupta from IPAN, another PR/public affairs consultancy doing CSR on behalf of various clients was quoted saying that when companies engaged outside expertise in their CSR works, it would bring about "objective, holistic view of business and environment." IPAN, he said, had developed India-specific initiative of Levi Strauss on its AIDS project and for Amway in its Amway Opportunity Foundation that works for education of visually disabled persons.

Commenting on the entry of PR in the social sector, Malini Mehra of Center for Social Markets opined that PR was long synonymous with slick marketing and image polishing and CSR, she commented, "is certainly not about just looking good."[27]

Many scholars and social commentators have questioned the real intension behind the façade of CSR. Many reckon it to be lip service and a smart public relations manipulation. British Petroleum received adverse comments from many on the spilling of oil in the Gulf of Mexico in April 2010. Here is what the Pulitzer Prize-winning journalist John McQuaid on science, environment, and government had to write:

> This is a constant drumbeat, but thinks about it: Isn't it remarkable how transcendently awful BP's approach to the Gulf disaster has been? At each and every turn, with the stakes impossibly high, BP has always chosen to do the wrong thing. There's the substance—having no emergency worst-case contingency plans for a blowout, disingenuously refusing to estimate the amount of oil flowing. There's the politics and image stuff, including CEO Tony Hayward's lies and self-pity and the platoons of lawyers and PR people trying to keep cleanup workers silent and choke off media attention. It's been an awesome display of every kind of 21st century corporate dick-itude.

British Petroleum's "Beyond Petroleum" campaign, portraying the organization as a forward-looking, responsible corporate citizen commented McQuaid, fell flat, as there seemed no substance in it. On BP's PR strategy, he commented,

Here's one thing I genuinely don't get. Just from a PR standpoint, BP's tactical, hectoring approach makes no sense. If I were BP (which in fact I'm not) I would simply roll over, conceding everything the critics are saying, promising to make everything whole again to the fullest extent possible, acknowledging the profound wrong that it has committed here at every opportunity, in words and actions. I'd call off the lawyers and PR people. The nickel-and-diming media interference is futile, after all. The story is simply too big—geographically, environmentally, and historically—for it to have any appreciable effect other than to make BP look bad. But BP's honchos either cannot recognize this, or they don't care, or they have no overarching strategy for the company's corporate and social responsibilities going forward—other than minimizing them.

Many environmentalists seem worried that if the oil spill is deep down in the sea, the company may not really know how to contain it and the extent of damage it may cause to environment, besides human and marine life.

It makes so much sense, only if the PR strategists understand that covering up, concocting, and telling half-truths would do more damage than keeping it truthful and getting it off the chest.

Social Development Monitoring/Social Audit

Social audit is seen as an important tool for conception and implementation of effective CSR projects. SDM is defined as a social audit process with

[P]eriodic observation activity by socially disadvantaged groups as local citizens who are project participants or target beneficiaries. It could also take the form of action intended to enhance participation, ensure inclusiveness, articulation of accountability, responsiveness, and transparency by implementing agencies or local institutions, with a declared purpose of making an impact on their socio-economic status.[28]

The erstwhile Planning Commission of India commissioned a research study on social audit of panchayati raj institutions (PRIs). Vision India, which conducted the study, in the context of social audit said that considering the difference in the interpretation of social audit in

Western Countries and India, the definition "useful" for Indian conditions would be

> Social Audit is a process in which, details of the resource, both financial and non-financial, used by public agencies for development initiatives are shared with the people, often through a public platform. Social Audits allow people to enforce accountability and transparency, providing the ultimate users an opportunity to scrutinize development initiatives.[29]

According to Tata Sustainability Report 1999–2001,

> The term is ubiquitous, yet contentious, with diverse connotations. To some, it may mean preparing a publicity document in the form of a glossy report highlighting organizational achievements on social performance, for many others it serves as a tool for preparing and verifying the social balance sheet of an organization based on social costs and benefits.

The annexure to the chapter carries highlights of Tata Sustainability Report 1999–2001.

Examples of Social Accounting/Audit

Social audit in Jharnipalli Panchayat, Agaipur Block, Bolangir District, Orissa

In October 2001, the Gram Sabha members of Jharnipalli Panchayat conducted a one-day social audit of development works carried out in the panchayat over the preceding three years. This audit took place with the active participation of many individuals and agencies, including block and district administration officials, Mazdoor Kisan Shakti Sanghatan (MKSS), National Campaign for People's Right to Information (NCPRI) and ActionAid India.

The audit found that:

- Although the works were not carried out, the sanctioned funds were shown in the records as having been utilized.
- Contractors were banned under government guidelines, but 31 contractors were working on the project.

- Muster rolls were not maintained by the contractors.
- Instead of the target of 100 man-days of employment for families below the poverty line (BPL), only 12 half days of work were generated.
- The BPL families could not buy subsidized food from the public distribution system (PDS) shops as partial wages because they did not possess the needed ration cards.

Micro-development Planning as Part of Social Audit

A voluntary development organization Samarthan and Society for Participatory Research in Asia (PRIA) collaborated in a participatory micro-planning exercise with local officials, panchayat members, members of different castes, etc. The process was a way to bring resources to the local community and to increase its involvement in Gram Sabha meetings which took place four times a year. This led to the identification of several goals. One was to construct a drain. Inspired by the participatory local planning process, the community contributed half the cost of the drain (₹50,000). Those who could not give money offered their labor. The rest of the money came from the district office and was mobilized by the Gram Panchayat and its proactive woman president, the Sarpanch.

Every member of the Gram Sabha developed a sense of ownership of the project.

The Gram Sabha monitors the work. Gram Panchayat representatives also hold regular ward-level meetings. The relationship between people and their local representatives developed quickly into one of mutual support.

Planning a CSR Project

Now that CSR has become mandatory for large companies, especially in the public sector, here we provide the following checklist for initiating a CSR program:

1. **Decide on the Area for CSR:** The first step, ideally, is taken by the board of directors to decide on a CSR initiative. It has to be

a well-thought out decision, based on a sound economic model so that there is no going back. This can begin with the preparation of "social responsibility inventory" of what the company may be doing until then. DPE guidelines may be referred to for keeping the "Big Picture" in view.

2. **Select the Right Person to Head the CSR Team:** Select a person for the CSR who would prepare a proposal on various areas that ideally would go well and fulfill the company's vision and mission. This needs to be based on a clear picture of the country's socioeconomic matrix, the Planning Commission's Five Year Plan outlay, and, if possible, a good look at the UN Millennium Development Goals (MDGs) of which India is a signatory. A CSR program that is not embedded in the social reality may not be of much relevance. Select the area of operation around your projects or at places that need to be reached on priority.

3. **Undertake Social Audit:** Every organization leaves an impact on the society's ecosystem that would be positive or negative, but rarely neutral. The company needs to know about it and make amends, if necessary. Before embarking on a CSR plan, it will be a good idea for a PSE to commission a social audit on its organization to map the effect of its various processes and decisions on the society, especially the neighborhood where it is located. The exercise will also make clear the gap between organization's vision and reality and people's expectations from it.

4. **Baseline Survey:** The social audit then can be followed by a baseline study to analyze the existing situation before embarking on a CSR initiative. A baseline study can cover many things. A baseline study aims at researching only those factors that one expects can change after the project is implemented. It provides insights against which changes can be measured after a developmental project is completed. For example, the board may be contemplating to open say 100 schools in 10 villages. One way is to go ahead and open the schools, the other is do a baseline study to look at the current status vis-à-vis demand, the futuristic demand, the facilities available, the facilities required for a school, number of teachers available against number of teachers required, if one were to go by ideal student–teacher

ratio, books in the library, the gaps, among other things. The baseline study may bring forth many insights, one of which could be that there are plenty of schools already, but the infrastructure could be in a shambles, or the local administration has dearth of funds for paying teachers' salary. So, prudence would lie in not reinventing the wheel but picking up from existing reality and strengthening it, rather than opening new schools.

5. **Make It Participative:** Involve the concerned ministry, the local government, and the grassroots-level institutions such as the Gram Sabhas in designing the project.

6. **Make Employees Participate in CSR Work:** Involve various levels of employees in your CSR initiative. This could be voluntary and not necessarily mandatory. It would not only be fulfilling for those who are inclined toward this activity, it will also help create a sense of pride in them for the company. This can be done in the following manner as many global and private companies are doing:

   • The employees who volunteer for CSR work can be attached to company's CSR projects with NGOs/research team, etc. for a term.

   • Decide on the number of hours/days in a year, the company would be allowing such an employee to do the social work (say one week/two weeks in a year). The employee would be at liberty to select an NGO of her/his choice to work with it. The report at the end of the project work then can be called from the NGO.

   • Senior people can be encouraged to be on the board of NGOs of their choice and lend consultancy/training/domain knowledge. The organization will be kept in the loop.

7. **Make Your CSR Initiative Quantifiable:** A CSR plan needs to translate into concrete action by identifying the team that would be responsible and accountable for making it happen as envisaged through well-laid out goals, financial resources, deadlines, and sorted out priorities. The objectives need to be measured at the end of the project.

8. **Leverage CSR for Building Brand Equity:** It is important that the CSR initiative reflect the company's ethos and not dilute its brand name value in any manner.

9. **Third-party Monitoring:** A continuous appraisal is required to sustain the CSR initiative through an independent research

agency. A suitable audit methodology needs to be made a part of the program.

10. **Archiving CSR Activities:** It is important that companies keep a record, both written and through suitable multimedia format on its CSR projects. Small films can be shared with various stakeholders on the activities to boost their morale as also to learn for future endeavors.

Case Studies of CSR in India

We shall look at a few case studies in CSR to understand the strategies and implementation of such schemes by some well-known business houses.

Bharti Airtel

Bharti Airtel, one of the well-known mobile service providers, is a well-known name in CSR also. According to its CSR Policy document, 2014, the CSR policy of the company revolves around the following cardinal principles:

1. Promoting education including special education, employment enhancing vocational skills, especially among children;
2. Eradicating hunger, poverty and malnutrition by promoting preventive health case and sanitation and making available safe drinking water;
3. Provision of funds to technology incubators located with academic institutions which are approved by the central government.

Besides these, the policy has provision for inclusion of any project as specified in Schedule VII of the Companies Act, 2013, subject to the approval of the CSR committee, which comprises of at least three directors, one of whom would be an independent director.

The CSR Committee is empowered to invite members of senior management, representatives of Bharti Foundation and any other person, it feels necessary for its meetings.[30]

Some glimpses of Bharti's CSR initiatives

The philanthropic arm of the company, Bharti Foundation runs over 250 schools across Bharti Foundation has adopted a three-pronged implementation strategy to reach out to and impact more number of children in the rural pockets:

1. **Green Field Schools:** Of the 254 operational Satya Bharti Schools, 200 primary schools are Greenfield Schools built and run by Bharti Foundation on land either donated or leased-out by the community.
2. **Adopted Government Schools:** The Foundation manages and operates 49 government schools are adopted government schools in Rajasthan.
3. **Public-Private Partnership Model:** Five Government Satya Bharti Adarsh Senior Secondary Schools are being run in partnership with the Punjab State Government under the Public-Private Partnership Mode.[31]

Bharti ACT Ambassador Initiative

Bharti enterprise initiate an innovative programme by the name ACT (A Caring Touch) in 2006 that encourages employees to empanel themselves and donate to the Bharti Foundation and other identified NGOs that focus on education. Later in 2010 ACT Ambassador awards were initiated in 2010 to recognize all those employees across the Bharti Group who helped steer the ACT Program- an Employee Philanthropy Program in their respective Group Companies.[32]

- **Bharti Centre for Entrepreneurial Initiative:** Set up in partnership with Entrepreneurship Development Institute of India in 2000-20002, it promotes entrepreneurship and motivates young people to become entrepreneurs.
- **Bharti School of Telecommunication Technology and Management at IIT, Delhi:** The school has been set up with an objective of creating tomorrow's telecom leaders.

- **Bharti Computer Centers:** To provide computer-aided learning to children (6-14 years) from the under-privileged sections of society.
- **Bharti Library Program:** The program aims at helping in improving the reading and learning habits of underprivileged children.
- **Bharti Scholarship Schemes:** Under the scheme meritorious children from underprivileged families pursuing Higher Technical Education get scholarships.
- **Mid-day Meal Program:** Bharti Foundation has partnered with Akshaya Patra Foundation for providing nutritious food to underprivileged children in Vrindavan under the mid-day meal program.

Post the new Companies Act 2013, which stipulates compulsory CSR for the public enterprises and expects the private sector to also pledge funds for CSR, the company's policy document underlines that it would support CSR activities as permitted by the Act.

The company monitors the CSR activities through periodic third party assessment, impact assessment of the areas of operations and regular review by its CSR committee.

Bharti CSR has received wide acclaim and awards for its activities in the CSR domain. Among many awards, it has been the recipient of the Global CSR award, 2008, Asian CSR Award, 2008, Golden Peacock award, 2006, The Economic Times Corporate Citizen of the year award, 2010, and World Education Award, 2011.[33]

The company is able to garner a lot of positive publicity through its CSR activities, if media coverage is any indication. Experts believe that CSR can subtly help build brand equity for an organization, if achievements in the social sector are shared with media and placed on the social media from time to time and there is no denying that many companies like Bharti do harvest the gains.

Coca-Cola Rainwater Harvesting

Coca-Cola India's CSR initiative covers areas such as health, environment, education, and livelihood. However, it is in the area of water harvesting that Coca-Cola is contributing the most in India. The aim behind it is "to return whatever water it has taken from the ground by 2009 through water conservation projects."

The company has wisely chosen water harvesting as its main CSR initiative in India because of growing criticism of the company from some advocacy groups for draining out scarce ground water from various states where it has its bottling plants. The company has also faced litigation in the state of Kerala where it had to shut the operations of its plant.

Coca-Cola partners with the Central Groundwater Authority (CGWA), local governments, and communities to help combat water scarcity and restore groundwater tables. Local government officials and NGOs identify critical areas, and then Coca-Cola sets up rainwater harvesting partnerships with local RWAs or communities in these areas to collect and recharge the groundwater tables. NGO specialists execute the project and mobilize community participation, while Coca-Cola facilitates the overall project and serves as the main funding arm. The partnership with CGWA ensures availability of technical expertise.

Some such initiatives included the restoration of *Kale Hanuman ki Bawari* and *Sarai Bawari* in Rajasthan in which the local communities were involved in the selection of project site, designing of the project, sources of supply for labor, material, and creation of awareness about the project. The work included removal of slit, rubble and algae, and repairs of the existing infrastructure in local Jaipuri style. According to company sources, thousands of gallons of water today flows into the wells from the underground pores and streams. More than 3,000 villages near each Bawari now have a sustained source of clean water.

In its new campaign with its tagline "Little drops of joy," Coca-Cola in its series has included its CSR initiatives. In one such ad a picture of Sarai Bawari brimming with water is reflected. The testimonial comes from a local person that comprises the headline and the body copy: "I cannot undo the past. But I help keep some memories intact." The copy goes, "I am Mohanlal Saini, a member of Coca-Cola team involved in the restoration of the Sarai Bawari. This 400 year old well was damaged and unfit for use…"

The Oil and Natural Gas Corporation

The Oil and Natural Gas Corporation (ONGC) is one of India's largest companies. Its CSR work encompasses various areas, such as the following:

Education

Promotion of literacy and higher education; grant of scholarships and assistance to deserving young pupils from weaker sections of society; facilities for constructing schools, renovation of school buildings, and other infrastructure include some of the activities under its CSR initiative.

Health Care and Family Welfare

The company has opened medical camps and mobile dispensaries, thus supplementing the efforts of already existing health centers in the rural areas. Health care for women, children, and disabled are areas of special consideration.

Community Development

Providing civic amenities: sanitation, clean drinking water facilities to panchayats, Gram Sabhas etc.; development of agriculture and other cottage industries; environment protection; animal husbandry; woman and child development; support to vocational training institutions for upgrading the skills of the local people form part of its community development initiative.

Tata Chemical Limited (TCL)

The CSR themes encompass micro-finance, education, environment, health, and livelihood.

The company undertakes participation appraisals, open discussions, conducts surveys, and takes input from national and global concerns to include areas of intervention in its CSR initiative.

Through correlation of needs with specific projects, the CSR program ranks them in order of importance and maximum impact on larger sections of communities.

The community development program encompasses natural resource management, income generation program, and health education infrastructure. Under their initiative "listening and learning" the company undertakes evaluation of various initiatives, third-party audits, community satisfaction, and CS practical process followed by the Tata Group throughout.

Bennett Coleman & Co Ltd

The CSR initiative of this media company, run largely by its Times Foundation, encompasses education, environment, livelihood, women empowerment, disaster management, climate change, and capacity building. The company believes that CSR has always been an inherent part of its governance, reporting on issues of social relevance is the character of a media organization, which it fulfils.

Times Foundation was set up as a "strategic organization working on a macro canvas-connecting, highlighting, facilitating, and creating effective bridges among stakeholders of civil society."

The Times Foundation mainly catalyzes through public–private partnership on public policy, advocacy, CSR, capacity building, and information dissemination. The Times Foundation, according to company sources, "is a point of convergence for government agencies, NGOs, the corporate sector and individuals to synergize initiatives for inclusive and equitable socio-economic development." It chooses partners on defined mandates.

ITC: Connecting the Hinterland Digitally—The Concept of e-Choupal

ITC's sustainability reports reflect its pioneering effort in connecting digitally rural India that has won the company international accolades and myriad awards.

An interesting example of linking business goals with a larger societal cause is ITC's e-Choupal initiative, which has proven to be a digital revolution and is believed to be reshaping the lives of farmers in many remote Indian villages. The model has been taken up for a course at Harvard's Business Management School.

What Is e-Choupal?

The e-Choupal concept is the brainchild of ITC's Agri Business Division, created to serve as a more efficient supply chain aimed "at delivering value to its customers around the world on a sustainable basis," given the typical feature of Indian agriculture, characterized by fragmented farms, weak infrastructure, and the involvement of numerous intermediaries, among others.[34]

Gathering of the elders in a village to deliberate on important issues is referred as Choupal in India. By using the same nomenclature, ITC was able to bring in familiarity among its desired target audience about the aim of its venture e-Choupal.

The Model

The model followed by ITC, appreciating the imperative of interme-diaries in the Indian context, "e-Choupal"

> [L]everages Information Technology to virtually cluster all the value chain participants, delivering the same benefits as vertical integration does in mature agricultural economies like the USA. "e-Choupal" makes use of the physical transmission capabilities of current intermediaries—aggregation, logistics, counter-party risk and bridge financing—while dis-intermediating them from the chain of information flow and market signals.

Launched in June 2000, "e-Choupal," has already become the largest initiative among all Internet-based interventions in rural India. According to official sources, "e-Choupal" services today reach out to over 4 million farmers growing a range of crops: soybean, coffee, wheat, rice, pulses, shrimp in over 40,000 villages through nearly 6,500 kiosks across 10 states (Madhya Pradesh, Haryana, Uttarakhand, Karnataka, Andhra Pradesh, Uttar Pradesh, Maharashtra, Rajasthan, Kerala, and Tamil Nadu). Encouraged by the response to "e-Choupal" from the end-users, ITC plans to spread it altogether to 15 states across India over the next few years. On the anvil are plans to channelize other services encompassing micro-credit, health, and education through the same "e-Choupal" infrastructure.

As said earlier, corporates choose their own method of supporting social causes. Many banks have been supporting NGOs in collecting funds as well as contributing themselves for certain social causes. For instance HSBC, a global bank, supports World Vision in India. The bank sent direct mailers to its clients giving information on how they could support children through sponsorship and the cost involved. The amount, it said, could be sent through HSBC credit card on DD/check which also would enjoy income tax rebate. Citi Bank's CSR programs include following Dow Jones Sustainability Indexes and FTSE 4Good Index. The Bank has awarded more than $ 88.8 million in grants to nonprofits and NGOs around the world through the Citigroup Foundation and group businesses (for example, when it entered India, it aligned with CRY). It led a coalition of financial institutions in developing and adopting the Equator Principles, guidelines based on the policies of the World Bank and the International Finance Corporation for managing social and environmental issues related to financing development projects. The bank also adopted a new global corporate and investment banking group and environmental and social risk management policy.

Notes and References

1. http://www.mallenbaker.net/csr/definition.php (accessed on February 15, 2016).
2. Archie B. Carroll, "The Pyramid of Corporate Social Responsibility: Toward the Moral Management of Organizational Stakeholders," *Business Horizons* 34, Issue 4 (1991): 39–48.
3. http://info.worldbank.org/etools/docs/library/57527/csr_mainconcepts.pdf (accessed on November 8, 2015).
4. http://www.mallenbaker.net/csr/definition.php (accessed on February 15, 2016).
5. See more at: http://indianexpress.com/article/business/business-others/direct-csr-expenditure-towards-toilets-for-schools/#sthash.q0BpWD3U.dpuf (accessed on December 11, 2015).
6. Doordarshan and Other TV Channels in a Direct Telecast from Red Fort, August 15, 2015.
7. Reeba Zachariah, "After Nano, Tatas' water purifier at ₹1k," *The Times of India*, December 8, 2009, 21.
8. K. Subramanya, CEO, Tata BP Solar, said while delivering the keynote address at the CII Conclave on Integrating CSR with Business Strategy in Bangalore on March 18, 2008.
9. Boli and Hartsukar, 2001, as quoted in ASSOCHAM and KMPG white paper 2008 on Corporate Social responsibility—Towards sustainable future, presented at the 1st international summit on CSR on January 29–30, 2008 organized by the Indian

Ministry of Corporate Affairs and Industry association Associated Chambers of Commerce (ASSOCHAM).

10. http://regulation.upf.edu/ecpr-05-papers/lsegerlund.pdf (accessed on February 15, 2016).

11. Bryane Michael at www.interscience.willey.com, October 10, 2002.

12. S. Kim and M. T. Ferguson, "Public Expectations of CSR Communication: What and How to Communicate CSR," *Public Relations Journal* 8, no. 3 (2014): 6–22.

13. Kim and Ferguson, *Public Relations Journal*.

14. B. B. Schlegelmilch and I. Pollach, "The perils and Opportunities of Communicating Corporate Ethics," *Journal of Marketing Management* 21 (2005): 267–290 and D. J. Webb and L. A. Mohr, "A Typology of Consumer Responses to Cause-related Marketing: From Skeptics to Socially Concerned," *Journal of Public Policy and Marketing* 17, no. 2 (1998): 226–238.

15. http://corporate-social-responsibility.ozg.in/2011/03/coca-cola-india-foundation-anandana.html (accessed on December 10, 2015).

16. http://pepsicoindia.co.in/purpose/pepsico-foundation.html (accessed on December 12, 2015).

17. http://www.theguardian.com/business/2010/aug/24/vedanta-mining-industry-india (accessed on November 2, 2015).

18. http://www.thehindubusinessline.com/economy/govt-rejects-vedantas-niyamgiri-mining-project/article5570028.ece 12 January 2014 (accessed on November 2, 2015).

19. *Economic and Political Weekly*, http://www.epw.in/web-exclusives/analysis-corpo-rate-social-responsibility-expenditure-india.html (accessed on December 10, 2015).

20. http://www.academia.edu/419290/The_Business_Case_for_Corporate_Social_ Responsibility_A_Review_of_Concepts_Research_and_Practice (accessed on February 15, 2016).

21. http://www.business-standard.com/article/companies/an-overview-of-csr-rules-under-companies-act-2013-114031000385_1.html (accessed on December 9, 2015).

22. S. Bider, "Offering Solutions or Compromises?" https://www.uow.edu.au/~sharonb/ Greenpeace.html (accessed on December 10, 2015). //homepage.mac.com/herinst/ sbeder/home.html as quoted in Jaishri Jethwaney, Corporate Communication: Principles and Practice (New Delhi: OUP, 2010).

23. http://timesofindia.indiatimes.com/india/Foreign-funding-of-NGOs-Intelligence-Bureau-report-bid-to-stifle-dissent-activists-say/articleshow/36514310.cms (accessed on February 15, 2016).

24. httpwww.indianet.nlCSRIndia_CREMfinal.pdf

25. "The Role of NGOs in CSR: Mutual Perceptions among Stakeholders," *Journal of Business Ethics* 88, no. 1 (August, 2009): 175–197.

26. http://www.questia.com/googleScholar.qst;jsessionid=LfjQR4W4g2yGTPw6s8 NTtwMcJ0WFTGKzyLv7qymDZKzbXCYdN9mx!-791355714!527935978?do cId=5002559227 (accessed on November 19, 2015).

27. http://www.thehindubusinessline.com/2002/11/26/stories/2002112602210600.htm

28. S. P. Jain and Wim Polman, *A Handbook for Trainers on Participatory Local Development The Panchayati Raj Model in India*, 3rd ed. (Bangkok: Food and Agriculture Organization of the United Nations, 2003), http://www.fao.org/ docrep/006/ad346e/ad346e09.htm (accessed on December 1, 2015).

29. http://planningcommission.gov.in/reports/sereport/ser/stdy_sagspr.pdf (accessed on February 15, 2016).

30. http://www.airtel.in/wps/wcm/connect/fd7b3172-02e5-4e25-af7e-51d64cc17534/CSR+Policy.pdf?MOD=AJPERES&ContentCache=NONE (accessed on February 15, 2016).

31. http://www.bhartifoundation.org/wps/wcm/connect/bhartifoundation/BhartiFoundation/Home/Satya+Bharti%20School%20Program/About%20the%20Satya%20Bharti%20School%20Program/PG_about_bharti_program (accessed on February 15, 2016).

32. http://www.bhartifoundation.org/wps/wcm/connect/bhartifoundation/bhartifoundation/home/media+kit/news+events/honouring+those+who+matter (accessed on February 15, 2016).

33. http://www.bhartifoundation.org/wps/wcm/connect/bhartifoundation/Bharti Foundation/Home/About+Us/AwardsRecognitions/PG_AwardsandRecognitions (accessed on February 15, 2016).

34. ITC portal.

4
Advocacy, Communication, and Social Mobilization

Introduction

Advocacy, communication, and social mobilization, commonly referred to as the ACSM form the trinity of the development arena and can truly be called its lifeline. Any change that involves people requires advocacy to not only bring the issue in the public domain but also influence policy to facilitate the desired change. The various stakeholders need to be mobilized to participate in the advocacy process around an issue. In the following paragraphs, we shall understand all the three concepts individually and also look at the need for synergy, which scales up efforts for change and put pressure on the legislature and policy-makers to bring in the required legislation and policies for the proposed change, followed by analyzing various case studies.

Defining Advocacy

Advocacy is defined as making use of information and communication strategies to bring an issue in the public domain for discussion and debate with the ultimate objective of bringing about the desired change. Advocacy has a very specific role in mobilizing public opinion for change. An advocacy campaign is designed to be proactive in nature, seeking specific change unlike an information campaign. Advocacy targets a disparate set of target audience using various, strategies, tactics, and instruments to create awareness on the issue for seeking the necessary change.

The origin of the term advocacy historically located with the movement around the release of John Wikes who objected to the Treaty of Paris and was imprisoned for so doing. He was also released and rearrested for obscenity and slander. A group called the Society for the Support of the Bill of Rights was formed which aggressively began promoting Wikes' policies. Later movements using advocacy were largely political, like the Abolitionist Movement against slavery that organized the boycott of sugar in 1791. So much was public opinion against the sugar harvested by slaves that a law came into effect that abolished slavery in 1806 in the Great Britain. Similarly movements for People's Charter, universal suffrage, and secret ballot were all political movements with a view to ensure the rights of the people.[1]

Advocacy Practice: How It Works

For an effective advocacy practice it is important to have a careful planning about the process, a proactive agenda, and an elaborate activity plan. No advocacy can succeed unless people are involved at various levels. An effective advocacy program must address the following key questions:

1. What do you want to change?
2. How can change come about?
3. Who can you help to bring about the desired change?
4. What methods would you use?
5. Who will do what and when?
6. How effective is your strategy?
7. Where do you need to adapt?[2]

Advocacy is seen by activists as a multiple of many strategies woven together. In the post-World War scenario, some new social movements emerged around women's rights, gay rights, civil rights and protecting environment, against nuclear power, among many more.

It is generally agreed that advocacy as practiced today by independent advocacy organizations evolved from the Citizen

Advocacy Movement in the West in the mid-1960s which stemmed from Bengt Nirge, Wolf Wolfensberger's, and John O'Brien's work on normalization. This fact is endorsed by many as fundamental to advocacy development in a number of countries, most notably the USA, Canada, Australia, and the UK.

Amnesty International founded in the early 1960s is believed to have been set up on the belief that ordinary people were capable of making extraordinary changes. In 1961, British lawyer Peter Benson wrote a newspaper appeal, "The Forgotten Prisoners," calling for an international effort to protest against the imprisonment of people for their political or religious beliefs. Within six months, the argument developed into a permanent, international movement, speaking up for the human rights of prisoners of conscience. As they grew, their focus expanded to take in not just prisoners of conscience but other victims of human rights abuses such as torture, "disappearances," and the death penalty—throughout the world.[3]

The 1990s witnessed the emergence of global social movement against globalization per se. Globalization was seen by critics as capital imperialism of rich nation thrust on the poor and developing countries with an eye on expanding their markets. A number of pressure groups emerged in developing countries. In India the Swadeshi movement was one such pressure group. The 1990s also saw an increasing acceptance of the fact that advocacy was political in nature and character. Hence, it came to be defined as a political process which aims to influence public policy and resource allocation decisions within political systems and institutions.

Some of the tools of advocacy include media campaigns, public speaking, and mobilization of groups for reaching at public places to raise their voice, picketing, signature campaigns, and distribution of literature based on data from credible sources.

In the West, lobbying is also seen a form of advocacy. Many known ex-members of US parliament represent in various lobbying groups. In lobbying, the lobbyists directly approach legislators. In India lobbying is not legal but is practiced, albeit surreptitiously.

The development promoters have added another dimension to advocacy and defined it as when a person or an organization helps individuals or groups to have their opinions and concerns heard by others. Advocacy is seen as a means for those people who otherwise find it difficult to get their opinions reflected on the issues they feel strongly about. Advocacy is seen by development activists as giving people a real control over their lives to help them make their own choices and informed decisions. Advocacy, according to this view, was not about acting in what is perceived to be the person or group's best interest but it is about standing with the individual or group to ensure they are able to say and try to get what they want and need, thus clearly identifying the role of change agents. Advocacy was seen as relevant where people were being treated unfairly as a result of other people's prejudices or because of their own vulnerabilities: where services provided do not take into account their needs or requirements. It is in this context the question why do we need advocacy is situated. Experts believe that, in general, people in authority are not good listeners, especially while responding to the disadvantaged and vulnerable groups. Being at the fringes, it is difficult for such individuals and groups to articulate their voice and concerns to those who wield authority, be they bureaucrats or politicians. Advocacy groups which often come from the nongovernmental and civil society arena therefore take up the causes and concerns of these individuals and groups. Two cases in point in the Indian context that saw relentless advocacy followed by legislation include the "anti-dowry" and "anticorruption" movements.

Advocacy, Activism, and Awareness

Advocacy posits voicing one's concerns or beliefs to people or institutions that matter in order to affect changes on behalf of others or one's own self. Advocacy can also mean arguing in favor of a cause, idea, or policy through active support and involvement. Doing advocacy requires an avid understanding of the realities and dynamics of power and decision-making process in a society. Advocacy can focus on any issue, any group of people, or any cause.

Activism is about an engaged citizenry charged with an effort to promote, impede or direct social, political, economic, or environmental change. Activism is kind of a civil engagement for collective action.

Activism is about individuals or groups or organizations taking concrete steps to affect change in the wider community, state, nation, and the world at large.

Activism adopts varying methods that include advocacy, agitation, civil disobedience, lobbying, boycott, strikes, fasting, *dharnas* (sit-in protests), protests, rallies, demonstrations, and direct action, to name a few. Activism can entail challenging the status quo, questioning authority, and employing critical thinking skills, and using media strategically and innovatively. Today, the social media has become an articulator of the voice of the voiceless and the marginalized. Advocacy and activism are closely related. Both advocacy and activism involve giving voice to those who are otherwise ignored, empowering the marginalized, and working to change the structures, policies, and practices that dehumanize people. Awareness-raising is an important part of advocacy and activism, and all the three practices are deeply linked. The goal of awareness-raising activities is to build understanding in the wider community about an issue, to highlight a particular work and its importance, and to persuade others to become involved as concerned individuals, allies, and activists themselves.[4]

It has come to be believed that the issue of the victims of the 1984 Bhopal Gas Tragedy has been kept alive by activists for three decades by using innovative means to remind the world what still remains to be done. The media is normally abuzz with articles and features a few days ahead of the anniversary day on December 2–3 every year. In the article titled "PR Push- NGOs innovate to keep Bhopal issue alive," Vidya Krishnan commented, "If activism is an experiment in innovation, Bhopal is the perfect lab. Ask any journalist who has been to the city."[5] Thanks to the efforts of some NGOs, scores of journalists from India and overseas make their "annual Bhopal pilgrimage." Translators are facilitated for those who do not speak English. Krishnan commented that it was not uncommon to find that journalists were provided with story angles also. Unlike other places, NGOs in Bhopal worked in sync with each other, despite the differences in their approaches and day-to-day squabbles.

Another interesting example is the simmering issue of stopping the use of checks in the UK that has the potential of snowballing into a major advocacy and social mobilization issue. British banks have been drawing up plans to halt the use of paper checks in favor of electronic transfer of money latest by 2018. Media has reported that several consumer groups and small business organizations have voiced their concerns and attacked the proposal spearheading "save the cheque" campaign to protect three-century-old method of payment.

It is a matter of fact that more and more people do not use checks anymore. The past two decades have reflected the use of checks being given up by two-third people, but many older people and traders still use checks. A payment council set up for the purpose is working toward that. The move is going to save hundreds of million pounds to banks. Quoting a source close to the council, media reported that a lot of work has gone into getting ready to do this for 2018 and it is pretty certain to go through. "The only thing that might delay this is politics," commented the reporter, "After all, you may have noticed bankers are not exactly popular at the moment."[6]

Process of Advocacy

Advocacy is seen by activists as a multiple of many strategies woven together.

A successful advocacy program must begin with defining the issue threadbare, followed by setting of measurable objectives, definition of target audience, and measurable research parameters. Let us look at the process of advocacy.

Today most nonprofit organizations use professional communication agencies to promote their issues and causes through well-heeled multiple-media campaigns. Such campaigns appearing on prime time television and mainstream newspapers, besides social media, and manage to get the right eyeballs and readers from among policy and opinion-making community. Some of the well-known national and INGOs such as Plan India, OneWorld, Cry can be cited as forerunners of campaigns ranging from child rights to empowering communities in distress and environment protection. Then there are advocacy portals such as Change.org and Avaaz, among others, which mobilize public opinion online.

Identifying the Issue

The program team as a first step has to identify an issue related to the development problem that seeks debate and policy intervention. The institutions and individuals that can help in culminating the process then need to be identified. This would also include those institutions and individuals who are expected to oppose and the extent to which they could go.

Let us take the instance of refugee infiltration in a country. It is obvious there would be two kinds of advocates: one that would like policy intervention in expatriating them; the other may take the human rights approach and the existing national policies and international conventions to help such groups. A broader issue then may help focus on specific advocacy issue.

Target Audience Segmentation

Once the advocacy issue is identified, target stakeholder analysis would be the next step. Who are going to be the facilitators from among various groups such as bureaucracy, politicians, NGO groups, civil society organizations, development writers within the media, and international organizations? As said earlier, possible adversary institutions and individuals would also have to be identified and worked upon to ensure that the issue is not derailed by their efforts. The program team after segmenting the target stakeholders would work on the strategy on how to reach out to them and who could facilitate the process. It may range from some social, political, economic, or religious institutions such as the church, the mosque, or temple representing interests of these groups or a media story, a talk show that could trigger action.

Determining Priority Actions

The advocacy team needs to make a list of priority actions for advocacy and rate for the complexity on parameters of cost, consequences, and impact on the policy problem. Experts suggest that those that rate poorly should be eliminated from the list or modified.

When Is the Right Time to Use Advocacy as a Tool?

Advocacy can be used when there is one of the following situations:

1. When an issue needs debate for clarity and consensus of various players, such as Article 377 of the Indian Constitution on gay rights in India.
2. When it becomes necessary to break the status quo on an issue for the desired change such as the anti-corruption movement.
3. When political support is necessary to bring about the necessary enactment like the Criminal Amendment Act.
4. An emergent situation that creates earth-shattering public opinion, cutting across narrow sectarian divide such as the Nirbhaya rape case in December 2013. An ordinance was promulgated by the government immediately to sooth frayed nerves and extreme anger among people.

The passing of the "Right to Information Act," ban on cigarette and liquor advertising, public smoking, indecent portrayal of women, and gay rights have been some of the campaigns that were long drawn and went on for decades before the national and international bodies gave them recognition in some countries.

The issue of giving 33 percent reservations to women in the Indian Parliament has been a contentious one for long. The issue has been discussed and debated by most of the political parties within and outside the parliament in India for years, but it seems a long way. Analysts believe that the biggest hurdle in this case are the parties themselves. While on the one hand some of the mainstream parties publicly support 33 percent reservations for women, but when it comes to allocating tickets to women within their parties to contest election, they don't adhere to that percentage- a first step to demonstrate their belief in what they profess. On the other hand, one-third reservations for women in gram panchayats and the voluntary efforts of many states to allocate 50 percent reservations in panchayats has not really been a result of any advocacy but a robust political will that truly has not only empowered women at the grassroots level but brought about the necessary paradigm shift.

Advocacy often is the outcome of research on developmental issues. Communication and social mobilization become the important ingredients in the trinity to reach the goal.

The W.K. Kellogg Foundation handbook on advocacy provides interesting tips on methods and strategies that the nonprofit organizations could make use of. Policy-makers, it reiterates, choose among competing policy options, therefore it serves the cause of the NGO sector to craft and evaluate options for putting before the policy-makers. Here are some of the tips articulated by the Kellogg Foundation:

Compare your preferred option to those of your opponents.
Make each option mutually exclusive.
Keep the list of options short. Include the option of doing nothing.
Present politically feasible choices.
Remember that policy issues and options are time sensitive.[7]

Opportunities to change policy do not always come with the precision of a clock. Sometime an incident may propel the long-desired change. An unfortunate incident of the gangrape of a young college girl in Delhi on December 16, 2012, can be cited as an example that hastened the passing of legislation due to the mounting of a gargantuan public opinion against the laid back attitude of the government in securing safe life for women in India. The incident relating to the 23-year-old woman intern who came to be known as Nirbhaya (the fearless), in a private bus in which she was travelling with a male friend, stirred the conscious of the city and elsewhere to such an extent that thousands of people especially the youth gathered at vantage places demanding justice for the victim who did not survive the assault. The incident gave a window to women activists to press for better laws to protect women. The issue had been pursued for over two decades, but this unfortunate incident provided an opportunity to mobilize a large section of society. This resulted in the setting up of the Justice Verma Committee and finally the passing of the Criminal Amendment Bill. After considering thousands of suggestions, the committee submitted a report which indicated that failures on the part of the government and police were the root cause behind crimes against women. In 2013, the Criminal Law (Amendment) Ordinance, 2013, was promulgated by the President of India; several new laws were passed, and six new fast-track courts were created to hear rape cases.

Message Development

An appropriate advocacy message works as the goal around which revolves the strategies, tactics, and actions. The message has to be clear and persuasive that captures the essence of what the advocacy group wishes to achieve.

A message is a concise and persuasive statement about the advocacy goal that captures what advocates want to achieve, why and how. Since the underlying purpose of a message is to create action, the message should also include the specific action participants are to take. Thus, message content should include the following:

The actual message can be brief, even in the shape of a slogan—but it would generally require technical information to convince participants to take action.

The Jago Re campaign by Tata Tea with just two words *Jago Re* (wake up) conveyed the essence of the advocacy movement that exhorted the youth to participate in the election process to register their voice. The statement also went with its tea brand.

In the second series while "Jago Re" remained the basic slogan, the issue was to sensitize the citizens not to pay bribes for getting the work done.

The *Times* campaigns Teach India and Lead India can also be cited as other examples.

In retrospect, "The Quit India" was an advocacy issue that turned into a movement exhorting the British to leave India in the 1940s.

After liberalization of the Indian economy in the early 1990s emerged the "Swadeshi lobby" that advocated support and policy intervention on things Indian.

Media Selection

Advocacy often has to reach out to a disparate set of target audience who can be accessed through a variety of media that would include mass media, interpersonal, and social media. The advocacy group will have to work on a proper media mix to get the multiplier impact. Experts believe that media selection should be the last step in the advocacy process, that is, after the issue has been decided, stakeholders segmented and their behavior analyzed so that it fits into the program and message and not the other way round, when media are decided before the messages are coined. In order to match the target groups with message and media the following need to be addressed:

1. The information sources accessed by participants to know about policy matters.
2. The credibility of the information sources with the participants.
3. The media habits of the participants.
4. The media reach and access.
5. The best communication channels to reach out with best cost and time opportunity.

Vigorous Use of Social Media for Advocacy

With a huge proliferation of social media, the Internet now seems to be an obvious choice for advocacy. Many organizations are engaged full time in advocacy of various issues. In fact, all major movements in recent times that include the Arab Rising, gay rights, and human rights have used social media vigorously to create worldwide movements. Change.Org is an interesting platform that spearheads issues on behalf of individuals and organizations. Advocating for allowing the defense force personnel to vote during the 16th parliamentary elections held in April–May 2014, Change.org ran the signature campaign and collected thousands of signatures and made it happen! The armed forces personnel indeed voted in the election. Change.org is a website operated by Change.org, Inc., based out of the USA that provides a free petition tool for over 60 million users and hosts sponsored campaigns for organizations. Its mission statement is "empower people everywhere to create the change they want to see."

Change.org is the fastest growing social change platform in the world, empowering more than 60 million people to create change in their communities.

We wake up every day knowing that our work is changing lives: helping kids to stop bullying in schools, communities to protect wilderness from mining, and citizens to hold corrupt officials to account. And we are just getting started.[8]

Avaaz, supposedly world's biggest online advocacy organization, operates in 15 languages. It claims 34 million people in 194 countries as its members. Avaaz.org was cofounded by Res Publica, a "community of public sector professionals dedicated to promoting good governance, civic virtue, and deliberative democracy" and MoveOn.org, an American non-profit progressive public policy advocacy group. It was also supported by Service Employees International Union, a founding partner, and Getups! An Australian nonprofit campaigning organization.[9] *The Guardian* once commented, "Avaaz is only five years old, but has exploded to become the globe's largest and most powerful online activist network."

Some of their Victories

For over two decades, the Tanzanian government was evicting the Maasai community from its traditional lands to make room for a big game hunting company to bring in tourists to shoot wildlife. Seized of the issue, Avaaz spearheaded a campaign calling on the Tanzanian President to stop the evictions. As a part of the strategy, in a gargantuan effort 1.7 million people signed the petition; along with the Maasai, it involved the international media, getting CNN and Al Jazeera to visit the area and break the story to the world. This was supplemented by hard-hitting advertisements in local papers calling out the government. The expenditure on ads was funded by Avaaz members. Prominent members sat on *dharna* outside the prime minister's office. The media covered the stories. Pressure was built on the prime minister to listen to the call to which he at last relented, and orders were passed that the community will not be evicted.

Defining Communication

Communication can be defined as the two-way process that involves a sender and a receiver, the former sending a message through a channel to the latter. By communication we share our ideas and views with others. If the message is commercial then the basic purpose of communication is to sell a product, service, or idea. If it is advocacy, then it aims to inform, educate, initiate a dialogue, or debate on a relevant issue. In advocacy the communication has a specific goal, that is, a rights-based approach in favor of those for whom the advocacy is undertaken. Advocacy communication is meant to be based on appropriate research that seeks to influence the behavior of the program participants in order to achieve the predetermined advocacy objective. A mix of various communication channels is selected to reach out to various target segments.

One does not have to refer to any books to know the role communication has played in bringing about social change in the world. The civil liberties movement in the USA and France, the apartheid movement in Africa, and the Independence movement in India, and the Arab Spring in recent times are fresh in the memory of people to understand the value of connecting with communities.

The domestic violence against women, the indecent portrayal of women in the media, female feticide, and the right to information are some of the top-of-the-mind movements in India that used communication to bring about social movements of sorts that provided necessary policy directions and appropriate laws and enactments in India. In the development sphere, however, communication is complex as it involves a disparate set of stakeholders, some of whom may be working in the opposite directions; hence, it requires a well-orchestrated strategy to reach the desired goal.

Communication needs to be focused on the issue at hand. Defining it broadly does not help. For instance, environment protection is very general and may mean different things to different people, such as forestation, water conflict between two states, litter management, air pollution, industrial emissions, global warming, etc. Therefore, it is imperative that the issue is defined clearly before working on its communication plan. Clarity about the issue would also help in defining the role of communication in addressing the issue and its activity plan. Research-based material and expertise lend credibility to the position taken on the issue.

In any development project, unlike the commercial endeavor, in which a specialist agency is selected to produce a campaign which may or may not be pretested in a focus group, for a development issue, the communication has to be participatory because any development project is addressing an issue that needs to be resolved. To illustrate it further, if the issue is water conservation through rain harvesting for domestic use, then not only would it need the communities or the neighborhood to agree to the common cause but also share resources, both manpower and financial (if the help is not pledged from an outside source) to achieve the goal. The communication would work as a facilitator that besides informing and educating people would also empower them to realize the value of the collective initiative.

Before any communication content or material is produced and shared through any channel, namely, interpersonal, mass media, or social media, it is important to pretest them. The process helps in getting the feedback of a cross section of the audience who would be exposed to the communication. Program implementers should not hesitate in revising the materials based on the feedback.

It is important to know through research whether the objectives set up have been achieved or not. Very often when movements take place as a consequence of an event, policy decision, or any other action immediate response is required and such planning and implementation processes are not possible and most research and evaluation is post facto. Therefore, it is important for social activists and advocacy agents to study historically how movements were built and advocacy used to promote their causes. This enables them to draw from the experience of other movements to meet immediate contingencies. On the other hand, for issues like women's empowerment long-term well-planned strategies can be developed and experimented with local communities keeping in view their issues.

For instance, in Kerala, an NGO facilitated a dialogue in the school parent–teacher association (PTA) meetings, when it was realized that the lack of toilet blocks dissuaded girls from going to school. Once the reason was discussed and understood, some schools, parents, and NGOs pooled in the financial resources to build toilet blocks in many schools.

Communication experts believe that undue importance is often given to the use of mass media, which may not always be useful. For reaching out to the mind space of the people with a goal of changing their attitudes and behavior, mass media may not be adequate. Interpersonal media and now the new age media, that is, the social media may prove more appropriate. Mass media has the great capability to inform and educate, but for large groups of people to adopt new practices for long term, other means of motivation and support would also be required.

Program implementers need to decide on various communication channels to connect with communities and other stakeholders. Many

NGOs are empowering communities in media facilitation so that they could articulate their issues themselves.

The Deccan Development Society (DDS), for instance, showcased the video production by rural women on developmental issue to Delhi audience in 2008. It looked so amazing real that the workshop in Delhi was also being videographed by some women who had come for the workshop. P.V. Sateesh, the moving spirit behind the venture, is a proud man today, having helped many such women articulate their stories through the medium. The stories regularly appear in regional news channels.

It began as a series of video workshops a few years ago. Spread over eight months, each workshop was for four days. The workshops have trained a total of seven women, of whom four are illiterate. Of these seven women, two are students, four are farm laborers, and one is a DDS worker. All of them are dalits in the age group of 16–35 years. The workshops started with a total of 11 persons, 10 women, and one man. Out of them, four dropped out during various phases of the workshops and seven have made it to all the workshops. The training objective was to familiarize the participants with the grammar of television, with the operation of video cameras, and in editing their shoots and making their own stories.

Mobilizing Public Opinion through Print Media

The print media has been a precursor in bringing developmental issues to the forefront. If one newspaper is to be mentioned for its pioneering and continued efforts, it undoubtedly is *The Hindu*. Over a period of time, other newspapers have also joined the bandwagon. It is not uncommon to find developmental stories in mainstream newspapers.

For instance, in a story in *The Tribune* titled "UP Refuses Deaths during Childbirth," the writer Shahira Naim, quoting an official from the Registrar General's office, said, "The situation in UP is very grim. Only 0.7 percent of the total registered deaths were medically certified." The reason here is interesting, the kith and kin of the deceased "create an environment that threatens free reporting." The fear of departmental inquiries, attack by relatives, and disciplinary action against alleged negligence are cited as some of the reasons for nonreporting. The story quotes one staff nurse who said, "I am naturally scared of reporting death. I am only human. Over here if something goes wrong, they will first suspend and only then will they find out if we did anything wrong."

The story then touches upon caste-based discrimination. Quoting a UNICEF study of 2007 conducted in six northern states, the writer mentioned that 61 percent women who died during pregnancy were from the dalit or tribal communities. For instance, in Chitrakoot, all the health functionaries such an anganwadi worker, two accredited social health activists (ASHAs) and an auxiliary nurse midwife (ANM) were from the upper castes, who had never visited any any person from the Kol community as they were considered untouchables.

During immunization days, the so-called high-caste health functionaries brought a dalit to administer polio drops to children belonging to dalits and tribal communities. Quoting from a report, she writes:

> A complete lack of political will to address the issue of maternal deaths and a devious collusion between state-level and district health officials not only to deny these dying women their basic human rights to survive but also the dignity of making their death part of the official statistics.[10]

On its opinion page, *The Hindu* carried the article "Drought of Justice, Flood of Funds" by the foremost development writer P. Sainath befittingly on the Republic Day, August 15, 2009. Sainath lambasted the government for doling out concessions to the corporate world, while it pleaded lack of enough resources when it came to catering to development funds. He estimated the concession that worked out to ₹30 crore an hour to the corporate sector. To quote him:

> Income foregone in 2007–08 due to direct tax concessions was ₹62,199 crore. That foregone on excise duty was ₹87,468 crore. And on customs duty ₹153,593 crore. That adds up to ₹303,260 crore. Even if we drop export credit from this, it comes to well over ₹200,000 crore. For 2008–09, that figure would be over ₹300,000 crore. That is a very conservative estimate. It does not include all manner of subsidies and rate cuts and other freebies to the corporate sector. But it's big enough.

On the other hand, he writes ruefully, "Ask for expansion of the NREGS, universal access to the PDS, more spending on health and education—and there's no money. But there's enough to give away to the corporate world in concessions."[11]

Talking about the social responsibility of business, Kanika Datta in her insightful article, "Needed a Social Regulator," refers to India's human development which is only a little above those of sub-Saharan Africa, suggesting that the government has a huge challenge on its hands.

What is the role of business? She argues that these problems may not be the private sector's making, but can business be isolated from the social milieu in which it operates? "So, instead of searching for partial stop-gap solutions to an enduring problem," she suggests:

> It might be to the private sector's advantage to suggest a kind of "social sector depreciation charge" in the form of compulsory financing of primary schools and health centers and hospitals in targeted areas. This would differ from the current set-up in that these schools and hospitals could be administered by independent institutions, not associated charitable trusts, and audited and monitored by independent regulators.

As India has insurance and telecom regulators, which have facilitated growth, despite the hiccups, she suggests for independent social sector regulators who monitor the quality of education and health delivery systems and work at the sorely needed "capacity building." "Indian trade and industry has proved that it is quite capable of being globally competitive. Now, it is time to demonstrate genuine good corporate citizenship and prove to the doubters that social justice can be embedded in market dynamics," she writes on an optimistic note.[12]

Writing on gender discrimination and gender equity can make better sense if put in an interesting manner and contextualized. In a very inspiring story, Dinkar Vashisht wrote how in Haryana that has the most shameful data on sex ratio, three sisters, daughters of a former professor of political science not only made it to the coveted administrative services decades ago, but two of them have risen to the level of chief secretaries to the State of Haryana, while the third may be waiting in the wings. The story was about Meenakshi Chaudhary, who retired in 2006 as the chief secretary to the government of Haryana and Urvashi Gulati, the present chief secretary, who brought the state international laurels under her stewardship as commissioner and principal secretary of rural development and panchayat department. Haryana successfully implemented the Nirmal Scheme, an initiative to improve sanitation in villages. The state received the UNDP recognition and an award from the president of India and an entry into the Limca book of records. The third sister Keshni Arora is also an IAS officer in the Haryana Government.

The story then quotes one of the sisters, who said they were not really born with a silver spoon. They had to struggle hard to reach where they have been today.[13]

If we look at the above stories in various mainstream dailies, it sure makes a lot of impact. Development programmers and development writers therefore must synergize their efforts to mobilize public opinion by working in partnership with the media.

Electronic Media in the Developmental Saga

The electronic media plays an important role in engaging with the viewers on issues that concern the viewers. The past few years have seen on the one hand crass commercialism to gain the eyeballs, but on the other, an increase in the people-centric programs to engage with the audience, adopting a participative approach. CNN-IBN was the first one to initiate a citizen journalist program in 2005. Its sister Hindi news channel IBN 7 also started the program in the same year: The program that allows nonprofessionals in researching, gathering, and presenting news. CNN-IBN's *Be the Change* program bagged the News Television Award in 2012 endorsed by the Ministry of Information & Broadcasting. Some of the themes of the program encompass official negligence, law violation, against corruption, and lack of civic amenities. Supported by media such programs hopefully are expected to have an impact on the concerned agencies in putting their act together.

The "Tribal Drum": The Radio

With the coming of FM in India, the monopoly of the government on entertainment channels has broken, but it still monopolizes news on radio. The third alternative, the community radio has been gaining currency, albeit slowly in India. Some committed nongovernmental organizations have been pushing the agenda of voicing the concerns of the marginalized communities through participative approach via the community radio in some distant places and hamlets. The proponents of the community radio feel that the medium holds the key that could address the linguistic, cultural, and economic diversity of India, which the government-owned All-India Radio or the FMs would never be able to do.

Some of the community radio initiatives that are being talked about for their participative work include the VOICES in Budhikot in Karnataka, the DDS in Pastapur (Andhra Pradesh), the Alternative for India Development (AID) project in Daltonganj in Jharkhand, and the Kutch Mahila Vikas Sangthan (KMVS) project in Bhuj, Gujarat.

The Increasing Footfalls of Cinema and Television Programs in a Convergent World

Cinema—both through the theatrical circuit, and now via television and Internet viewing, not to forget its access on hand held iPads and mobile phones has a greater reach than it was ever conceived. Some sensitive filmmakers have picked up developmental issues including health in their films with tremendous impact. Manthan, a film on cooperative sector that changed the lives of thousands of families taking them to the road to development; *Phir Milenge* and *My Brother Nikhil*, films that addressed the issue of stigma attached to HIV/AIDS; *Black* aimed at the issue of blindness and dementia; and *Tare Zameen Par*, addressed the issue of dyslexia among children. Each of these films created the necessary debate and sensitized the stakeholders. Aapki Antara was a television serial based on autism among children. The episodes ended with a real-life situation, the parents talking about how their children were dealing with autism. It also reflected a helpline number to know more about the diseases. One of the popular teleserial Balika Vadhu that started with the issue of child marriage picked up many issues in its long journey including sensitizing very young kids on sexual abuse, but later the storyline got lost, given that the serial ran for years with generation change among protagonists and many leaving the serial in between.

Enhancing Brand Value through Social Interface

The brand value of a social issue can be enhanced when it becomes a talking point. The media for such an interface could range from inter-personal to social media and even advertising. When Lowe created the "What an Idea, Sirji!" campaign, little did it realize where its campaign for Idea Cellular would lead to. The hypothetical "Purmi-Thumihar" caste conflict, village children learning their lessons straight from a high-brow public school, or a woman minister trying to touch the pulse of public opinion through SMS and voice mail, the protagonist, cine star Abhishek Bachchan telling her, "Public ki sunoge, toh public aapki sunenge, nahin toh bahut maaregi. Yehi hai democracy" (If you listen to the public, the public will listen to you, or else you would have to pay dearly. This is democracy) or the latest "aap hamein ullu nahin baana sakate" (You cannot befool us), emphasizing the access of information via the Internet instantly on a mobile.

Mobilizing Communities through Social Media: A World *sans* Boundaries

The Internet has created a flat world where communities cutting across the barriers of space, time, color, caste, and socioeconomic divide can join on issues that concern the human race. It is not uncommon to receive e-mails on issues that may touch the hearts and minds. *What Would You Do?* is the moving story of a father with a mentally and physically challenged child, circulated widely through the e-mail. Here is the reproduction:

What would you do? You make a choice! Don't look for a punch line; there isn't one!
  Read it.

Anyway. My question to all of you is: would you have made the same choice?
  At a fundraising dinner for a school that serves learning-disabled children, the father of one of the students delivered a speech that would never be forgotten by all who attended. After extolling the school and its dedicated staff, he offered a question:

(continued)

(continued)

"When not interfered with by outside influences, everything nature does is done with perfection. Yet my son, Shay, cannot learn things as other children do. He cannot understand things as other children do.

Where is the natural order of things in my son?"

The audience was stilled by the query.

The father continued. "I believe, that when a child like Shay, physically and mentally handicapped comes into the world, an opportunity to realize true human nature presents itself, and it comes, in the way other people treat that child." Then he told the following story: Shay and his father had walked past a park where some boys Shay knew were playing baseball. Shay asked, "Do you think they'll let me play?" Shay's father knew that most of the boys would not want someone! like Shay on their team, but the father also understood that if his son were allowed to play, it would give him a much-needed sense of belonging and some confidence to be accepted by others in spite of his handicaps. Shay's father approached one of the boys on the field and asked if Shay could play, not expecting much. The boy looked around for guidance and said, "We're losing by six runs and the game is in the eighth inning. I guess he can be on our team and we'll try to put him in to bat in the ninth inning."

Shay struggled over to the team's bench put on a team shirt with a broad smile and his Father had a small tear in his eye and warmth in his heart. The boys saw the father's joy at his son being accepted. In the bottom of the eighth inning, Shay's team scored a few runs but was still behind by three. In the top of the ninth inning, Shay put on a glove and played in the right field. Even though no hits came his way, he was obviously ecstatic just to be in the game and on the field, grinning from ear to ear as his father waved to him from the stands.

In the bottom of the ninth inning, Shay's team scored again. Now, with two outs and the bases loaded, the potential winning run was on base and Shay was scheduled to be next at bat. At this juncture, do they let Shay bat and give away their chance to win the game? Surprisingly, Shay was given the bat. Everyone knew that a hit was all but impossible 'cause Shay didn't even know how to hold the bat properly, much less connect with the ball. However, as Shay stepped up to the plate, the pitcher, recognizing the other team putting winning aside for this moment in Shay's life, moved in a few steps to lob the ball in softly so Shay could at least be able to make contact. The first pitch came and Shay swung clumsily and missed. The pitcher again took a few steps forward to toss the ball softly towards Shay. As the pitch came in, Shay swung at the ball and hit a slow ground ball right back to the pitcher. The game would now be over, but the pitcher picked up the soft grounder and could have easily thrown the ball to the first baseman. Shay would have been out and that would have been the end of the game. Instead, the pitcher threw the ball right over the head of the first baseman, out of reach of all team mates. Everyone from the stands and both teams started yelling, "Shay, run to first! Run to first!" Never in his life had Shay ever ran that far but made it to first base. He scampered down the baseline, wide-eyed and startled. Everyone yelled, "Run to second, run to second!" Catching his breath, Shay awkwardly ran towards second, gleaming and struggling make it to second base. By

(continued)

(continued)

the time Shay rounded towards second base, the right fielder had the ball, the smallest guy on their team, who had a chance to be the hero for his team for the first time. He could have thrown the ball to the second-baseman for the tag, but he understood the pitcher's intentions and he too intentionally threw the ball high and far over the third-baseman's head. Shay ran toward third base deliriously as the runners ahead of him circled the bases toward home. All were screaming, "Shay, Shay, Shay, all the Way Shay." Shay reached third base, the opposing shortstop ran to help him and turned him in the direction of third base, and shouted, "Run to third Shay, run to third." As Shay rounded third, the boys from both teams and those watching were on their feet were screaming, "Shay, run home! Shay ran to home, stepped on the plate, and was cheered as the hero who hit the "Grand Slam" and won the game for his team.

That day, said the father softly with tears now rolling down his face, the boys from both teams helped bring a piece of true love and humanity into this world Shay didn't make it to another summer and died that winter, having never forgotten being the hero and making his Father so happy and coming home and seeing his Mother tearfully embrace her little hero of the day!

AND, NOW A LITTLE FOOTNOTE TO THIS STORY:

We all send thousands of jokes through the e-mail without a second thought, but when it comes to sending messages about life choices, people think twice about sharing. The crude, vulgar, and often obscene pass freely through cyberspace, but public discussion about decency is too often suppressed in our schools and workplaces. If you're thinking about forwarding this message, chances are that you're probably sorting out the people on your address list that aren't the "appropriate" ones to receive this type of message. Well, the person who sent you this believes that we all can make a difference. We all have thousands of opportunities every single day to help realize the "natural order of things." So many seemingly trivial interactions between two people present us with a choice: Do we pass along a little spark of love and humanity or do we pass up that opportunity to brighten the day of those with us the least able, and leave the world a little bit colder in the process?

A wise man once said every society is judged by how it treats it's least fortunate amongst them!

You now have two choices:

1. Delete
2. Forward

Note: An e-mail that was received and forwarded, (but hopefully not deleted) by millions of Internet users in August 2008.

Social media has become a huge hub for brand promotion by marketers.

Many NGOs and national and international organizations in the development sector have befittingly used the social media space to reach out their stakeholders. In the following paragraphs, a case study in the public service category which used social media has been critically examined.

UNICEF

UNICEF India's campaign of "Take Poo 2 Loo" on Facebook, Twitter, and YouTube to spread the message of the harmful effects of open defecation is interesting, but in terms of target audience strategy, a bit misplaced.

About 595 million people defecate in the open in India. The fictional character Poo in the shape of feces is funny and whacky. The Facebook page has many videos like "The singing Poo" and the "Poo dabba dance" in animation. Over 1.5 lakh people have pledged "to take the Poo to the loo." Poo made it to the *Times* "15 most influential fictional characters in 2014."[14]

When we look at the presence of this campaign on the social networking sites, one cannot help but question the logic behind the use of social media for an issue like this. The kind of people who access Facebook in India in all probability would not be defecating in the open; such people will also in any way really be influencers to people in the villages defecating in the open. The only thing Poo could do, if at all, was to create a buzz in the media without any tangible gains for the people whose behavior it was supposed to change. For truly taking the *Poo to the Loo*, motivating people to construct toilets would be the first step especially at the grassroots-level in thousands of villages. Interestingly, a campaign in the legacy media like radio and television, "Jahan Soch Wahan Shauchalya" (Wherever there is an application of thought, there would be toilets), with cine star Vidya Balan has been getting critical acclaim for its hard-headed commonsensical narrative.

Defining Social Mobilization

Social mobilization is defined as:

> The process that engages and motivates a wide range of partners and allies at national and local levels to raise awareness of and demand for a particular developmental issue through face-to-face dialogue. Members of institutions,

community networks, civic and religious groups and others work in a coordinated way to reach specific groups of people for dialogue with planned messages. In other words, social mobilization seeks to facilitate change through a range of players engaged in interrelated and complementary efforts.[15]

One of the interesting practices of social mobilization came from Colombia in the 1980s, what came to be known as the Juanita Campaign in 1988. This initiative used the image of a 10-year-old girl to represent all Colombian children. Called Juanita for the purposes of the campaign, the girl's photograph and letter appeared in various mass media that included the press, radio, and television. Her large posters could be seen on squares all over the country. Her letter was also printed as a leaflet with information to sensitize all the mayoral candidates and their immediate political colleagues to the problems faced by children in Colombia. The underlying premise of the slogan was that democracy is fundamentally local and that effective action and accountability can be assured only when issues and actors are rooted locally.

The second example came a decade later from the same place, when peace efforts were still fragmented and the peace movement remained weak. In 1996, the Children's Movement for Peace emerged with young people working as individuals or in small groups, often at great risk. It led to the UNICEF supported Children's Mandate for Peace and Rights in which 2.7 million children voted overwhelmingly for their rights to life and peace. In 1997, the Citizen's Mandate that brought 10 million adult Colombians to the polls, who backed the Children's Mandate and pledged their own commitment to peace making. In 1998, with a manifesto based on both mandates, Andres Pastrana swept the polls in the Colombian presidential elections.[16]

As per the handbook for trainers on participatory local development of the panchayati raj from the Food and Agriculture Organization's (FAO),

[Social mobilization] is the cornerstone of participatory approaches in rural development and poverty alleviation programs. It is a powerful instrument in decentralization policies and programs aimed at strengthening human and institutional resources development at local level. Social mobilization strengthens participation of rural poor in local decision-making, improves their access to social and production services and efficiency in the use of locally available financial resources, and enhances opportunities for asset-building by the poorest of the poor.[17]

Hamaara Paisa, Hamaara Hisaab (our money, our account), a social mobilization movement initiated by Mazdoor Kisan Shakti Sangathan (MKSS), Rajasthan in 1990 has become a large grassroots organization that grew out of a local struggle for minimum wages and its belief that change for the local people would only come through the political process. Despite promises by the politicians of all parties and hues, the poor struggled for decades to get their rightful wages from contractors even on government jobs. The campaigners realized that they had to obtain the relevant documentation, in particular, the muster rolls to expose the truth about the predicament of gullible workers. The right to information and the right to survive thus became the driving force in peoples' minds.

The campaign of MKSS in Rajasthan befittingly branded as *Hamaara Paisa, Hamaara Hisaab,* initially demanded to see the muster rolls. The requests obviously were met with refusal on the grounds that these were "secret documents." These refusals led to a long agitation for the right to access information. By 1994, the MKSS hit upon a new, empowering strategy, based on the idea of a Jan Sunwai or "public hearing." The MKSS brought people together and simply read out official documents that they had procured, either through surreptitious means or from officials who had no idea of their import. The documents related to construction records for school buildings, panchayat bhawans and patwari bhawans, dams, bridges, and other local structures. The government boycotted the first few hearings. To ensure openness and publicity, anyone could attend and an independent outsider chaired each hearing. Local officials and public representatives were invited, including those likely to be at the receiving end. The proceedings were videotaped, which deterred the speakers from misrepresenting information. When the records were read out it, was sometimes immediately obvious that they contained false information. Some such instances included presentation of false conveyance bills or payment to people who were long dead. The documentation also proved that corrupt officials and others were siphoning off money and that minimum wages were being paid only on paper. It became evident that the poor were being exploited in two ways, namely, by denial of their minimum wages and through corruption by officials.

The poor people, who were intimidated for long, now had a platform where they could speak out fearlessly. Soon the movement received support from the middle class that spoke openly against corruption as it hurt them too in many ways.

The MKSS in Rajasthan demanded and got information on minimum wages and government infrastructure programs, leading to, in the process, a national movement for freedom of information. After a long battle, the government announced a change in the Panchayat Act, so people could inspect local documents pertaining to development works. This also led to the national movement for Right to Information Act, led by Ms Aruna Roy and others finally the enactment of a legendary Right to Information Act 2005.[18]

Role of Gram Sabha and Public Information in Social Mobilization

The 73rd Constitutional Amendment has empowered the village council, the gram sabha, into being a very powerful tool of social mobilization. Many types of neighborhood groups, health and literacy programs, *Mahila Mandals* (village women's groups) are becoming active, thanks to the growing awareness, the presence of the voluntary sector and to an extent the efforts of the government. Social mobilization can be successful only when people are involved in issues that affect their lives and livelihood. Access to information is the first step.

Here are a few case studies on the success of social mobilization that in turn empowered the local governing bodies in the southern states of Kerala and Andhra Pradesh.

Total Sanitation Program in Avanur Gram Panchayat, Kerala, India

This example of successful mobilization of the entire community by a gram panchayat to meet a basic need has been widely recognized. It has brought national honor and a cash prize of ₹1.2 million to the Panchayat.

In 1996, a survey held by the Avanur Gram Panchayat in Kerala State found that over 2,000 of Avanur's 5,000 households were too poor to afford basic sanitation facilities. The gram panchayat president convened a series of awareness-building meetings for all families below the poverty line. As an outcome of these meetings, it was agreed that the gram panchayat would provide all these families building material for sanitation units, with the condition that each beneficiary family would complete 20 percent of the work on its own. The meetings focused on awareness-building of women as main beneficiaries. Much to the surprise of all, the campaign was successfully completed within three months. The gram panchayat spent only 20 percent of allocated resources because 80 percent of the work was done by the beneficiary families themselves. In this way, a total of about ₹12 million in assets could be mobilized for the poorest families.

Total Housing Scheme in Avanur Gram Panchayat, Kerala State, India

The Avanur Gram Panchayat used the cash award of ₹1.2 million to start a Total Housing Scheme for families below the poverty line. This led to 500 houses being built during 1997–2000. The gram panchayat gave each family an amount of ₹20,000 in three stages, as a grant. The beneficiary families contributed their own labor and material worth ₹30,000 for each unit. The scheme created assets worth more than ₹25 million. The gram panchayat has also successfully implemented a drinking water scheme and neighborhood units in Avanur and was declared the Best Panchayat' in Kerala for its innovative work.

The Janmabhoomi Program in Andhra Pradesh: A Learning Model for Capacity-Building for Participatory Local Development Planning

Janmabhoomi was inspired by South Korea's *Saemaul Undong* program and launched in January 1997 as a mass mobilization effort to involve people in rural development planning and decision-making through PRIs in Andhra Pradesh. It aims to take the administration closer to the people, make it more responsive to their felt needs and to promote transparency and accountability in public affairs. It is also directed against the caste system. It has specific programs for disadvantaged groups such as women, the Scheduled Castes and Tribes, and people with disabilities to integrate them into mainstream development.

Janmabhoomi has activated the gram sabha, which is convened every three months and presided over by the Sarpanch, the Mandal president, the ward member, and the government.

Case Studies in Social Audit

Social Audit in Delhi

Parivartan (a nonprofit organization) initially began its journey about a decade ago by helping people get their work done in government departments without having to pay bribes.

It started out as a people's movement in June 2000, to provide relief to taxpayers from corrupt income tax officers, who would demand a percentage from the refund amount of tax paid in excess. Taxpayers in Delhi through its public information campaigns were exhorted not to pay bribes but to approach Parivartan with their grievances.

Parivartan, however, soon realized that although its role as troubleshooter provided immediate relief to people, it neither empowered citizens to resolve their grievances directly nor helped bring about permanent systemic changes.

The organization then began to make use the Delhi Right to Information Act 2001 to resolve public grievances. The Delhi Right to Information Act, which came into effect on October 2, 2001, empowers citizens to access government files by simply filling out a form and submitting it to the concerned department. However, implementing the law has not so easy and needed lots of honest efforts to put it into practice.

Some of the major cases initiated by Parivartan in Delhi include the social audit of the Municipal Corporation of Delhi that reflected that public money was routinely redirected away from the purposes it was intended for. Another social audit conducted by this NGO was a citizen's initiative, along with the local residents of two resettlement colonies of North East Delhi, namely, Sundernagri and New Seemapuri, for development works undertaken by the Engineering Department of the Municipal Corporation of Delhi (MCD). It was found that in these two resettlement colonies between April 1, 2000 and March 31, 2002, only works pertaining to construction of roads, lanes, and drains, and installation of hand pumps were taken up for a total of 68 contracts worth about ₹1.42 crore.

It was also found that ration shopkeepers were not willing to divulge their records, food department officials were not filing complaints, and the police were not acting on their own or accepting complaints from the public. After the initiatives of Parivartan, more than 250 people from different parts of Delhi filed applications under the Delhi Right to Information Act and sought the records of their ration shopkeepers. They succeeded in getting the records in Kalyanpuri, R. K. Puram, Bhatti Mines, and Anna Nagar. The crusade continues.[19]

Social Audit in Bolangir District of Orissa

Initiated by ActionAid, an INGO, and assisted by the gram sabha members of Jharnipalli Panchayat, Agaipur block, a one-day social audit of development works was carried out in the panchayat to cover three years preceding October 2001. The audit took place with the active participation of many individuals and agencies, including block and district administration officials, MKSS, NCPRI, and ActionAid India.

ActionAid undertook the task of collecting information, sorting and filling, analysis and tabulation, and information sharing and physical verification. Many rounds of discussion on the plan for the entire action training project preceded the work.

As a first step in the process, a street play (*Geeth Natya*) was created by the villagers of Adendungri and Kudopalli and an organization, informing people through the folk form familiar to them about their right to social audit, and the fact that such an audit is going to be taken up soon in their village.

As a next step, the local administration was met with and appraised about the plans. The district collector expressed his full support and cooperation in the effort. The same feelings were reflected by the local MLA, who wanted similar processes to be taken up in as many gram panchayats as possible in his constituency. At a later date, the local police officials were also informed about the plans for the social audit. The last four weeks preceding the social audit saw the efforts on many fronts intensifying as a run up to the audit.

With the help of the district collector's introduction letter and instructions, a team of people started collecting information related to various works in the panchayat for three years (1998–1999, 1999–2000, and 2000–2001).

Information sought covered various development works that had been taken up by the block office in Agalpur and works taken up directly by the Panchayat. The audit brought to the fore the development projects that were sanctioned, the state of works, and glitches.[20]

ACSM Strategies with Case Studies

Having looked at the concepts, role, and scope of ACSM individually, it is clearly understood that all the three are interdependent and must be synergized for any developmental project. In the following paragraphs a number of such projects would be discussed that required the coordination of ASCM.

"Stop TB" Partnership

One of the larger ACSM strategies in the past few years at the international scale concerns the control of tuberculosis (TB). In the *Global Plan: Stop TB Partnership 2006–2015*, a significant scaling up of ACSM was envisaged to achieve the global targets for tuberculosis control. In 2005, the ACSM Working Group (ACSM WG) was established as the seventh working group of the Stop TB Partnership to mobilize political, social, and financial resources; to sustain and expand the global movement to eliminate TB; and to foster the development of more effective ACSM programming at the country level in support of TB control. This work plan focuses on those areas where ACSM has most to offer and where ACSM strategies can be most effectively synergized to help address four key challenges to TB control at the country level. Some of these included the following:

- Improving case detection and treatment adherence
- Combating stigma and discrimination
- Empowering people affected by TB
- Mobilizing political commitment and resources for TB.[21]

The program identified the following strategic objectives:

- By 2008, at least 10 endemic countries will have developed and will be implementing multisectoral, participatory ACSM initiatives, and generating qualitative and quantitative data on ACSM's contribution to TB control.
- By 2010, 20 priority countries implemented multisectoral, participatory-based ACSM initiatives, and monitoring and evaluating their outcomes.
- By 2015, multisectoral, participatory ACSM methodologies will be a fully developed component of the Stop TB Strategy.
- By 2015, all priority countries will be implementing effective and participatory ACSM initiatives.

These objectives were envisaged to be achieved through a mix of five key strategic components:

1. Building national and subnational ACSM capacity
2. Building inclusion of patients and affected communities
3. Ensuring political commitment and accountability
4. Building country-level ACSM partnerships
5. Learning, adapting, and building on good ACSM practices.[22]

India is said to bear the highest burden of TB with 2.3 million cases of TB out of a global incidence of 9 million as per WHO data for the year 2013. It is estimated that about 40 percent of the Indian population is infected with TB bacteria, the vast majority of whom have latent rather than active TB.[23]

Creating Awareness Through ACSM to Eradicate Tuberculosis in India

Adventist Development and Relief Agency (ADRA) made use of the ASCM strategy to address the Revised National Tuberculosis Control Programme (RNTCP) at the grassroots level in eight districts of Bihar. The agency claimed to have brought down the incidence of TB by reaching out to people though the rigor of ACSM. The focus of this initiative was to educate the communities about the symptoms of the diseases that have resulted in higher rate of detection, bringing down lower infection numbers.[24]

ACSM on National Immunization Day

Polio, which affected millions of children in India, was envisaged to be eradicated by the year 2000, but that was not to be. India was declared polio free in 2014.

In retrospect, a gargantuan effort was undertaken every time the children had to be taken for polio drops. Pulse polio probably is one of the longest run campaigns involving thousands of crores of rupees in informing, educating, and communicating with various stakeholders through ACSM.

The ACSM becomes particularly important during and leading up to National Immunization Days.

Posters, banners, TV and radio spots, road shows, rallies, and public address system were some of the activities undertaken to announce the campaign. Movie stars and national sports personalities wholeheartedly lent their support in advocating the importance of polio eradication.

Many NGOs and UN organizations, particularly the UNICEF, have played a crucial role in the entire exercise. Social organizations, such as the Rotary International, also participated enthusiastically in the endeavor.

The UNICEF has an extensive network of 3,300 community mobilizing coordinators (CMCs) in place, whose sole role is to get the word out among communities that the polio immunization activities are being conducted and reminding parents on the importance of having their children immunized.

The engagement of local influencers and religious leaders helped reduce any potential resistance to the polio vaccine among communities. "Special teams" of local influencers or local community or religious leaders visit homes of parents who may have concerns about the safety of the polio vaccine. Vaccinators carry written statements such as religious fatwas with them, to reassure parents that polio vaccination is the right thing to do for their children.

All these activities contributed to ensure reaching out to the desired target audience on the national immunization day.[25]

In the box (as follows), a run on the pulse polio campaign strategy would highlight the need for creativity and celebrity endorsement in connecting with the target audience.

Celebrity endorsement in pulse polio campaign

In the 1980s and early 1990s, one saw ads on pulse polio drops on government owned television's national hook-up exhorting the parents to take their children for polio drops to camps especially organized for the purpose. The communication was directed mainly at the economically weaker section, which probably had to sacrifice a day's wages to take leave from their casual job to get the child immunized. One of the ads had a woman asking her husband, if she could take their child for polio drops, to which he quipped as to what would happen to her day's wages. Pointing to an adolescent child on crèches, she reasoned out with her husband that it was a small sacrifice to avoid disability to their child as the boy in the frame had. The ad was hard hitting, one that used a rational approach to get the desired response.

A number of creative agencies over a period of time have been involved to make commercials more persuasive and saleable. Shahrukh Khan and other male celebrities endorsed the social product for some time. In one of the TVC, Shahrukh Khan was shown saying that he was not going for his shoot on that day as it was the day to take his child for pulse polio drops. The ad would appear on the designated day to also serve as a reminder to the target audience.

One of the ads in the series had cricketing sensation Virendra Sehwag being nudged by some of his cricketing team members that since he forgot his son for polio drops, they brought the child.

Over a period of time it was seen that although more and more people were coming for pulse polio drops but it was long way to go. One of the TVC had Amitabh Bachchan cribbing about people not listening to him, probably because they wanted to listen to a beauty queen instead. And there came Miss World Aishwarya Rai, who pleaded with the viewers not to annoy Amitabh Bachchan and take their children for polio drops.

It was felt that there was a general perception among people that pulse polio drops had to be given once. In order to dispel that myth and tell people that pulse polio drops had to be given many times, till the child reached the age of two years, the strategy was changed to bring home the point. When India and Pakistan were engaged in the Cricket series in April 2004, yet another ad in the series was added, which this time had Amitabh Bachchan with the famous "master blaster" Sachin Tendulkar. The ad had Bachchan telling the viewers that he was surprised to see that people thought they were the best judges about how many times the drops had to be given. Then he went on to say that the drops had to be given every time there was an announcement for pulse polio drops till the child turned two years. He made an analogy with Sachin who was sitting next to him saying that if Sachin walked off the field after a few runs to say it was enough, could India win? "No" gestured Sachin exhorting the viewers with his soft voice "Do boond zindagi ki" (Only two drops for life). The camera then cut to the irrepressible Amitabh Bachchan, seen picking up the cricket bat in a gesture as if he was going to hit those, who did not listen to him (a friendly gesture elders generally indulge in when warning youngsters to listen to them, else…!).

Some analysts feel that a rigorous campaign has resulted in creating not only the right environment but also awareness among the targeted group.[26]

Mobilizing Grassroots Communities to Be Self-reliant: Case Study of Post-tsunami Occurrence in India (An Effort at ACSM)

On December 26, 2005, a tsunami triggered by an earthquake off the coast of Sumatra devastated several countries in South and South East Asia, and even as far as East Africa. In India, the tsunami caused massive destruction and casualties in the coastal regions of Tamil Nadu, Andhra Pradesh, Kerala, the Union Territories of Andaman & Nicobar Islands, and Puducherry. More than 10,000 people lost their lives and many were injured. In addition, the tsunami caused the destruction of infrastructure, housing, and livelihood. The environmental impacts were severe, including large amounts of coastal land being contaminated by sea water. Beyond the visible effects of the tsunami, the lives and livelihoods of countless people and communities were severely impacted and may take years to rebuild.

Many organizations and NGOs responded very quickly to the situation and provided emergency relief and supplies to help the affected people. However, beyond this immediate assistance, a number of long-term issues emerged. These issues affect the coastal areas in general and would need to be addressed in the future. The tsunami underscored the vulnerability of coastal regions, which are also susceptible to other natural disasters such as cyclones and/or floods.

Partnership

OneWorld South Asia (OWSA), in association with Plan International and the Indian Institute of Mass Communication, initiated a multimedia campaign for tsunami-affected people in some select areas of Tamil Nadu.[27] The objectives were as follows:

1. To help people overcome tragedy;
2. To provide relief and to help bringing attitudinal and behavioral change in adapting to new a life pattern;
3. To sensitize them on improvising health requirements;
4. To bring behavioral change in accepting the services;

5. To address the related social issues; and
6. To facilitate economic uplift and livelihood.

To design the campaign, it was necessary to take stock of the situation and analyze the trauma of the affected people and areas of intervention keeping in view the needs of different age groups; to gather insights about various issues brought in by the tragedy; and the access to communication media and tools.

Field Visit

A field visit was made in February 2005 to gather insights into issues referred above and map the perceptions of grassroots communities in three villages, namely, Nagapattinum (Akkaraipettai); Puducherry (Periyakalapet and Veerampatinam); and on the Chennai–Puducherry national highway (Pattipulum Kuppam) in anticipation of the media campaign.

The tsunami brought with it some issues, which had long-term effect on the lives of the concerned. Some of the insights from the field visit included the following: Many men who lost their family members received a lot of compensation money, leading them to drinking. Those who lost wives remarried, however, there were not many instances when women who lost their husbands remarried. Many children lost both their parents. Long-distance relations in many cases came in for adoption, which many believed was not for children's sake but the compensation money. Some men tried to get their minor daughters married from the compensation money after losing their spouse to get over the responsibility of the girl child and resettle themselves.

Dependence on relief for long could have a telling effect; hence, they needed to be nudged to get back to their routine in life.

A Year After

Realizing the importance and role of the grassroots communities' involvement in carrying on the task further and empowering them for future disasters, if any, OWSA, in association with Plan International

(India), introduced the concept of building communication opportunities for community communicators on how information could be converted into knowledge and how knowledge could be shared with communities through various media tools, namely, radio, comics, photography, written communication and the Internet, and to groom some from among the communities as change agents, who would eventually become community knowledge leaders.

Capacity-building workshops were initiated in the month of November 2005 with select children and youth from various areas such as Sirkali, Dindigul, Kanchipuram, and Marakanam. The blocks were chosen from the coastal areas of Tamil Nadu and Puducherry. During this process, around 500 children were trained in communication through various media tools on various issues identified by them in their communities with a wider canvas of life-cycle approach. The week-long training modules in various areas as indicated above gave them intensive understanding on the development issues; how visual media like comics and photography can communicate, especially on issues that concern the communities. During the training workshops, community communicators were introduced to ICTs such as radio and the Internet, and how the process of using radio and the Internet enhances the communication opportunities among grassroots communities on development issues. They were also exposed to the community software developed by OWSA, called ENRICH, and how they could share the local/global contents among the communities. Experts were drawn from various areas of communication specializations to anchor various modules in the said workshop.

The participants, in the age group that varied from 13 to 35+, expressed their concerns about the communities to which they belonged through various media such as comics, radio programs, photographs, and computer graphics.

Comics made by them reflected their concerns that included factors such as nonavailability of doctors in their villages, children not going to school because of one or the other reasons, lack of safe drinking water, nonavailability of transport for commuting from one village to another, etc. Photographs depicted the issue of water logging, children working for their own survival, and poverty-stricken men and women. The stories on the one hand narrated the trauma faced by communities losing their homes and hearths, children who lost their parents in tsunami-affected communities; on the other hand, some reflected the grit and determination of people who made the most of what was left in their lives.

During this process, they learnt why community voices were important, how they could be recorded and transcribed, and how radio could be used to address issues such as these. With the concept of situational analysis, the participants were exposed to the process of understanding issues (why were they there and what was ahead) and how the analytical process could help build the community mentorship in converting information into knowledge; building knowledge-seeking behavior, and finding solutions.

Through storytelling, youngsters were encouraged to reflect their innermost feelings relating to tsunami. It was interesting and very insightful to find that children were able to articulate not only the issues concerning the tragedy but possible solutions.

Prabhakaran, a young child from one of the villages of tsunami-affected areas wrote the following story (edited for language clarity):

> *My friend studied +2. On her X-Mas holidays on 26 December 2004, she lost her mother in tsunami. That Sunday turned out to a black Sunday for her. So, My friend stopped her school education and was missing her mother's love and care. The village elders and classmates explained to her the importance of education. She continued her studies and scored good marks and topped in the school. From the compensation money received after her mother's death, the family members arranged for her marriage. Now, she has conceived a child. If her mother would have been alive, she would have not become a mother, but continued her education. Her life style has changed with more responsibilities because of tsunami.*

The workshop included input on the potential of local folk media in communicating with communities. Vellopattu, a folk form prevalent in Pondicherry, based on storytelling to a gathered audience was used as pedagogy for that module. The participants learnt it and gave a sterling performance weaving the tsunami story.

In Puducherry during the radio training, the young participants were enabled to speak with the union minister for information and broadcasting in Delhi on November 12 that incidentally is celebrated as the Public Broadcasting Day in India. On that day in 1947, the Father of the Nation, Mahatma Gandhi, spoke to the public through All India Radio. Participants from Pondicherry, who probably had never spoken Hindi, sang Gandhi's favorite prayer *Raghupati Raghav Raja Ram, Patita Pavan Sita Ram* that was broadcast live from AIR Pondicherry, thus symbolizing the power of radio in reaching out to a large audience.

The concept and importance of community knowledge centers was introduced and how the knowledge could be collected, collated, and disseminated through various media tools and through the community software solutions. Communities were connected and empowered through the whole process.

This exercise was aimed at creating an environment for the Right to Information and Knowledge through the vibrant grassroots media and to bring in the synergy among grassroots media and the mainstream media. This effort has visibly ignited the spark within the young community communicators, thus empowering them to think and act for their own development and for the communities to which they belong. Through radio and the Internet, they connected with the outside world to share their thoughts, concerns, learning, and vice-versa.

During the orientation program, various stages of disaster management were discussed, such as (a) pre-disaster; (b) disaster; and (c) post-disaster (long-term planning), and the need for making disaster management committees in villages.

After every module, the participants were given simulations and role plays to ensure the learning of various communication tools.

Participants' Input on Disaster Management after Learning the Concepts

1. A Disaster Management Committee (DMC), comprising the youth, panchayat representative, and an opinion maker from within the village may be made.
2. Terms of reference of the DMC should be worked out.
3. Information on possible kinds of disasters should be shared with the community.
4. Seasonality of possible disasters, if any, should be prepared and a calendar could be maintained.
5. Preparedness in advance was important irrespective of whether the disasters come or not.

A List of Dos and Don'ts Articulated by Participants

1. Constructing houses away from the seashore
2. Prevent sand dunes
3. Plant trees near the shores
4. Impress the government to create a wall along the coast
5. Check on rumors
6. Names of the disaster committees will be made available to everybody with their telephone numbers. The lists can be pasted on walls, temples, and other prominent places
7. Safe places should be identified in advance so that entire village should know where they have to run for safety
8. Planning could be done according to the availability of the safe shelters nearby. (This information should be made available to everybody so that they know where they have to go for safe shelters in the time of disasters.)
9. Disaster committees should use various modes of communication such as public address system, loudspeakers from places of worship, schools, cable television, mobiles, and word of mouth so that public could be addressed with no loss of time. The building authorities should be informed in advance so that they are prepared to provide shelter to the community.
10. The names of the NGOs, government persons, and volunteers should be painted on the walls and reflected at prominent places, so that in emergency they can be contacted.
11. All valuables could be kept in one place, maybe in a box, so that at the time of disaster, these could be picked up fast and shifted to safer places. (In fact, a box/bag containing a change of clothes, first-aid kit, money/checkbook, valuables, and contact number/address of a relation need to be always kept ready per person for any eventuality.)
12. Mock drills to be practiced every three months so that people could be prepared well in advance to do the real exercise at the time of disaster.
13. Youth to join the volunteer team so that they could later join the DMC.
14. Pool resources every month to meet the needs at the time of disaster. Otherwise, this money would be available at the end of year for some community welfare scheme.

15. Review the committee's performance after two years and change the members.
16. Skills could be built on alternative jobs so that at the time of disaster, these skills could be utilized for alternative livelihood.
17. Micro-credit society to be formed wherever not available, so that money is available at the time of disaster.
18. When actual disaster strikes, the disaster management committee to meet immediately and designate work to volunteers as decided in the plan, such as:

- Evacuation of people
- Opening of emergency call centers
- Helping people shift to various places
- Provision of food and water
- Getting in touch with medical community for attending to the injured
- Making the list of dead/injured
- Arranging burial of dead
- Networking with NGOs and other bodies
- Social audit with community interventions to make a list of issues to be taken immediately
- Calling clinic psychologists/psychiatrists for trauma counseling
- Communicating important notices to community
- Use of various media including public addressing system/radio/cable/ for immediate interface with the community
- Check gossip mongering by providing immediate facts and figures

Participants' Activity Plan on What They Would Like to Do on December 26, 2005, After One Year of Tsunami:

1. Mobilize the area community and do a program with them.
2. Visit all the villages and console the affected, especially those who lost their kin.
3. Do not want to observe the day because during Diwali everybody wept. Any activity would make them remember tsunami. It is better to forget.

4. To make posters with the help of youth.
5. Tree plantation to generate awareness about tsunami on the same day.
6. Monument in remembrance of those who lost their lives during tsunami.
7. Medical camp to give services to those who are still suffering.
8. Mobilize the village community to observe silence on that day.
9. Prayer meetings: light the candle on the black day.
10. Events should be created so that people should forget tsunami.
11. Conduct programs for children: members of children's club to visit every child and talk to children on how to come out of the tsunami-thinking process.
12. Programs with positive thinking.
13. Seminar for thanking various stakeholders who helped during tsunami.

The whole exercise enabled the local communities to think, plan, and act while managing the disasters themselves.

Mainstreaming ICTs was one of the agenda explored. The participants were exposed to the use of the Internet and radio. A desire was expressed by many to have the knowledge centers manned by the youth. [28]

Social mobilization coupled with participative approach is important to bring about the desired change and achieve sustainability. Team members who articulated the ACSM also sensitized media through their writing as the article in the annexure to the chapter will reflect.

Annexure

The 2004 tsunami has been called as one of the deadliest natural disasters of the world killing 230,000 people in fourteen countries. The countries most affected were Indonesia, Sri Lanka, and Thailand. India, being a part of the Indian Ocean ring, too bore the brunt of the tsunami. The massive ocean earthquake created havoc with not just property and lives but had a devastating effect on the psyche of survivors, especially the children. Though the rehabilitation process began instantly and to a large extent succeeded in providing succor to the victims, it failed to address one key issue, that is, the psychological trauma undergone by the survivors.

During disasters, children are the most vulnerable who not only lose their loved ones but relive the trauma on a day-to-day basis and are in urgent need of psychological care. According to experts, Post trauma control after disasters need special efforts and require immediate treatment.

"Even Disasters Have Limits: Post Tsunami Trauma Control-The Need of the Hour" is a story of human grit and determination to overcome the most powerful natural disaster, involvement of various governmental-non governmental agencies in the rehabilitation process and the post trauma care of the survivors..[29]

Notes and References

1. https://thehistoryofparliament.wordpress.com/2013/04/23/the-treaty-of-paris-john-wilkes-and-north-briton-number-45/ (accessed on November 7, 2015).
2. http://www.hakikazi.org/tcdd/newpage14.htm (accessed on November 7, 2015).
3. http://www.advocacyresource.org.uk/History-of-Advocacy (accessed on November 17, 2015).
4. http://www.readwriteact.org/node/25 (accessed on November 29, 2015).
5. Vidya Krishnan, "PR Push—NGOs Innovate To Keep Bhopal Issue Alive," *The Mint* (December 1, 2014):1.
6. Robert Watts, "Cheques to Bounce into History?" *Sunday Times*, London, as appeared in *The Times of India*, November 24, 2009, 16.
7. https://www.bja.gov/evaluation/links/WK-Kellogg-Foundation.pdf (accessed on Februarey 16, 2016).
8. http://www.change.org/careers?lang=en-GB (accessed on December 4, 2015).
9. http://en.wikipedia.org/wiki/Avaaz.org (accessed on December 14, 2015).
10. Shahira Naim, "UP Refuses Deaths during Childbirth," *The Tribune*, October 17, 2009, 11.
11. P. Sainath, "Drought of Justice, Flood of Funds," *The Hindu*, August 15, 2009.
12. Kanika Datta, "Needed a Social Regulator," *The Business Standard*, July 13, 2006.
13. Dinkar Vashisht, "Family of Chief Secretaries: Past, Present and Future," *The Indian Express*, November 8, 2009, 1 and 2.
14. https://www.facebook.com/poo2loo (accessed on November 4, 2015).
15. www.unicef.org/cbsc/index_42347.html (accessed on December 4, 2015).
16. www.unicef.org/cbsc/index_42347.html (accessed on December 4, 2015).
17. www.fao.org/docrep/006/ad346e/ad346e07.htm (accessed on December 4, 2015).
18. Social audit: Gram Sabhas and Panchayat Raj—Final report submitted by Vision Foundation for Development to the Planning Commission in October 2005. Full report may be accessed at: social audit-plng commi-httpplanningcommission.gov. inreportssereportserstdy_sagspr.pdf (accessed on December 21, 2015).

19. A team comprising the author and a representative each from OWSA; A British NGO; and MS Swaminathan Research foundation visited a number of villages affected by the tsunami in Nagapattmun and Pondicherry to make a communication needs assessment program on February 15–17, 2005.

20. Ibid.

21. http://www.stoptb.org/assets/documents/global/plan/tb_globalplantostoptb2011–2015. pdf (accessed on February 16, 2016).

22. Ibid.

23. http://www.tbfacts.org/tb-statistics-india.html (accessed on December 5, 2015).

24. http://www.tbpartnershipindia.org/documents/tb%20report%20media.pdf. pp. 35–36 (accessed on February 16, 2016).

25. http://www.iple.in/category/index/media-advocacy-1 (accessed on February 15, 2016).

26. Jaishri Jethwaney and Shruti Jain, *Advertising Management* (New Delhi: OUP, 2006), 438.

27. The three institutions, namely, One World, Plan International, and Indian Institute of Mass Communication were represented by Mr Kannan, Dr Geeta Malhotra, and Dr Jaishri Jethwaney, respectively.

28. Based on the monograph brought out jointly by the three organizations referred in endnote 2.

29. Jaishri Jethwaney. 2005 "Even Disasters Have Limits: Post Tsunami Trauma Control-the Need of the Hour ," *Mainstream* XLII, No. 18.

5

Grassroots Communication

Defining Grassroots

Grassroots in the past was defined as the masses; the proletariat, as an antonym to nobility, or the classes. Over a period of time, grassroots communities are seen as the vulnerable groups of people who have fewer resources and often none or less access to literacy and mass communication. Grassroots communication is put to use to influence policy in favor of those who often are on the fringes of the social, economic, and political system of a society. The process is multilayered, multifaceted, and challenging, yet with great results if handled with empathy and honesty. Many agencies generally are involved in grassroots communication that include three tiers of government, namely, local, state, and central, the nongovernmental organizations, international nongovernmental organizations, and, in a limited manner, also the corporate sector with its CSR initiatives. According to the *Commission on Risk Perception and Communication* in the USA, grassroots communication system works in partnership which enables public health and emergency preparedness practitioners to involve grassroots organizations such as community based, faith based, and business organizations serving low-income groups in risk communication activities during an imminent danger, response, and recovery phases of a disaster.[1]

In the face of a disaster and in the aftermath, the rumor mill and the grapevine generally get activated. There is a limited access to valid information. Media is often alleged to sensationalize such events, making it difficult for the communities to take a stock of what is happening to their lives. The other fallouts are a general distrust in political leadership and heightened public emotion. In such times, a grassroots communication system creates a partnership with grassroots communities and organizations that include NGOs, faith-based organizations, community groups, self-help groups, and business organizations operating at the grassroots level to participate in the information dissemination and providing succor to the affected communities. A few cases in point are the Katrina Hurricane in the USA, the tsunami in India and Sri Lanka, and the devastating floods in Bihar and Srinagar that had thousands of people losing their lives or becoming homeless.

Post-Katrina Hurricane disaster, it emerged through research that the concerned population had negative perceptions of disaster efforts, especially on the fronts of rescue, evacuation, and delivery of services. Participants in a survey felt that racism and class played a role in how the relief efforts were carried out. The respondents felt that media in general perpetuated negative images and delayed in reflecting the positive aspect of the aftermath of the hurricane. An overall lack of trust and confidence in the government was displayed. The respondents said they felt scared about such disasters including floods, tornadoes, hurricanes, and terrorist attacks hitting their communities. Participants of a focus group discussion in the USA revealed that their own communities were not prepared to deal with such emergencies. In terms of social support in an emergency situation, respondents by and large said that the family was the primary source of support followed by religious organizations, volunteers, the government, and the people in that order. The organizations that agreed to participate in the grassroots communication expressed their willingness to display posters and other printed materials (96 percent), add disaster awareness information to their websites (16 percent), and participate in radio talks over the issue (28 percent). The grassroots organizations shared that they had the capability of reaching out to 500 low-income residents in a day.[2]

Emotions were not different during the Srinagar flooding in October 2014. The devastating earthquake in the Himalayan state of Nepal on April 25, 2015, killing thousands of people, saw tremendous response from many countries, India being at the forefront. There were some murmurs about an Indian news channel focusing on its efforts to cover the news, rather than bringing succor to people. (It was rumored that the team arrived in a chopper, the story began with the cameraman's showing the interior of the chopper and a journalist alighting from the helicopter. The critic rented that the team could have brought in some doctors!) This is a slightly tricky issue, and the media sometimes finds itself being judged as news-crazy at the cost of being empathetic to victims of a disaster.

In developing countries such as India where traditional information infrastructure like the power supply to access electronic media and telephones is not evenly distributed, the mobile telephony and the Internet are trying to bridge the gap in connecting the vast grassroots populace with the mainland. When Rajiv Gandhi gave an impetus to the telecommunication sector during his premiership in the 1980s, his critics ridiculed him, little realizing that he was laying the foundation for connecting the people at the grassroots level and establishing network among peoples cutting across the geographical and economic divide. With over 90 crore mobile phone connections in India as in 2014, the little handset indeed has become a game changer in grassroots communication.

According to Kenneth Keniston, Professor at MIT, billions of dollars are being committed in the developing world to enable the poorest to leapfrog traditional problems of development such as poverty, illiteracy, disease, hunger, unemployment, corruption, and inequities and to move them into the modern information age through the information and communication technologies, commonly referred to as the ICTs, but a lot remains to be done.[3] Based on his field visits to certain projects in India and discussions with program implementers and others, Professor Keniston observed that there was more talk than action. He felt that while there was no dearth of plans (international, national, and local); the ground realities were very different. Every project that he overviewed ran into time overruns, with unexpected difficulties. The goal of financial sustainability, he wrote, was hardly met. The scope of IT, he commented, need not be restricted to computers; some of the innovative uses could be made through radio, television, embedded chips, and satellite inventories. He referred to the classic example of the White Revolution at Anand in Gujarat, where automated butter fat assessment equipment simplified the process of evaluating milk and paying dairy farmers according to the extent of fat in the milk.

In development projects, top-down approach rarely succeeds, so it is important that consultations must begin at the grassroots level. It is important to know what information is required by the people before supplying something which may or may not be of much relevance or of interest to them. People may change their information needs in time, which also needs to be factored in. For instance, in the M.S. Swaminathan's ICT project in Puducherry (formerly Pondicherry), the farmers initially said they needed information relating to agriculture, but interestingly soon it was found that they were mostly accessing information on government schemes from the information kiosks.[4]

With a sort of information revolution hitting at the grassroots level, albeit at a limited level, access to information among some groups has created a credibility gap for various schemes as some projects start with a huge hype but may either not kick start in real terms, or run at a sluggish pace with scant regard to time and cost overruns. There is, however, no denying that some projects are running extremely well, thereby bringing the fruits of development to communities in far-flung areas.

Participatory approach at the grassroots level is seen as the imperative for sustainable rural development. Familiarized by the approaches of Saul Alinsky, Ceaser Charaze, and S.L. Kahn, and in popular education, the approaches suggested by Paula Frère, participatory development is seen by experts as the possible answer to involving communities in the development saga.

Experts suggest the following steps in participatory change:

1. Formative research through community immersion and talking with community leaders.
2. Outreach activity to include talking with grassroots leaders on a one-on-one basis to understand the community needs, goals, and strengths. At this stage the programmer need not have any predetermined objective. One needs to go with an open mind to listen empathetically and openly.
3. From the above two steps would emerge the idea for an issue that needs addressing from the community's perspective.
4. Having identified the issue, the next step is to meet up with a group of 5–10 persons to work on the vision and measurable goals. This would help in charting the future course of action and strategy to accomplish the goals.
5. At this stage, the project is defined and planned and would encompass: (a) defining the community development project; (b) making connections with people and groups who would support the proposed project; (c) conducting a feasibility study to make sure the project can be accomplished.

6. The group then can work as an organizational structure, which can either be a loose community association or a formal non-profit organization with work assigned to various people and teams. This is followed by leadership development.
7. Funding is a major area of consideration for such projects. It can come from the government, an NGO/INGO, or with contributions from the community or in partnership with one or more funding sources.[5]

Principles of Grassroots Communication

Like any communication, grassroots communication can be effective if founded on a set of robust principles. Here are a few:

- Identify stakeholder population that needs to be reached, and find out their communication habits and the media they access.
- Identify right grassroots organizations, partners to carry forward the job of information dissemination.
- Identify opinion leaders from among the community and organizations. In case of differing views on the subject matter, the differences need to be sorted out and consensus reached before undertaking the task.
- Find out their predispositions about the issue to be tackled.
- Create appropriate messages keeping in view the social and cultural sensitivities. Find out what is relevant to the needs of the target audience and their literacy levels.
- Work out a plan that ideally should be flexible to be adapted to the need of the hour.
- Keep a provision for quick and effective response to any unexpected situation.
- Provide updated information through various media that are accessed by the target audience.
- Motivate the team in charge of grassroots communication, especially when dealing with disasters. It is not uncommon to receive unwarranted criticism and allegations when dealing with emergency situations as human emotions run high.

Identifying Grassroots Organizations

As said elsewhere in the chapter, a combination of grassroots organization encompassing charitable trusts, NGOs, civil society organizations, and business organizations is imperative in grassroots communication as all put together these would cover the entire spectrum of target audience.

Typology of Grassroots Organizations

Community-based Organizations (CBOs)

1. Organizations that provide social service and outreach
2. Charitable trusts
3. Job-training centers
4. Health centers
5. Schools and colleges
6. Resident welfare associations
7. Social clubs (such as Rotary and Lions)

Business Organizations

1. Departmental stores/malls
2. Beauty salons and barber shops
3. Drug stores/medicine shops
4. Child care centers
5. Petrol stations

Faith-based Organizations

Churches, temples, mosques, and organizations are run by spiritual gurus (in the Indian context, the Radhasoami, the Nirankari, Baba Ramdev, Anandmayee, Ramakrishna Paramhansa Math, Yogoda–Self Realization Society, and similar organizations that draw millions of followers).

In 2009, when Virus H1N1, commonly referred as the swine flu spread, a country like USA made a good use of grassroots communities to reach out with the message constantly. In retrospect, on June 11, 2009, the World Health Organization (WHO) raised the global pandemic alert to phase 6 in response to the global spread of the influenza virus H1N1. A phase 6 designation meant that a global emergency was under way. The decision for high alertness was calculated on the basis of the spread of the virus and not the severity of the illness caused by the virus. As a result, the Center for Disaster in Maryland partnered with 20 faith-based organizations and several business organizations to serve the low-income population in the country. Formal agreements were signed to ensure that these organizations would serve as the points of distribution of risk communication materials in the event of a disaster or public health threat. Each such organization identified one contact person and two alternate names to assist the state with this effort.[6]

In India the scare continued unabated as the mainstream national and regional media carried stories of deaths in hospitals day after day. The electronic media included emotion-surcharged sound bytes of family members, who often complained of negligence in hospitals. The then Health Minister Ghulam Nabi Azad found himself in the dock when he spoke about a young girl from Pune who succumbed to the virus that she would have spread the virus to many as her family went on taking her from one hospital to another. As soon as a few television channels carried the sound byte, within an hour or so, the family's angst and disgust appeared on news channels, forcing the minister to apologize for his insensitive remarks.

People in general in India were not sure of the symptoms till the various state governments issued ads that also included the names of the hospitals that were equipped with necessary medication. The Ministry of Health and Family Welfare came out with a TVC that had the scene of a bus. One person kept holding his sneeze till he was able to take out his handkerchief from the pocket of his trouser. As he sneezed into the kerchief, all the fellow travels got up and clapped. This was followed by a voiceover that cautioned the people to be careful when coughing or sneezing in public (The key communication preposition of the TVC was "*Swine flu ko phelene se bachao or bano Hero!*"). To cash in on the situation, a number of FMCG companies came out with ads suggesting people to wash hands with their brand of soap for a number of times to avoid H1N1 flu!

Tools and Strategies in Grassroots Communication

Communication is a great facilitator in changing the perceptions and attitudes of people, if handled effectively. It can boomerang, with serious consequences, if care is not taken especially in the social and cultural contexts. Grassroots communication, in a country like India where the penetration of mass media is low, generally boils down to various forms of interpersonal communication in a participative mode. India has a great repository of folk forms that can be befittingly used to connect with the communities, but at the same time the role of mass media in providing the big picture cannot be denied.

Working with NGOs at the Grassroots Level

Civil society organizations, including the NGOs have become an important aspect of change management at the grassroots level for various reasons, including the following:

- They give voice to people.
- NGOs provide a platform for citizen participation.
- NGOs use appropriate technologies.
- NGOs form a bridge between the government and the community.
- The size of the problem is enormous and government cannot handle it alone.
- They are familiar with community approach.
- NGOs are generally strong in interpersonal approach.
- They have access to "apathetic" population.
- They are sensitive to local needs.

- The generally command good credibility.
- They work out cost effective when compared to government infrastructure to carry out similar works.
- They are less bureaucratic so provide support systems faster, especially in emergencies.

Role of NGOs in Grassroots Projects

It is increasingly believed that in developed economies, the states have in a large measure withdrawn from welfare activities and grassroots communication. NGOs have filled in the gap in reaching out to communities living on the fringes, despite the developed status of such societies. There are millions of NGOs operating in such countries. In developing economies, NGOs have emerged as a matter of dire need and have become an important part of the political fabric and social milieu. NGOs here are seen as critical agents in addressing myriad issues that the governments have neither the capacity nor capability to handle. NGOs also work as the conscience keepers of the powers that be, if seen in the supporting vein. NGOs, however, can sustain their missions if constant funds pour in for them. In fact, this sometimes becomes their priority area and often a cause of much worry. This also leads to attrition and losing of experienced manpower. In many developmental projects, a number of agencies are seen pitching in to get the project. There are varying views about the capability of the NGOs in handling development projects independently or in partnership with the local, state or central government, and corporate sector, or international organizations. What role can best be suited for NGOs? It is important to prioritize their involvement? NGOs can be very useful in handling the following areas at the grassroots level:

- Advocacy
- Targeted intervention with vulnerable audience
- Working with caretakers
- Working with influencers

There are instances when NGOs have been entrusted with the task of implementation of actual task, like running of primary health centers.

Choice of Media in Grassroots Communication

There are many media to choose from at the grassroots level. In India, a general suggestion cannot be given as the various states have different kinds of reach and access to media. With cable and satellite television and Direct to Home (DTH) technology available in the entire country, all the regions can have the reach of the mass media, but due to varying economic conditions, a large number of people may not afford to own a television or radio set, or an individual dish or afford to pay the cable operator; hence, they remain untouched by mass media.

In the late 1970s and 1980s, the GOI had made television sets and video recorders available to a large number of villages under its program "Margdarshan." The equipment was kept in the house of the village head, where the men would go and watch television for a couple of hours. Women were invariably left out from this. The innovative project, however, did not succeed in the long run for various reasons, including frequent power cuts and lack of local facilities for the repair of the hardware.

In a five-state study undertaken by The Media Foundation between June 2012 and July 2014, the findings revealed that the poor in rural India were adversely affected by the cost of digitization. The findings also have implication for the content strategy by news channels, especially, the public broadcaster Prasar Bharti. Some of insights, especially through the focus group discussions, revealed that there was a demand from people on programs on career advice, health, farming, etc. When one looks at the program bouquet of the regional channels of the public broadcaster Doordarshan in the five states in which the research was conducted, namely, Andhra Pradesh, Chhattisgarh, Delhi, Gujarat, and Odisha, there is no content on careers, very little on health, and one or two sundry programs on agriculture that are scheduled in the morning and day time, when most of the men are away to their fields.[7] It is important for programmers to not only devise those programs that meet the unfulfilled aspirations of the viewers, but the scheduling strategy also has to be in keeping with the viewing habits of the target audience.

Despite that the research study was conducted in a handful of states, but being qualitative in nature, it does reflect some interesting facts and consumer insights. Based on one of the takeaways from the findings, it is felt that the programmers need to match the program needs of the Indian youth vis-à-vis the program choices and use of innovative strategies. For instance, India has a huge aspirational class of young rural and semi-urban Indians who somehow have cobbled together degrees but are still looking for job breaks: an idle workforce waiting to explode in terms of frustration and demoralization. Once educated, most of them do not wish to go to farming. On the other hand, there are many jobs which are advertised from time to time by Union Public Service Commission (UPSC), Staff Selection Commission (SSC), the armed forces, and hundreds of public sector undertakings, which an average rural youth is not aware of. The public sector data reveal that thousands of posts remain unfilled in the reserved category year after year because there are not many and, at times, no applicants. One of research insight was the demand for career advice. Once in a while one sees ads reflecting "special drive for SC/ST candidates," but these mostly appear in mainstream English language newspapers which are not accessed by the rural youth. News channels, especially Doordarshan, can fill this gap by creating interactive phone-in programs based on the advertised jobs and connect the job seekers with companies and departments seeking people for jobs. Television channels, especially the public broadcaster Doordarshan, can befittingly engage with the youth in this very important area.

India has a rich cultural tradition. Folk media can be used to reach out to grassroots communities, especially in the rural India. In the following paragraphs we shall take a look at the folk media in India.

Folk Media

India has a rich repository of folk art farm, which can be befittingly used to adapt the social themes with community participation. The MacBride Commission was established by UNESCO to study, among many issues, the importance of communication in the development arena. One of the significant recommendations of the commission regarding the traditional folk forms included the following:

> Even when modern media have penetrated isolated areas, the older forms maintain their validity, particularly when used to influence attitudes,

instigate action and promote change. Extensive experience shown that traditional forms of communication can be effective in dispelling the superstitions, archaic perceptions and unscientific that people have inherited as part of traditions and which are difficult to modify if the benefits of change are hard to demonstrate. Practitioners of the traditional media use a subtle form of persuasion by presenting the required message in locally popular artistic forms. This cannot be rivaled by any other means of communication.[8]

It has been observed that many countries in the South Asian regions are making use of the traditional folk form to reach out to people, especially in their hinterlands. The Chinese puppetry made a comeback in Hong Kong partly because of its inclusion in the Hong Kong Arts Festival. The governments of Indonesia, Malaysia, and the Philippines, according to observers, have increased their emphasis on resuscitation of folk media. For instance in Indonesia, studies and inventories are being made on indigenous communication forms such as *BeberWayang Orang* (traditional opera of masked characters in live performance), *WayangKulit* (leather shadow play), *WayangGolek* (wooden-puppet show), *Ketoprak* (Japanese opera), *LobrukZ* (opera of men). The Malaysian Government in the 1970s used the folk media to communicate development messages to rural audiences. The Ministry of Information and Broadcasting since the early 1970s has used folk artist groups to present the classic Ramayana figures of *WayangKulit* (shadow play) to rural people with themes of anti-Communism, the advantages of the New Economic Policy, Second Malaysia Plan, the national ideology, and birth control. The Penang Information Department hires a Chinese drama troupe to perform skits which include government messages couched in humorous dialogue.[9]

Bordenave holds an absolutely opposing view on the use of media for development issues. To quote him:

Developmental thinkers' obsession with goal achievement and not with human growth may take up these folk media as another set of instruments for changing people's way of thinking, feeling and behaving. And this is not the purpose and the function of the traditional communication media! I am afraid that as soon as the people realize that their folk songs, poems and art are being used for subliminal propaganda they will let them die.[10]

In some countries, folk media is being preserved through the mass media. For instance, the National Iranian Radio and Television (NIRT) have established a center since 1971 for the preservation of traditional music, among other things such as festivals of the arts, etc. Another center financed by Iranian television collects music from all over the nation and encourages active preservation by offering grants to old musicians who cannot earn a living by their music. The live performances of such musicians are recorded and made available to broadcast. Similarly, the South Korean broadcasters visit various villages to tape record folk songs. The Malaysian broadcasters have brought folk performers to studios to preserve their arts.[11]

In Thailand, the folk art form most successfully adapted to radio and television is locally known as *Mau Lum*, a folk opera or folk story drawn from the Thai tales and myths. "The rhyming songs of *Mau Lum*," observe critics, "allow for improvisation." According to Katz and Wedell, efforts over the years have been made to expand the repertoire of *Mau Lum* singers to "take account of campaigns of rural development, anti-communist propaganda, and other contemporary and development topics." The earliest days of Thai television were based on much wider use of traditional art materials, such as shadow plays, puppets, dance, theater, etc. However, with the onset of satellite television and a variety of entertainment programs available to choose from, the traditional folk form may not be as popular with the listeners.[12]

UNESCO's document "Folk Media and Mass Media in Population Communication" reflects that behavior change directly attributable to mass media is not more than 10–15 percent. The percentage increases to 54 percent when mass media is integrated with extension efforts. It was possible that if folk media was included, it would further increase the percentage of "desired behavior change."

Following an experts' meeting (organized by UNESCO and the International Planned Parenthood Federation (IPPF) with United Nations Fund for Population Activities (UNFPA) support) in London in 1972, which recommended guidelines for the integration of folk media and mass media, UNESCO, as a follow-up, invited communication specialists in folk media from 20 countries to study the way in which folk media in India have been mobilized for "motivational" purposes. The workshop was organized with the following objectives:

1. To discuss and discover the potential of various folk forms in communication work;
2. To afford the participants the opportunity to study both the steps involved and the factors to be considered in the production of the various folk forms; and
3. To study and evaluate the finished product.

Eight folk forms were chosen for study that included Harikatha, a discourse with story and song; KaviGaan, or the poet's song; puppetry; Tamasha, a popular folk entertainment form which is a harmonious blend of music, dance, and drama; ballad singing; Yakshagana, a kind of dance drama; and Khayal, a folk theater form. Folk troupes from throughout India converged in New Delhi for the purpose. The event constituted an India case study for the participants. A rural setting was provided for the demonstration and staging of the folk media. Experts presented background papers before these forms were demonstrated.

The seminar, based on participants' input concluded that folk form in conjunction with mass media, could be befittingly used in channeling motivational messages to rural audiences. However, there was a need for caution to ensure that the forms did not become unacceptable by overloading the message content. Ten guiding principles on the issue were suggested, some of which included the following:

- The folk media should be an integral part of various motivational programs for rural development;
- The prerequisites to the use of the folk media would be an avid understanding of the rural audiences and the use of these media to provide rural people with recreation;
- To attract their attention and to ensure sufficient motivation for their participation in developmental activities; and
- The utilization of folk media in modern motivational programs should be viewed from the perspective of socioeconomic development and cultural development.[13]

The following table reflects some of the popular folk forms in different Indian states.

Folk form	Region	Description
Alha	MP and UP	Song form: requires a four member team, two singers, and two instrument players (it is a popular narrative on the heroic deeds of Alha brothers)
Bhopa	Rajasthan	Song and dance form: team husband, wife, and child. The wife and child sing and dance, and the husband plays the instrument.
Birha	Eastern UP	Song form: requires a team of four to six persons
Burra katha	Andhra Pradesh	Drama form
Dandya and garba	Gujarat	Dance form
Jatra	West Bengal	Stylized folk drama of Bengal and Odisha, originally of devotional nature, now increasingly used for social awakening.
Kabbigaan	West Bengal	A musical arrangement between two teams of skillful artists, improvising for and against a given message.
Kathakkali	Tamil Nadu	Dance form
Lavani	Maharashtra	Dance on romantic songs. Originated during the Peshwa period. (It is a ballad on historical and social themes sung by two artists.)
Tamasha	Maharashtra	Similar to nautanki. It is robust, topical, musical, and humorous.
Burrakatha	Andhra Pradesh	An ingenious folk performance, presented by three artists with Burra, the talking drum.
Bhavai	Gujarat	It truly represents Gujarat's colors and costume, well known for its skills in improvisation, humor, and satire.
Longa and Maganyar	Rajasthan	Drama and song form: requires a team of four, out of who two are generally tribal.
Naca	Madhya Pradesh	Dance and drama form; requires five to six member teams.
Nautanki	UP, Bihar, and Haryana	Drama mixed with folk songs; requires a team of 4–10 performers.
Puppetry	Northern India	Drama and song form; requires use of puppets, they could be string puppets, glove puppets, shadow puppets, or rod puppets.
Pabojiki pad	Rajasthan	Pad (phad) is a scroll of sequential panels of figures and situations, painted in color. The stories are scriptural. The curtain is stretched out between two poles. An earthen lamp illuminates the panel from behind as the narrators unfold the story by singing.
Qawwali	MP and UP	Songs of descriptive nature, adapted from sher-o-shayari

(continued)

(continued)

Folk form	Region	Description
Ragini	Haryana	Telling stories of legends in song form
Rasa lila	UP	Based on Sri Krishna Rasa lila form that has one male and a few female dancers; based on shringar rasa
Swang	Haryana	Drama form dialogues mixed with songs; requires a team of five who play *nagara* and folk tunes to attract crowds. It is very popular in east Punjab.
Yakshgan	Karnataka and Tamil Nadu	Southern counterpart of nautanki
Vellupaattu	Tamil Nadu and Kerala	The "bow song" is sung by six to eight artists plucking the string of a large bow, placed in the front center, for keeping the rhythm.

Source: Communication and the Traditional Media: IIMC, 1981.

Explaining the use of the performing arts during the freedom struggle in India to rouse sentiment against the British, H.K. Ranganath writes,

[T]he communication potential of Indian performing arts has been proved time and again by many instances of national consequence. *Alha*, the popular ballad from the Uttar Pradesh and its counterpart *Laavni* of Maharashtra, *Gee-Gee* of Karnataka, and *Villupattu* of Tamil Nadu/Kerala and Kabigaan of Bengal…roused the conscience of the nation against the British rule. But the same arts became counter-productive in the hands of the British.[14]

Looking at the power of folk communication, the British government deployed some famous folk artists who composed *Swaang* during the First World War recruitment drive resulting in thousands of Indian youth joining the armed forces. To quote Ranganath,

[T]hese native media of "sung communication" and "enacted information" proved more than a match to the government-controlled mass media during the many political and social campaigns launched by Gandhiji. In the later years, the Union government continued to utilize these arts to bring awareness of many development programs in rural areas.[15]

The 1972 UNESCO meeting referred to the outlined criteria (as mentioned earlier) for the selection of folk media for use in family planning communication programs and discussed the cultural, sociological, and practical contexts of their use. The experts classified folk media on the basis of various factors such as music, song, drama, skit, puppet shows, poetry, speech, sound, gestures, gossip, and costuming including patterning and coloring of materials and the use of head gear. The following general guidelines were prepared for selecting a particular folk form:

1. Concern for "plasticity" of the medium, or capacity to be "loaded" with specific innovative messages. An examination of religious or social functions attributed to the; medium so that it does not distort its special role. In some cases, it may be found totally unsuitable.
2. It should be seen whether the medium has an "ego" or "individuality." If it has then there is a possibility of a positive identification of audience with the actor/anchor who could prove to be a change agent. Some forms may however be impersonal as in the case of puppets and giant figures.
3. It need to be seen whether a particular form or any aspect of its tradition and features can be used by or extended to the mass media. If yes then it needs to be debated whether it is desirable in relation to both the medium and the message.
4. It needs to be established if the required resources, talent, materials, texts are available for extensive utilization to both the medium and the message.
5. To establish if the selected form has the entertainment value and artistic appeal.
6. To be sure that the selected form has the uniqueness to prove its value as a communication vehicle.
7. To establish whether the form allows the flexibility to incorporate a sufficiently broad range of content material such as family planning and other developmental messages.
8. To ensure that the form is versatile enough to cater to various target groups.
9. To be sure that the chosen form is relevant to the intended target audience.

The guidelines also suggested that the folk artists need to be properly oriented to the developmental issue so that they could develop their own understanding of the tasks required of them: their role as change agents.

The guidelines recommended the creation of national and regional organizations in the country, which would be responsible for selection of appropriate forms and for development of methods and structures to utilize the resource.

Some other tips included the following:

- It was expected of the administration to give proper respect to artistic integrity and tradition of a form.
- Local communities to be encouraged to participate in the development of such programs.
- The form should not be used as a propaganda vehicle.
- The sensitivity surrounding a folk form towards a developmental issue to be established by the artists.

On the use of selecting a folk form for development communication, Eapen writes that care has to be taken to ensure:

> Their social authenticity has to be retained, the integrity of their forms have to be kept. Purists are touchy about pouring new wine into old bottles. Mutilations of the form have occasionally happened and one has to be wary on this score. Some of the folk media do not depend basically on spoken words. For example, the traditional drama is a cocktail of gesture, mime, music, poetry and limited dialogue. Is the non-verbal aspect a deterrent to purposeful communication?[16]

Traditional artists are generally very talented who can be assigned the work of adapting their storyline to a certain social issue that the program implementer is addressing. Because the characters in the folk form are familiar to the people, a good adaptation has the requisite effect on the audience.

In a seminar organized by the Indian Institute of Mass Comm unication in collaboration with the Film and Television Institute in 1981, Giri Prasad, one of the folk artists invited to participate in the proceedings, expressed his angst on the treatment received by his ilk by the so-called folk media specialists and organizers of such programs. To quote him,

> I am in the midst of specialists. And it seems to me that they have no thought for the folk artists. Even today we are called for various functions and when the function is over no one even bothers to see us to the door. I would request these specialists to think of our welfare as they thought of their own. After all it is our art you specialize in and got your PhDs and after your work is finished, you forget us…if the link between the artist and the specialist is broken the folk artist as well as the specialists also suffers.

Taking the argument further, Prasad commented, "We are thinking of developing folk theatre when we should be thinking of human development. We cannot impose an idea on the performer. He must be convinced."[17]

The Ministry of Information and Broadcasting has an independent unit called the Song and Drama Division that has hundreds of troupes on its panel representing various folk forms in India. The services of these troupes are taken by the government in disseminating information on various developmental activities undertaken by it. The ministry's Directorate of Field Publicity has the mandate of covering the vast land periodically and propagates information on development projects. They go to the grassroots communities with what is called the "Talking Points" that suggest the agenda of their discussion from time to time. They also show films and audio visual programs to various audiences from village to village. The field officers are required to bring back feedback to the government. The critics believe that such efforts are nothing but propaganda for the party in power.

In his well-researched article on the use of folk media in various Third World Countries, Lent comments that when the governments use folk media and interpersonal communication channels to transmit the developmental message to rural people, it becomes apparent that "they have in their hands a truly grassroots propaganda machine capable of being harnessed to also promote non-developmental interests." To quote him,

> [B]ecause the dividing line between developmental, governmental and political ends can be hair thin, it is possible (and is happening) for folk media to be misused to promote the development of national leaders, rather than the development of national policies and programs. That, indeed, would be unfortunate in a world where governments already control so many mass media used to promote their own ends.[18]

With the onslaught of mass media through its 24×7 entertainment channels, some experts believe that these commercially driven models have little by way of connecting with the millions of people who live in the villages in India. *Abhivyakti Media for Development*, a Nasik-based Indian development communication organization is encouraging the use of folk media for development issues. It seeks to identify grassroots organizations that are already using some media forms in order to support them to participate in a loose informal network. The network aims at mobilizing their creative energies to focus on the local and, in doing so, brings a host of "diverse realities into public awareness and generate alternative nodal centers to distribute these voices and images."[19]

Development experts for long have debated the efficacy of community radio. Many experiments especially in developing countries suggest that community radio has been of immense value to grassroots communities in improving their lot, especially when they have been in charge with the active assistance of development experts and scientists.

Community Radio: An Innovative Medium to Reach Out to Grassroots Communities

There has been a lot of academic and policy discussion on the role and potential of community radio in the development saga of developing societies. It is believed that the landmark ruling of the Supreme Court in 1995 that airways was for public good sowed the seeds of community radio in India. Immediately after that many civil society groups got together and formulated the Bangalore declaration, articulating the need for a third tier of broadcasting, namely community radio. The Pasteur declaration on the year 2000 asserted that community radio has to be a community owned, nonprofit venture. Between 1999 and 2001, some of the initiative included *Namma Dhwani* in Karnataka, *Sangham* radio in Andhra Pradesh (now it is part of Telangana), *Chalogaonmein* in Jharkhand, and Radio *Ujjas* in Gujarat. These community radio stations either used cable radio or bought time on All India Radio to broadcast local content.

In retrospect, the UPA government's Community Radio Policy 2004 defined "communities" to include only educational institutions; later, however, in 2006, its new policy allowed agricultural universities, educational institutions, and civil society institutions, who now could apply for community radio broadcasting license under the FM band 88–108 MHz.

Community Radio India 2007 was introduced as a new track in the country's biggest ICT event, *eINDIA2007*. The event was partnered by UNESCO, UNICEF, UNDP, and the Ministry of Information & Broadcasting (MI&B), GOI. The event was supported by OWSA,

Commonwealth of Learning (COL), and AMARC. The consultation brought together experts from various specialist field, policy-makers, and community radio users from across many countries who shared their experiences in using the community radio in grassroots communication, thus, empowering marginalized communities.

The Ministry of Information & Broadcasting as of March 2015 has issued 409 permissions to set up community radio stations in the country, out of which, 179 stations have become operational while others are in the pipeline.[20] The ministry has been conducting workshops in various parts of the country to create awareness about community radio. To streamline the process of applications and approval, online facility has been made possible. The applicants now can also track the status of the approval process.

The Ministry of Information & Broadcasting in association with OneWorld Foundation India organized the Fifth National Community Radio Sammelan at Vigyan Bhawan, New Delhi, from March 16 to 18, 2015. The national-level annual conclave of community radio stations aimed at providing a platform to operational stations for networking, exchange, and sharing of good practice.[21]

What Use Can Community Radio Be Put to?

Community radio can be befittingly used for various things, such as the following:

1. It can bring the laboratory innovations and research and development to the common folks, especially in the field of agriculture in the rural areas.
2. It can help create awareness about people's rights and mechanisms to get their grievances redressed.
3. It can make the local government and implementing agencies accountable for various projects, expenditure, time schedules, etc.
4. It can inform the people about various government schemes, thus benefiting communities.
5. It can help create a social network among socially and economically disadvantaged communities.
6. It can alert them about price of their products, and about locations and dates for various haats and fairs where they could sell their produce.[22]

What Are the Challenges in Community Radio?

While the process of getting license for community radio has been made efficient, sustaining the radio on a long-term basis without proper infrastructure, professional manpower, and financial support; and content creation are areas of challenge. As the medium grows in popularity and listenership, it is not uncommon to find local politics creeping in the management of community radio which often results in one-upmanship of the powerful lobbies. Working on the content and continuous training of manpower are other areas of challenge.

As per the UNESCO document "Grand realities-Community Radio in India, 2011," a large gap remains between policy and practice in India. It further comments that communities from the dark regions of India continue to struggle to get their voices heard and to receive critical and locally relevant information.[23]

To address the issue of content, Ek Duniya Ek Awaaz (EDAA: one world, many voices), a web-based open audio content and resource exchange platform for community radio broadcasters has been created that aims at facilitating meaningful utilization of resources overcoming geographical boundaries. Launched on September 1, 2008, the EDAA portal currently hosts more than 3,020 radio programs categorized under 36 different thematic areas in 28 languages. EDDA is a community-based audio content exchange for community radio broadcasters in India and South Asia.[24]

Despite all the teething troubles, some inroads have already been made, thanks to the untiring efforts of some NGOs and local communities involved in the effort. For instance, Medak, a tiny remote village in the state of Telangana can take the credit for first setting up of the Deccan Development Society (DDS) followed by formation of women groups, implementing public distribution system, creating awareness among them, cultivating lands in organic form, developing seed banks, and finally establishing the first community radio "Sangham" in 2008. A brainchild of DDS, an NGO based in Pastapur working with 5,000-plus dalit women in around 75 villages, it was created with the objective of helping the village communities vocalize their concerns, to give the marginalized a voice, and drive home a message that they too have a right to be heard. Moreover, there was a wealth of traditional knowledge about farming, biodiversity, and health that needed to be disseminated. Many villages and communities are now interested in replicating the model. During the two and half decades of existence of the DDS, the women folk have become totally independent and have been able to reverse the situation where landlords now are dependent on them for seed and other requirements.[25] The DDS women have also been trained in video production. It is not uncommon for news channels to source video clips and grassroots stories from the DDS. Professor Vinod Pavarala, dean, Sarojini Naidu School of Arts and Communication of the Central University of Hyderabad, terms the success of Sangham Radio, a first-of-its-kind model in India, to every woman member of the various Sanghams who contributed ₹5 each to make the dream of running their own radio station come true.[26]

OWSA, an INGO, has initiated the use of ICTs for the Millennium Development Goals (MDGs) in enhancing communication opportunities at the grassroots level through community radio and social media. Its community radio: Ek Duniya Ek Awaaz (one world, one voice), has been producing programs that are broadcast on a popular mainstream channel. The programs include capacity-building workshops for CBOs in the use of audio tools to achieve social and economic empowerment.[27]

Information and Communication Technologies

Most of the changes witnessed by the world in terms of the information revolution have been technology driven. While it is a matter of fact that the rich are the first ones to make use of technology and reap the benefits, unless technology touches the lives of all, including the poor and the aspiring class, not much can be achieved. There is a school of thought which feels that what the poor would do with technology when they do not have enough to live a life of dignity and how would they afford the cost of technology. In the following paragraphs we shall take a look at such debates and discuss how it is important to encompass all to the technology revolution.

Defining ICTs

The term information technology (IT) has recently been expanded to information and communication technology (ICT) in recognition of the growing significance of communications technology, especially to access the Internet, send email to other institutions, to video conference, and so on. ICTs, in fact, encompass telecommunications, computing, and broadcasting and cover any product that stores, retrieves, manipulates, transmits, or receives information electronically, including telephones, faxes, computers, and televisions.[28]

The ICT in retrospect was pioneered around the Second World War with the advent of computers, but its huge potential according to analysts was realized when a sort of revolution occurred in the semiconductors industry that brought about miniaturization of gadgets, first the transistors, then the walkman, etc., followed by the integrated circuit and finally the microchip. All this paved way for large-scale manufacturing of computers that were made available at economical cost.

Development experts, in general, are optimistic in believing that new ICTs offer ways to overcome the socioeconomic divide. Properly used, the ICTs can empower individuals and communities as no other strategy has done before. The critics, on the other hand, argue that in an unequal world, this may further lead to information "haves and have nots," through the digital divide, besides the economic divide.

Professor Keniston explained digital divide, a term used in the USA, for the first time in 1996 to define population that had telephones, computers, and the Internet and those who did not have. This term has gained worldwide currency in referring to the growing inequality in the world and a hope that the ICTs could be used to promote development. The various problems in India, according to Keniston, are both at technology and human levels. With many languages and fonts, the codes would need to be standardized and interoperation ability between programs involving distinct codes would need to be resolved. Some case studies do suggest that not computers, but local radio stations with regional language programming, concerning areas like agriculture, health, sanitation, etc. were useful and accessed by people.

The other problem is the lack of sharing knowledge and archiving achievements and failures, so that others could learn and do not reinvent the wheel every time a project is taken up. Where the government is in charge of a grassroots project implementation, it is not uncommon to transfer officials in between thus losing the tempo and the experience.[29]

The digital divide, write Rogers and Shukla, as vindicated in earlier studies also, widen the gap between those with higher socioeconomic status that acquire knowledge at a relatively faster rate than those with lower socioeconomic status, thus widening the knowledge gap between these segments. Currently, the knowledge gaps feel the authors are being created by the Internet.[30]

An important strategy that could bridge the digital divide, according to Rogers et al., is to encourage the setting up of telecenters, especially where people with lower socioeconomic indicators live. A telecenter typically offers public access to computers, the Internet, and other communication technologies, provides training, and supplies certain business services. The importance of telecenters lies in the fact that they provide *public*, as opposed to *private*, access to the Internet, so that each individual or household does not need to own their own computer and telecommunications equipment.[31] In India one witnessed the mushrooming of "cyber cafés" in the mid-1990s. The trend continues both in urban and semi-urban areas. Some spirited NGOs like the Swaminathan trust has set up "Knowledge Centers" in many rural areas of Tamil Nadu and Puducherry, thus addressing the issue of inclusive growth. The ICTs like any other technology are in effect a means and not end. ICTs are tools or facilitators to network/speed up and reach near and far constituencies. The ingenuity, improvisation skills, integrity of thought and purpose, keeping in view the stakeholders/right holders' needs and aspirations, is what will give the ICTs their true worth.

*PEOPLin*k, a nonprofit organization, employs a grassroots strategy to help artisans in over 22 developing countries to use the Internet to reach world markets. Working at a grassroots level, *PEOPLink* has opened doors for many aspiring artists the world over by providing them with digital imaging and Internet technologies. To demonstrate the effectiveness of the *PEOPLink's* e-commerce strategy, there are a few ongoing programs in Nepal and India that verily illustrate how producers and potential buyers interface together via the Internet, thus winning over the geographical barriers.

These two projects effectively reflect how technology can establish links at the community level to help them express the unique features of their culture, while helping the small businesses gain access to the global economy.[32]

Use of ICTs in India's Grassroots Development

India is a highly diverse country in terms of socio, economic, political, and cultural definitions. Many analysts talk about two countries within, namely, *India* and *Bharat*, which are very different from each other. Some have described India as an ocean of poverty with a few islands of affluence. The other reality is the inroads India has made in the fields of science, technology, agriculture, and education. The government, the UN organizations, and experts have long been debating on the use of ICTs in improving the lot of the rural poor. Most of the poverty, it is believed, is also due to lack of empowerment. Access to information through the ICTs is expected to bridge the gap.

In his paper "Mainstreaming ICT for Grassroots Planning," M. Moni from the National Informatics Center of the GOI argues that despite the 6.5 lakh villages in India governed by 2.3 lakh panchayati raj institutions (PRIs), where each village can be seen as a cognizable unit located in a specific agro-ecological and sociological environment, development planning is still a mirage. The reason is not far to seek. The various departments such as water, fisheries, power, health, education, culture, technology instead of working in tandem, often work in isolation. The village problems, argues Mani, are interrelated, so it only makes sense if both natural and human resources are integrated. People, he reasons, are both the "end and means" of development, an issue that he says needs to be addressed seriously by the planners.[33]

Upadhyay and Mani have presented a framework for community networking in the Indian villages that in their view aims at the "social inclusion" of the marginalized rural poor to access knowledge and information network library environment through *e-Granthalayas.* [34]

Former president of India Dr Abdul Kalam in his address to the Nation on the eve of India's 56th Republic Day talked about creating the Village Knowledge Centres (VKCs) in the entire 2.3 lakh village panchayats to serve as nodal points for knowledge connectivity.[35]

The major focus areas of a VKC are:

- **E-governance:** Information on entitlements and on methods of accessing the entitlements (for example, bank credit, inputs, etc.);
- **E-education:** Literacy and technocracy (that is, technical skills);
- **E-health:** Disease prevention, detection, and cure; nutrition with particular reference to maternal and infant (0–2 years) nutrition;
- **E-agriculture:** Crops, livestock, fisheries (inland and marine), agro-forestry, and forestry;
- **E-livelihoods**: Opportunities for on-farm and nonfarm employment, microenterprises supported by micro-credit, new skills, and training in agro-processing and agri-business;
- **E-commerce:** Producer-oriented marketing, quality management, and matching production with demand;
- **E-environment:** Conservation and enhancement of natural resources, with specific attention to land care, water conservation and sustainable use, conservation of flora and fauna, and management of common property resources;
- **E-disaster management:** Methods of managing drought, floods, cyclones, and rare events like tsunami.
- **E-judiciary:** Experts talk of various ICT models that could be used keeping in view the need, role, and scope of proposed ICT program vis-à-vis target audience. Here are some suggestions for some generic models.

Broadcasting/Wider Dissemination Model: Suited to national and local governments in developing countries to encourage participation of citizens in the governing process.

Critical Flow Model: Different organizations can use it differently depending on the aspect of governance they wish to address. By focusing on the critical aspect of information and locating its likeable users, the model corrects information failure, raising awareness about the bad governance practices, and acts as a hindrance to bad governance practices.

Comparative Analysis Model: Developing countries could very effectively use this comparative model as ICT opens their access to the global and local knowledge products at a relatively low cost. The model, however, becomes ineffective in absence of a strong civil society interest and public memory that is essential to force decision-makers to improve existing governance practices.

E-advocacy/Lobbying and Pressure Group Model: The model enhances the scope of participation of individuals and communities in debates, which affect them and help them, build a global alliance.

Interactive Service Model: The potential of ICT for governance is fully leveraged in this model and can help bring about greater objectivity and transparency in decision-making processes. This model facilitates establishing decentralized forms of governance (G2C2G or G4C4G).[36]

Reaching out to grassroots communities, especially the marginalized section in far-flung areas, poses both structural and sociocultural challenges, especially the literacy barrier and social conditioning of women. Canadian International Development Agency (CIDA), in collaboration with the Guyanese Ministry of Education, helped operate a basic teacher training model using audio and video cassettes to reach out to remote areas in Guyana, comprising Amerindian communities.

In Afghanistan, CIDA supported a BBC World Service initiative called Radio Education for Afghan Children (REACH). The program is aimed at both children and youth and provides a wide range of issues such as landmines, agriculture, and safe motherhood.

In Jordan, CIDA in partnership with the Jordon Ministry of education began a project in 2001 that introduces ICTs by connecting all the schools to the Internet.[37]

ICTs, as said earlier, do not need to involve complicated technology. Social entrepreneur Rose Shuman from California, USA has innovated the use of ICTs by creating what she has named the "Question Box" a project of Open Mind. The question box works like an Internet search engine. It is made of a metallic box with a cell phone fitted inside. If for instance a farmer wishes to get information, say on the price of a particular farm product in the market, he would press the green button on the box and his call would be connected to an operator who would look at the database on the Internet and relay back the reply to the farmer. The question box has arrived in some remote villages of Maharashtra. *The Indian Express* carried the story of the remote Loni village in Maharashtra where an assorted mix of people are getting empowered by accessing information that helps them in their business, including school children who can check their examination results or travelers who can confirm their reservations. The entire operation is driven by volunteers. The project is not connected to any call center that can handle the queries. Anyone with a cell phone and net-enabled computer can take the calls. Over a period of time some more innovations have happened. The boxes now are connected to the solar panels to keep the power back-up during frequent power cuts.[38]

According to a media report, government spending on its various social sector schemes has created opportunities worth over ₹10,000 crore for the IT industry. As per a study conducted by industry association FICCI and Ernst & Young, the government has become a big buyer of ICT in education, rural employment, and power reforms. The three schemes, namely, the Sarva Shiksha Abhiyan, The Mahatma Gandhi National Rural Employment Guarantee Scheme, and the Accelerated Power Development & Reform Program could alone generate $1 billion worth of business, media quoted Milan Seth, from Ernst & Young.

Role of ICTs in Health Promotion

The ICTs have enabled connectivity and access to knowledge and information at the touch of a button. Can ICTs help in health promotion of millions of people, especially in the developing world where the statistics defy all the logic? The state of health is an important indicator of a country's well-being. The percentage of expenditure spent on the health sector vis-à-vis the GDP reflects the seriousness that a country imparts to the health of its population. The per capita expenditure on health in India remains one of the lowest in the world. When we address ICTs and health promotion issues, we need to look at the various stakeholders to understand the need and scope of IT to reach various segments of population.

Stakeholder Segmentation in Health Sector

1. Policy-makers
2. Ministries in charge of health and family welfare
3. Medical colleges
4. Medical research and development labs
5. Government/district hospitals/private hospitals/nursing homes
6. Doctors' associations
7. Pharmaceutical companies
8. International organizations dealing in health issues
9. International and national donors
10. Right holders (people at large)

If we look at the above-mentioned stakeholders, they already have access to one or the other form of ICT. What possibly is needed is working on the areas that will build partnership, enable access, and build synergy among various stakeholders on a continuous basis through appropriate ICTs.

A Virtual Medical Environment

The advent of the Internet and World Wide Web has increased its foothold in the past about two decades cutting across geographical boundaries and socioeconomic divide. IT has made the access of knowledge about medical breakthroughs, research, and development easier for the concerned stakeholders. The free access to most of the sites has helped create a global knowledge community. The latest fact and figures, knowledge about the invention of various drugs, and the general state of world health at the touch of a button has facilitated not only the providers but also consumers of health products and services. Many hospitals the world over have strategic relationships across countries to share the benefit of the best medical practices and inventions. In India especially in the NGO sector some hospitals have collaborated with the best ones globally for sharing of knowledge and expertise. It is not uncommon to see advice sought through teleconferencing when dealing with difficult cases.

India is one of the countries that can claim not only some of the world's best brains in the medical field but also world-class facilities at an economical cost when compared with the Western countries. IT has made it possible for the world to know about it, and India is fast becoming a medical destination for people from various countries.

Virtual Libraries

The Internet has created virtual libraries of database on various areas of health. The seekers can access most of the information free of cost. Many practicing doctors and scientists have their sites that can be accessed and a dialogue initiated with them by like-minded people. People especially from the urban areas are increasingly surfing the Internet not only to access information on health-related issues but also information on the composition of various life saving drugs before using them.

The various sites of government departments, especially the Ministry of Health's National AIDS Control Organisation (NACO) and other institutes of excellence have their websites that facilitate viewers to not only access the latest information but also get their queries answered. A number of telephone helplines exist to facilitate people seeking information on various issues that they may not be able to discuss with their families otherwise.

E-health is an upcoming area which looks at the utilization of electronic communication and IT to transmit, store, retrieve digital data for clinical, educational, and administrative purposes at the local site and at distance. Among digital technologies, Internet-based solutions are fast changing the way health providers, policy-makers, regulators, donors, and customers are accessing information, acquiring health-based products and services, delivering care, and interfacing with each other. The philosophy behind e-health is reliable transaction delivery at a fast speed involving people, systems, and health infrastructure with both the seekers of medical intervention and healthy individuals.

The emerging applications are oriented to professional networking, integration of clinical process management, and availability of web-based health information, health care, and monitoring.

Use of Mass Media in Health Promotion

Mass media by its nature is ICT-driven. A lot of health promotion is done by the mass media to reach millions of people in India. Television has a reach of more than 50 percent households. Some of the success stories include the campaign on eradication of polio. The campaign has been one of the longest ones in recent times and is claimed to be quite impactful in disseminating information and educating communities about the need to give polio drops to infants. The necessary hype created by the mass media is backed by media coverage, mobilization of community groups through district administration, and the NGO sector.

Use of ICTs in National Rural Health Mission Campaigns

The National Rural Health Mission (NRHM) has used mass media vigorously to reach out to communities on the availability of free services in various health areas. The campaign also educates the viewers about various medicines and vaccines that are required to be given to children. It also busts superstitions about health practices that are prevalent among many communities. The health campaigns have roped in some of the popular movie stars and cricket players to provide the necessary glamour and connectivity with the audience.

The success of the NRHM will also depend on not only making information available to people but also creating a database at local and national levels. India is a vast country with millions of impoverished people who may not have reaped the benefits of the ICTs till now, but it is catching up.

A silent revolution has already started in some states with the help of the NGO sector. One such research foundation (M.S. Swaminathan

Research Foundation) is lending its hand in creating IT hubs, known as Knowledge Centers in remote villages that are connected with its labs in various parts of some of the southern states. Software "open knowledge" developed by a few organizations including an international donor translates the information downloaded in local language that is then shared with local population during community functions that are organized for the purpose. Information that broadly encompasses agriculture, fertilizers, health issues like safe motherhood, AIDS, and livestock is frequently downloaded by "knowledge workers" (KWs) for spreading awareness. The KWs are generally local youth who are given training in computer, e-learning, and other related areas. They serve as a link between the lab and the village community. The knowledge centers are set up within villages at a cost that is initially borne by the donor but has to be maintained by the community. The village is expected to provide the infrastructure. In India, communities, especially in the rural hinterland, are very well connected at the village level. There is this sense of togetherness that needs to be harnessed for spreading knowledge about health issues through the ICTs. People in large numbers may not have access to IT individually, but collective ownership of facilities with the help of district administration, village panchayats, and the NGO sector can bridge the digital divide. The district health providers could consider linking up with such knowledge centers.

ICTs, believe many, can flourish in a society that is information and communication intensive. Development experts, however, have reason to believe that new ICTs offer ways to overcome the socioeconomic divide. Properly used, the ICTs can empower individuals and communities. The government according to some media reports is actively thinking to provide e-enabled computers to each gram sabha.

The cynics may have their reasons to question the affordability of ICTs in a country where a large number of people are "below poverty line," but the past experience of SITE pioneered by India did help in reaching out to farmers that helped in bringing in the Green Revolution. Such an experiment can be tried in the health sector too. The ICTs over a period of time have become so cost effective that one does not need intervention from the top. With over 90 crore mobile phones in the country, the devise can be used for activation and information dissemination at a personal level. A bottom-top approach can usher in a knowledge revolution of sorts.

Need for Synergizing Intra-organization Work

For any developmental work, a number of organizations may be working with their limited mandate and at their own pace. It can be challenging to synergy the goals of these organizations to achieve the common objective. However, a sustained effort through the use of the ICTs can help build synergies to reach a wider base of population.

ICTs: A Means and Not an End

ICT like any other technology is a means and not an end; it is the road and not the destination. ICTs are tools or facilitators to network/ speed up and reach near and far constituencies. What is required is the ingenuity, improvisation skills, and integrity of thought and purpose keeping in view the stakeholders/right holders' needs and aspirations.

ICTs, however, cannot attain much in a standalone situation. The following are critical for its success.

1. **The Human Resource Capital:** The seamless world of the Web has created heaps of information some of which is sociopoliti-cal and culture specific. What is relevant for one society may not be so for the other. Hence, societies and nations will have to develop their specific content to suit their constituencies and circumstances. Human resource training and skill development would not only sustain ICTs, but help develop content for infor-mation dissemination. The update of content on a continuous basis will make it relevant.

2. **Financial Investment:** ICTs need investment both while setting up the systems and for updating technology and maintenance. Who will bear the initial cost and its future sustainability is a crucial area that needs to be addressed. A private–public partnership/a donor-community partnership may be the answer.

3. **Coping up with Increasing Demand:** New research into ICT use and its impact have thrown interesting insights about its posi-tive and negative impact, depending on the intention and design

of policies. For instance, making systems efficient through ICTs may increase demand for the product or service. Hence, the systems have to be in place to cope up with the hunger for knowledge or access to services.

ICTs and Grassroots Connect

India can progress in a true sense of the term only if its vast rural population can reap the benefits of technology. The following issues remain crucial:

1. To establish and strengthen existing mechanisms and framework, especially to build capacity of community-based media network.
2. To create specific content to suit their constituencies and circumstances.
3. The need for creating ICT-centered communication media development programs.
4. Development of region-specific training modules that are target-group centered.
5. Initiate the youth in ICT training to ensure their sustenance.
6. Provision for such technology that suits the weather conditions/ maintenance and social structure.

ICTs and Interpersonal Communication

When communities are networked, the dissemination and sharing of knowledge even on one-on-one basis can help in achieving the goals. The ICTs need to be synergized with interpersonal communication and the rich folk form, specific to various communities. Communities can set examples for others to replicate success stories. Communities need to be involved in decision-making process. The examples of SEWA in Gujarat and DDS in Andhra Pradesh where women used IT to raise issues concerning them are some cases in point.

Public–Private Partnership

In order to achieve true success in health promotion, private–public partnership needs to be encouraged. The partners can use ICTs for knowledge management, documentation, facilitating discussions, networking, and promoting dialogue on health issues.

The story of how a multinational corporation, namely, Hindustan Unilever (HUL) created awareness through its Swasthya Chetna project about the need for cleaning hands with soap that changed the cleanliness habits of millions of villagers need to be replicated by many.

ICTs per se may not provide the panacea. One has to look at the entire set of ICT tools that include the Internet, radio, telecommunication technology (phones/mobile phones) electronic media (information kiosks, radio, and television) and choose the ones that are appropriate vis-à-vis the stakeholders.

Case Studies in Grassroots Communication

Integrated Media Training in Tsunami-affected Area

Plan India, an INGO in partnership with OneWorld and Indian Institute of Mass Communication, including other experts, organized three training programs at the grassroots level in 2005 in the aftermath of the tsunami in various areas affected by the disaster. The idea was to promote the use of various media and impart skills among a cross section of members of the affected communities so that they could voice their concerns and share their knowledge in a disaster situation. Convergence of all efforts was expected to establish the knowledge centers in every community so that there was both horizontal and vertical flow of the knowledge from and within communities. The training modules were organized at Sirkali, where participants from Karaikal district participated. In all, 120 members of the community were trained. Five different groups of the children and youth, 20–25-member strong group, joined media training on computers and the Internet, radio, print, comics, photography, and Villupattu (traditional media of Tamil Nadu).

One of the visible outcome of the training was radio coverage by Radio Karaikal and Live reporting to the minister of Information & Broadcasting in New Delhi on the occasion of Public Service Broadcasting Day.[39] The full case study appears in Chapter 4: Advocacy, Communication, and Social Mobilization.

"Soochanna se Samadhan" Project Using Phone-in to Interface with Grassroots Communities

The project initiated by OWSA, an INGO, is a telephone-based medium for disseminating information to reach out to grassroots communities. The service mainly aims at the agriculture sector to begin with. Farmers get their queries answered either immediately or within a span of 48 hours after consultation with the concerned expert.

How Does It Operate?

The caller is required to dial 0223911 6000, using his mobile phone or land line. The call reaches interactive voice response (IVR) where the caller registers the query with the help of a voice menu. The query gets recorded in the databank server. The (KW) then logs in to the application through web interface and views all the calls that are waiting to be responded to. The query is forwarded to the expert and no sooner the reply is received, the KW is alerted. The KW then retrieves the text answer, stores it in the audio database, and finally the answers in the voice mode are played when the farmers call to receive the answers. The farmer also has the option to access written answer from the information center near his village.

The phone line and the server are hosted by Reliance Infocom. The service called Lifeline India became fully operational in October 2006 and covers 600 villages across three states, namely, Uttar Pradesh, Madhya Pradesh, and Himachal Pradesh, covering 40,000 farmers from a total population of 2,225,000. The service on an average receives 175 calls per day. It is a paid service, costing the caller ₹5 per call. [40]

Grassroots Women Take Their Stories to the International Audience

Maud Hand for APC News reported:

> Like bright flowers in a grey space, the grassroots women of India livened up February's Prepcom proceedings and it wasn't just their stylish saris that did the trick. Undaunted by the suits and officialdom of Geneva's UN machinery, these Indian representatives vigorously demonstrated the value of ICTs in their working lives and made a cogent case for finances to build more equitable ICT infrastructures in developing countries like India.

These women from the grassroots communities were facilitated to attend the conference by OWSA in 2000. Pratima, a health and education coordinator from the mountainous state of Uttarakhand, narrated how she pioneered wireless alert system in her mountain neighborhood which is full of wild animals. There are no telephone or power lines in Pratima's community.

> I'd visit women in the mountain villages in the morning but if there was an emergency later in the day when the men folk were at work, the women had no way of getting help. That's when I figured we needed some technology to link up these isolated communities.

The system that works on walkie-talkies is powered by batteries and operates from four nodal offices in the region.

The local women have been trained in operating the system, which basically includes knowledge of frequency and switching on and off and talking clearly into the speaker and recharging the batteries.[41]

In summation, grassroots communication is both an indispensable tool and also a strategy in social sector communication. The choice of media can range from the folk form, community radio to the information and communication media that encompass radio, television, mobile phones, computers, faxes, cyber cafes, public address system, and the like. Grassroots communities, depending on where they are located, may or may not have access to the ICTs. Therefore, it is important for the program-implementing agency to do a target audience analyzes before deciding on the communication tools. If communities are reached and empowered, it remains only a matter of time when nations become empowered.

Swachh Bharat Abhiyan

Swachh Bharat Abhiyan is a national campaign (2014–2019) by the Government of India, covering 4041 statutory towns, to clean the streets, roads, and infrastructure of the country. It was launched by Prime Minister Modi with huge fanfare on the birth anniversary of the Father of the Nation Mahatma Gandhi on October 2, 2014. The Prime Minister invited public figures from various fields to join the crusade. He himself took the broom in a Valmiki colony in Delhi. Government offices were opened on that day, which is celebrated as a national holiday, to begin the cleanliness drive. People were asked to upload pictures of the drive. Media after six months into the campaign reported, "Work goes on without gloves, masks or aprons, but things are more organised."[42]

In Chapter 3 "Corporate Social Responsibility," we took a look at the responsibility the corporate Inc. feels towards the marginalized communities, and how much they feel is enough to go beyond their call of duty.

Notes and References

1. Commission on Risk Perception and Communication, *A Guide to Enhance Risk Communication among Low Income Population* (Washington, D.C.: National academy Press, 2006), http://serve.mt.gov/wp-content/uploads/2010/10/A-Guide-to-Enhance-Risk-Communication-Among-Low-Income-Populations.pdf (accessed on November 12, 2015).
2. Ibid.
3. Kenneth Kinston, "Grassroots ICT Projects in India: Some Preliminary Hypotheses," *ASCI Journal of Management* 31, no. 1 and 220 (2002): 1–9, http://web.mit.edu/kken/Public/PDF/ASCI_Journal_Intro__ASCI_version_.pdf (accessed on November 12, 2015).
4. Kinston, "Grassroots ICT Projects in India: Some Preliminary Hypotheses."
5. www.comminit.com/en/node/201039/36 (accessed on November 12, 2015).
6. Commission on Risk Perception and Communication, *A Guide to Enhance Risk Communication among Low Income Population*.
7. Sevanti Ninan and Aloke Thakore, "Impact of TV Digitization on Low Income Viewers and Public Broadcasting," (When the dish knocked down the antenna: Impact of TV digitalization on low income viewers and public broadcasting) A Five State Study by The Media Foundation, supported by Ford Foundation. The findings were presented in a workshop conducted by The Media Foundation, Delhi on August 22, 2015 at India International Center, New Delhi.
8. *Many Voices One World*, also known as the MacBride report, was a 1980 UNESCO publication written by the International Commission for the Study of Communication Problems, chaired by Irish Nobel Laureate Seán MacBride.

9. John A. Lint, "Grassroots Renaissance: The Increasing Importance of Folk Media in Third World Nations," in *Grassroots Renaissance*, 145–162. Full article can be accessed at folk media in the developing countries at https://nirc.nanzan-u.ac.jp/nfile/1119 (accessed on November 22, 2015).

10. Juan Diaz Bordenave, "The Role of Folk Media: A Point of View," *Instructional Technology Report,* (September 1975): 4. Quoted by Lent, "Grassroots Renaissance: The Increasing Importance of Folk Media in Third World Nations," 145–158, http://scholarworks.umass.edu/cgi/viewcontent.cgi?article=1001&context=cie_nonformal-education (accessed on December 8, 2015).

11. Tran Van Khe, "Traditional Music as a Living Force," *Communicator* XIII, No. 1, (January 1978): 44.

12. Elihu Katz and George Wedell, *Broadcasting in the Third World: Promise and Performance* (Harvard University Press, 1978): 171

13. http://unesdoc.unesco.org/images/0008/000805/080517eo.pdf (accessed on February 16, 2016).

14. H. K. Ranganath, *Not Relics of the Past, Communication and the Traditional Media* New Delhi: IIMC, 1981, 83.

15. Ranganath, *Not Relics of the Past, Communication and the Traditional Media*, 83.

16. K. E. Eapen, "Specific Problems of Research and Research Training in Asian/African Countries," in *Communication Research in the Third World: The Need for Training*(Geneva: Lutheran World Federation, 1976), 18–19.

17. *Communication and the Traditional Media*, a book based on the papers and proceedings of seminar organized by the Indian Institute of Mass Communication and the Film and Television Institute of India in 1981 (New Delhi: IIMC, 1981), 12.

18. Bordenave, "The Role of Folk Media: A Point of View," 4.

19. http://cdj.oxfordjournals.org/cgi/content/abstract/bsm036v1 (accessed on December 3, 2015).

20. http://southasia.oneworld.net/news/arun-jaitely-to-inaugurate-5th-community-radio-sammelan#.VsK5OyZunIU (accessed on February 16, 2016).

21. https://www.facebook.com/FactNewsindia/posts/1548441828756366 (accessed on February 16, 2016).

22. Dr H.O. Srivastava, President World Development Foundation. www.wdfindia.org

23. http://unesdoc.unesco.org/images/0021/002173/217381e.pdf (accessed on December 7, 2015).

24. http://edaa.in/campaigns/edaa-at-5 (accessed on December 19, 2015).

25. R. Avadhani, "Community Radio Celebrates 1 Year," *The Hindu*, October 16, 2009.

26. http://indiatogether.org/sangham-media (accessed on December 19, 2015).

27. http://lib.icimod.org/record/13770/files/4103.pdf (accessed on February 16, 2016).

28. www.pearsonpublishing.co.uk/education/samples/S_496132.pdf (accessed on December 14, 2015).

29. Kenneth Kinston, http://www.mit.edu/people/kken/PAPERS/ASCI_Journal_Intro__ASCI_version_.html (accessed on February 16, 2016).

30. Everett M. Rogers and Pratibha Shukla, "The Role of Telecenters in Development Communication and the Digital Divide," *The Journal of Development Communication* 12, No. 2, December 2001, httpwsispapers.choike.orgrole_telecenters-development.pdf

31. Rogers and Shukla, "The Role of Telecenters in Development Communication and the Digital Divide."

32. http://www.itu.int/ITU-D/ict_stories/themes/grassroots.html (accessed on December 23, 2015).

33. ftp://ftp.solutionexchange.net.in/public/emp/resource/res22050803.pdf (accessed on February 16, 2016).
34. P. R. Upadhyay M. Mani. "Community Information Networks in India—A Socio-technical Framework for Digital Opportunity." Paper presented at the International Conference on Information Management in Knowledge Societies, Mumbai, India, February 21–25, 2005.
35. Former president of India, Mr Abdul Kalam in his address to the nation on the eve of India's 56th Republic Day, Delhi Doordarshan, January 25, 2005.
36. www.solutionexchange-un-net.indecnresourceres_info_2800503.pdf. Also accessed at: http://www.digitalgovernance.org (accessed on December 14, 2015).
37. www.itu.intwsidocspc2roundtablesrt5zeitown
38. Uma Vishnu and Pranav Kulkarni, "Google in a Box? Just and Out-of-the Box Idea," *The Indian Express*, November 21, 2009, 1 and 2.
39. http://www.grassrootsvoices.net/events/event-reports/ (accessed on December 14, 2015).
40. http://www.mgovworld.org/topstory/soochna-se-samadhan-lifeline-india-knowledge-based-services-for-farmers-on-phones (accessed on February 16, 2016).
41. http://www.apc.org/en/news/access/world/icts-grassroots-women-south-asia (accessed on February 16, 2016).
42. http://indianexpress.com/article/india/india-others/6-months-later-returning-to-valmiki-colony-from-where-swachh-bharat-was-launched/ (accessed on December 26, 2015).

6

Planning and Executing Social Communication Campaigns: Case Studies

Many research studies in the past have adequately affirmed that bringing social change has never been an easy task. Bringing about change in the behavior of the people in a certain area that has been in practice for generations requires more than a smart communication campaign. It took decades before the abolition of Sati Pratha could even be accepted as an idea. Child marriage is illegal in India. The legal age for marriage in India is 18 years for girls and 21 years for boys. However, it is a fact that thousands of young children below the age of 10 get married under the very nose of the administration. In early July 2010 and later in October 2012, the khap panchayat of Haryana met to reduce the marriageable age of girls to 15 years. The khap believed that this would be the best way to address the issue of rape and molestation of young girls. Bizarre! But even the educated and young politicians from Haryana including the chief minister of Uttar Pradesh, Akhilesh Yadav, and Naveen Jindal, an MP from Haryana, would not like to take up cudgels with the khaps. There seems scant respect for the law.

Imperatives for the Success of a Social Campaign

For any social change campaign, Lazarsfeld and Merton have identified three conditions for its success, especially when mass media is used to reach out to a disparate group of TA.

Monopolization: An information campaign needs to enjoy a monopoly in the media with no contradictions to campaign objectives. Normally, any social campaign has many groups and institutions supporting it with varying objectives which sometimes create confusion in the minds of the people.

Canalization: Any social campaign depends a great deal on a favorable public attitude base. Commercial advertising in contrast is effective because the advertiser does not instill a new behavior but only channelizes the existing behavior of people in a particular direction of a specific brand. For example, people do not have to be convinced to brush their teeth; it is only to convince them about a particular brand of brush and toothpaste.

Supplementation: Social communication, according to this theory, can work best only when it is supplemented by face-to-face communication.[1]

It is believed by change-makers that unless a critical mass of audience, who matter, are convinced about the proposed change and how it positively affects their lives, not much can be achieved. At the same time, there is no one formula that can be applied to all behavior change campaigns to receive similar results. The concepts of effective communication and the process of social change campaigns have been adequately addressed in previous chapters, especially Chapter 2 on social marketing and Chapter 3 on grassroots communication. In this chapter we shall look at some case studies that would enable readers to understand the entire process closely.

Case Studies of Three Social Sector Campaigns Aimed at Behavioral Change

In this chapter three case studies have been taken up for discussion. All the three campaigns were the result of the team work led by the author for three different target groups. An effective communication strategy and plan is often the result of a clear "brief" from the client organization. The communication team should understand the brief, which could mean conducting a workshop with the client organization in order to get into the skin of the problem before going into secondary data analysis and baseline survey, and then take stock of the state of the problem. The word "problem" in communication parlance means "the issue at hand." The brief coupled with the research defines the problem for the communication team. The team ideally should comprise of a social sciences expert, creative writer, graphic designer, media planner, and public relations/advocacy expert.

Each one has a task defined in terms of output expected, but it serves the cause better if the group works as a close-knit team for synergy. It is important to ensure the participation of the client organization and target adopters all through the campaign process and implementation.

Case Study 1

Safe Injection Is Your Right: A Public Health Initiative by INCLEN

About INCLEN

INCLEN is an international network of health care professionals (clinical epidemiologists, biostatisticians, social scientists, and other health professionals) who:

> apply multidisciplinary approaches to identify best practices to improve "health for all" in local, national, regional and global settings. INCLEN achieves this by using the network to conduct collaborative, inter-disciplinary research on high-priority health problems, and to train future generations of leaders in health-care research.[2]

The network has a formidable presence in India. It has a functional and dynamic collaborative network of 185 Indian institutes including 160 medical schools, 10 public health institutions, eight research institutions, 12 non-medical universities, and nine nongovernment organizations across India, known as the INCLEN Program Evaluation Network (IPEN). INCLEN is also working with 15 Regional Indian Council of Medical Research (ICMR) institutes in India. This network has conducted 16 countrywide public health systems and program evaluation research for over a decade and a half.

INCLEN gave the following brief to the team for suggesting it a communication strategy to work towards safe injections in the country.

The brief: Suggest a holistic communication solution on safe injection practices keeping in view the state of the problem vis-à-vis the target audience, recommending a suitable strategy and media options.

The team, based on various meetings with the INCLEN members and its primary and secondary research, deconstructed the brief and the problem at hand as follows:

Problem Definition
Every one in two persons who is given an injection, receives unsafe injection, hence runs the risk of infection.

The Fallout
Every year at least 8–16 million hepatitis B cases occur due to unsafe injection practices. It is estimated that from 80,000 to 1,60,000 new cases of HIV infections happen due to unsafe injection practices. Seventy-four percent of the injections given in the immunization sector are unsafe, rendering infants and small children at high risk.

What Is an Unsafe Injection?
An injection becomes unsafe when it has the potential to transmit bloodborne viruses (BBV) such as HIV, HBV, and HCV. This occurs because of inadequacy of sterilized syringe/needle or using used injection. If the injection is administered using a faulty technique, this can result in local infection and possibly other reactions.

What Makes an Injection Safe

- Injection equipment
- Sterilization (when the syringe is sterilized as per prescribed procedure)
- Technique of administering injection

Which Ailments Attract Wider Injections Prescription?
Interestingly, common ailments do not really need injections, such as fever, cough, and diarrhea. (The organization's survey indicated that 53.3 percent patients who walked out of the OPDs were administered injections for one of the ailments referred above. The remaining 44.7 percent patients who received injections had symptoms such as swelling, injuries, and other infections.)

Regional Disparities
The research has revealed some interesting insights from various regions which would be addressed in the proposed communication initiative from the perspective of medical practitioners and clients.

The Reasons

- *Ignorance:* The injection dispensers often do not sterilize non-disposable injections the way it should be done. Disposable injections are often used repeatedly.
- *Economic issues:* Greed, disposable injections are reused either to save cost and/or because of shortage of injections when administered at mass level, especially in rural areas.
- *Lack of accountability:* The doctors and others often do not recognize the "rights" approach when handling patients.

What Can Communication Achieve?
Change of behavior among stakeholders as articulated below:

- To sensitize both the medical and paramedical fraternity about the lapses and the right procedure.
- To educate and persuade the rights holders (the patients and the kith) on reducing the demand for injections as an informed choice and their unquestionable right of safe injections.

The Challenges

- There are people who cannot be reached through mass media.
- There would be people who may not be interested in the issue; hence, they would not access information.
- People would be receptive if there is compatibility of information with their prior attitudes. If the information is conflicting they would avoid paying heed to it.
- People would interpret information according to their beliefs and value systems.

Communication Needs and Objectives
The needs of various target groups in terms of communication, information, awareness, learning new knowledge or new techniques, etc., has to be identified and prioritized. Based on the needs, communication objectives

have to be identified in a way that tell us what is to be accomplished with each specific group at the end of the communication initiative.

The Stakeholders
Primary:

- Doctors
- Paramedics
- Patients/kith
- People at large

Secondary:

- Medical administrators/policy-makers
- Pharma companies manufacturing injection equipment
- Medical and nursing colleges
- NGOs, civil society organizations
- Media

Safe Injections Campaign
The Ground Reality:

- Most of the times when an injection is prescribed or asked for, it can be avoided.
- People's faith in injections
- Complete trust in what the doctor says (This also often results in lack of vigilance about what side effects a medicine or prescription may have; doctors in India in a majority of cases do not discuss the ailment, prescription, and side effects with the patient or kin).

Communication Problem Proposed to be Tackled Through

- Information
- Education
- Communication

Let us see what and how we say under the three stages to various stakeholders:

1. Information

Our primary TA:
- Doctors/paramedics must know the state of the problem and whether it is critical to prescribe an injection.
- The patient/kin needs to have the big picture about safe injections.

2. Education

Our primary TA:
- Doctors/paramedics must know what a safe injection is, how to give a safe injection, and how to dispose of used injections.
- The clients/rights holders have to be educated on what a safe injection is, how to ensure that they are being administered a safe injection, and insist on a safe injection.

3. Communication

All TA groups to be brought on an even keel through various media to achieve synergy.

Communication Tasks
The "desired response" from the campaign:

- Reduced frequency of injection prescription and demand
- Enhanced safety in injection dispensation
- Scientific disposal of syringes (waste management).

Two-step Campaign
The critical TA in our campaign (given that GOI is convinced of the need for safe injections and the need for a campaign to inform, educate, and communicate with the TA), namely, the demand and supply side, would need to be addressed in two steps, namely, the doctors and paramedics, and the rights holders and the general public.

A. Stage I: The Doctors/Paramedics
   Communication Task: To convince them about the problem per se and reach out to them at two stages:
   - Prescription stage (when to prescribe injection; discuss with the client; convince him/her on the decision on why injection is being prescribed or not being prescribed)
   - Delivery stage (follow steps in injection administration and disposal)

B. Stage 2: Clients/Rights Holders
Communication Task: To convince them about the big picture and educate them on discretion on suggesting/accepting injection for quick relief

The Desired Response

Doctors: It's enough! No more prescriptions for injection (*Bahut ho gaya injection. Bas aab aur nahin dena*)

Client: It's enough! No more taking of injections (*Bahut ho gaya injection. Bas aab aur nahin lena*)

There are many motivations for adoption of a new behavior when a new social product is introduced. Some of these will include:

- Need to be different (innovator segment)
- Recognition of adoption (early adopters)
- Need to imitate (early majority segment)
- Joining the bandwagon (late joiners)
- Respect tradition/follow suit (laggards)
- What "desired response" is our campaign seeking?
- Be vigilant about safe injection procedure.

Partnership and Collaborations

Social issues need interdisciplinary approach and close collaboration with various organizations and institutions. For the safe injection advocacy, the following were identified:

- National Rural Health Mission (NRHM)
- World Health Organization (WHO)
- Syringe manufacturing organizations
- Civil society organizations (CSOs)
- Nongovernmental organization (NGOs)
- Medical and nursing colleges both in the government and private sector
- Government and private hospitals
- Media houses

Where to Reach Our Critical TA (Media Options)
The Doctors/Paramedics:

- Doctors (through sharing of policy/instruction, literature, conferences demos, over-the-counter [OTC] communication such as posters/instruction boards/collaterals [prescription pads, paper weights, etc.])
- Paramedics (through discussions, instructions, demos, and surveillance).

Clients/Rights Holders:

- Through mass media and OTC when visiting hospitals/health facility and social media.
- The campaign was suggested at a 360-degree communication solution that encompassed mass media, OTC, PR, social mobilization, and advocacy.

Suggested Media:

- **Television:** (genres such as general entertainment, news, etc. at national and regional level, particularly in states such as TN, AP, and Karnataka)—in talk shows like *We the People*
- **Radio:** Through radio jockey announcements
- **Mobile phone:** Alerts
- **Social Media:** Groups, games, viral marketing, etc.
  Outdoor: Hoardings, kiosks, wall paintings, bus shelters, mobile van
- **Direct Mailers:** Message on the postcards (Use the postmen in the rural hinterland to tell people. They can also wear the branded cap.)

Third-party endorsements, facility visits to model hospitals for media:

- OTC at Health Facilities
- Poster/instructions at health facilities
- Social workers/Anganwadi workers at interpersonal level

PR/Advocacy:

- Involve the clubs/RWAs (Rotary/Lion's, etc. in cities and towns) and school
- Teachers/students at rural level
- Gram sabhas/panchayats in rural India
- Convince corporate sector to include it in their CSR
- Branded content in popular TV serials such as CID
- Make media a partner in the crusade by sharing stories with them/taking them to model centers etc.

The Tone and Tenor of the Campaign
(The Route Recommended Was Rational)
The tone and tenor of the communication has to be such that it neither creates a scare nor does it accuse. Gender sensitivity, language, regional diversities, and cultural milieu would need to be addressed adequately.

Branding the Program
Creating Brand Elements:

- Objective: Create likability, meaningfulness, and easy identification with the program and memorability
- Mnemonic
- Slogan
- URL
- Advertising: jingles, colors, etc.
- Co-branding

Syringe manufacturers to endorse in their packaging and advertising, for example, "Dispovan supports the practice of safe injections" and carry the mnemonic

Injectible medicine (including immunization) manufacturers to endorse as above.

Considerations
When mass media is a suggested option, the communications team is aware that their message would be competing with various others such as news, views, editorials, entertainment, etc. therefore, the following questions need to be addressed while suggesting any media choice and strategy:

Who are we competing with in media and mind space?

- Seasonality
- Budget and evaluation

What Should Be Evaluated
Evaluation is a continuous, ongoing process throughout each stage of an activity. Therefore, the program has to cater to both stages, namely, to evaluate at the end of the activity and to assess during the course of the communication program implementation.

Measuring Effectiveness

- With the medical fraternity: Level of awareness of program; comprehension; memorability, and whether they have started practicing the right way of administering and disposing of.
- General public including administrators and policy makers: awareness; comprehension/knowledge.

Creatives: Some Glimpses
In order to bring home the point of vigilance, the creative team came out with the idea of Injection Inspector, thus making everyone responsible for one's own self. A pneumonic with male and female figures was created to lead the campaign.

Source: INCLEN Trust International.

Case Study 2

Communication Strategies for Peer-led Intervention for Drug Users (DU) and Intravenous Drug Users (IDU)

The project was sponsored by a well-known NGO, Society for Promotion of Youth and Masses (SPYM). Established in 1986, SPYM is a national organization working in the areas of "health: drugs,

HIV-AIDS, juveniles and for socio-economic development of the most marginalized population."

The issue of drug use is severe in our country. The youth is especially susceptible to the menace. There are mafia groups and peddlers involved in selling drugs to young children and youth. Many NGOs have been working in this direction. While the views of the government and NGOs may differ on the policy in this regard, SPYM has been propagating "harm reduction" among drug users as a first step.

The brief: To suggest a communications plan to reach out to drug users and facilitators along with prototypes that could be replicated locally.

The team began its work by doing secondary research to understand the state of the problem and the various laws and enactments in this direction.

Defining Harm Reduction

"Harm reduction," according to the International Harm Reduction Association, "is a comprehensive package of policies and programs which attempt primarily to reduce the adverse health, social and economic consequences of mood altering substances to individuals, drug users, their families and their committees."

What Is the Law?

The Narcotic Drugs and Psychotropic Substances Bill, 1985 was introduced in the Lok Sabha in August 1985 and was passed by both the Houses of the Parliament and subsequently assented by the President on September 16, 1985. It came into force on November 14, 1985, as The Narcotic Drugs and Psychotropic Substances Act, 1985 (shortened to NDPS Act). Under the NDPS Act, it is illegal for a person to produce/manufacture/cultivate, possess, sell, purchase, transport, store, and/or consume any narcotic drug or psychotropic substance.

Under one of the provisions of the act, the *Narcotics Control Bureau* was set up with effect from March 1986. The Act is designed to fulfill India's treaty obligations under the Single Convention on Narcotic Drugs, Convention on Psychotropic Substances, and United Nations Convention against Illicit Traffic in Narcotic Drugs and Psychotropic Substances. The Act has been amended three times: in 1988, 2001, and most recently in 2014. The Act extends to the whole of India, and it applies also to all Indian citizens outside India and to all persons on ships and aircraft registered in India.

Based on the brief from SPYM, the following goal and purpose were articulated by the communications team.

Goal of the Project

Goal: To improve quality coverage of substance using populations, especially injecting drug users, in order to prevent the spread of HIV among this population.

Purpose: The overall purpose was to improve both quality and coverage of drug demand reduction services in the country in order to:

1. Raise awareness of the adverse consequences of drug use including HIV/AIDS.
2. Reduce risky behavior among drug using populations to break the chain of HIV transmission.

Behavior Change Communication and Use of Appeal

According to UNFPA, behavior change communication is an intervention with individuals, communities, and/or societies to develop communication strategies to promote positive behaviors which are appropriate to their settings. This in turn provides a supportive environment, which will enable people to initiate and sustain positive and desirable behavior outcomes.

Creative writers, while working on campaigns, often make use of varying appeals, such as emotional, provocative, fearful, rational etc., keeping in view the target audience and the desired response sought from them. The choice of appeal depends on the demographic and psychographic profile of the targeted community. Behavioral change strategists many a time have tended to use the appeal of "fear" in the construction of messages especially for the "high risk" groups, which may not always work. Many research studies suggest that "fear," often creates dissonance and chances are that messages based on this appeal are ignored (many respondents interviewed during the field survey felt that emotional appeal would be a better option).

The communication strategy for the peer-led intervention (PLI) broadly sought to employ the behavior change communication model in order to engage with the specific communication requirements of the project. In short it sought to locate and identify the communication needs of different stakeholders in their specific context, and stage, in the process of rehabilitation with a focus on the urgent need to limit risky behavior in the context of the spread of HIV/AIDS. It also attempted to identify necessary communication tools required in the different stages of the process.

The fulfillment of the behavior change communication goals was expected to impinge on the following enabling factors:

- Address individual and social behavior
- Internalize behavior change communication as a community initiative and a continued movement
- Sensitize media to bring the issue to the public domain for discussion and top-of-the mind awareness
- Involve the political class to make policy changes to impact the program goals, implementation, and sustenance.

Behavior change communication, thus, was guided by the following broadly:

- Behavior change communication would be integrated with the goals of the program from its inception as an essential aspect of HIV prevention.
- All stakeholders, namely, clients, community, program implementers, and political class would be involved.
- At a broader level, a multimedia integrated approach would be adopted.
- All media messages would be pretested both at concept and deliverable levels.
- A continuous monitoring, documentation, and evaluation would be an integral part.

Identification of Target Population
The target population existed at different levels:

- The primary target group is IDUs and their partners.
- The secondary groups comprised the facilitators like the peer counselors, family, and community.
- Tertiary groups were regional centers and NGO partners.

Behavior Change Communication Goals

1. The program would aim at reducing high-risk behavior among IDUs.
2. Introduce and make available means of safe injecting practices.
3. Introduce and provide means of drug substitution.
4. Ultimately lead to abstinence from drug use.

Behavior Change Communication Goals

1. Increase perception of high risk of HIV among IDUs.
2. Create demand for information on risk factors, HIV/AIDS.
3. Increase demand for services.
4. Create demand for alternative/appropriate practices for use of syringes, needle, hygienic cotton swabs, and clean water.
5. Promote acceptance, support, and care within communities of IDUs, HIV, and PLHA.
6. Inform communities and IDUs, ensure safe injecting practices, availability of services, and referral details.

Framework for Behavior Change Communication Design
Strengthen Enabling Factors:

1. Providing effective communication through a multimedia strategy.
2. Creating an enabling environment through community networks and use of local communication and media practices.
3. Providing linkages, accessible services, and commodities through interpersonal/group communication processes.

Formative Research in Manipur and Delhi
Manipur:

Insights: The problem was enormous and the use of drugs widespread, youth being at the center stage.

- There was a lot of awareness and an increasing acceptance of the problem among families and communities.
- Lot of mobilization in place.
- Need to create materials, sensitize media, and political class.

Delhi:

Held in-depth interviews with a group of migrant workers

Insights: Awareness level high, despite not much literacy (Drug addicts on the fringes, may not necessarily be on the wish list of government, but a lot of work done by the voluntary sector).

Corporate adaptation: a ray of hope (Need for motivated peer councellors).

Pretest of Media Material with the Group

The creatives were pretested with a cross section of rights holders before submitting to SPYM. The strategy ensured that it was participative and carried a common string among various audiences and encouraged dialogue among audiences.

Campaign Objectives

- Introduce safe injecting practices
- Increase use of new disinfected syringes and needles by IDUs
- Alternative drug use
- Increase incidence of healthcare-seeking behavior (VCT, treatment for abscess, etc.)
- Address stigma against IDUs, HIV/AIDS
- Abstinence from drug use

Target Adopters (TA) for the Proposed PLI

- Target group for the PLI consisted primarily of males between the age group of 15 and 45 (as indicated by the field assessment).
- Women also fell into the same age group and consisted of IDUs as well as wives of IDUs, with and without HIV positive status.

Behavior Change Communication Materials

For Peer Educator:

a) Manual

Clear statement of objectives

Peer counseling methods and procedures:

- Methods of community mobilization
- Follow-up procedures
- Detailed illustrated information required by client for behavior change
- Related medical processes and procedures
- Referral sites
- Flipcharts, models, Av materials to support counseling

For male DU/IDU
Male
Safe injecting practices through:

- written material,
- flipcharts,
- audio-visual media
- games,
- quizzes, and
- reminder media that has shelf value.

Female (DUs/IDUs and HIV/AIDS positive)

- Storytelling with pictures
- Songs
- Street theater
- Games
- Flipcharts

It was proposed to be based on the folk forms to suit the cultural milieus prevalent in various parts of the country.

Message Content
What Do We Say?

1. A general run on drug use, intravenous drug use, and use of other substances and their connect with HIV/AIDS
2. Availability of syringes and needles

3. Identification of correct body parts for injecting
4. Rotation of injecting area
5. Where to exchange syringes and needles
6. Availability and how to use swabs and clean water
7. Where and which substitute drug to use
8. Abstinence from drug use
9. Infection from mother to child: Prevention and care
10. Life without drugs, etc.
11. Location of drop-in-centers, rehabilitation and referral hospitals
12. Helpline/AA/DA numbers

Monitoring and evaluation plan
A three-level research was proposed, namely:

- Pretest of all materials with a cross section of TA with the help of representative NGO partners
- A continuous appraisal and documentation of impact of the behavior change communication campaign
- A post-campaign evaluation

Benchmark studies covered three phases, namely:

1. Before mounting the campaign to assess knowledge on issues to be addressed by campaign,
2. When it is a high momentum campaign period to see exposure, comprehension, and recall as also trial safe behavior, and
3. After the campaign withdrawal to gauge the recall and sustenance of safe behavior.

Capacity Building
A three-pronged strategy was recommended:

1. Empowering the peer educator and counselors. (This would be through training them in peer education and counseling, which would be both from professional counselors and senior peer educators who have been relatively "successful" in the endeavor). Selection of peer educators would be very critical to the success

of this program. Some of the personality attributes could be as follows: a recovered DU/IDU, good communication skills, empathetic, well-read and informed, nonjudgmental, untiring, relentless, belief in self and client, a "never say die" spirit, and self-example portrayal to constantly motivate clients.

2. Creating a user-friendly peer manual (the manual has to be highly descriptive and graphically rich, and must contain everything that needs to be known, including inclusion of FAQs. The latest trends, innovations in ART and in treatment must be communicated to peer educators (PE) on a continuous basis, which can be added in the manual from time to time. (If we take the life of the peer manual as three years, we may keep about 36 pages at the end blank, which can be used by the PE for pasting the latest handout/s sent to him by the coordinating organization, say SPYM, as when required.) Hope is what is going to create a positive attitude, especially among recovering IDUs and HIV positive TAs.

3. Augmenting facilities at rehabilitation homes and drop-in centers. It was recommended to support these places with logistic support by way of audio-visual equipment like a desktop computer and an OHP projector to facilitate showing relevant audio-visual material; enhance extracurricular activities (a councilor at one of the DICS said that most of the drug users in transitory phase spent many hours watching television, playing games, and chatting with peer groups. All these hours kept them off drug use. Hence, the more the facilities, the more would the clients be attracted to visit DICs). It was recommended to SPYM to consider involving corporate sector organizations in the field of computers or other youth-related merchandise to partner in the venture.

Linkages and Partnership

Networking with various NGOs, national, and regional AIDS control societies, cultural organizations, religious organizations such as churches, local community clubs, schools and colleges, panchayats at grassroots level, bureaucracy and political class at policy framing levels, and corporate sector would synergize efforts. That the proposed behavior change communication strategy would be used by more than 300 NGOs working in the field is reflective of the need to make linkages and partnerships.

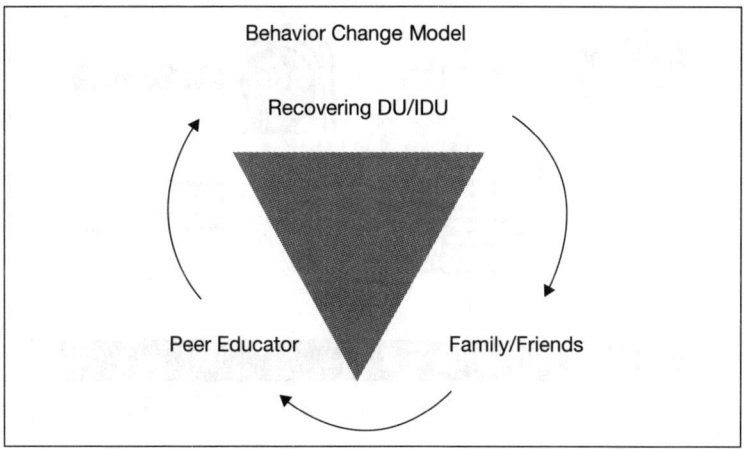

Leaflet

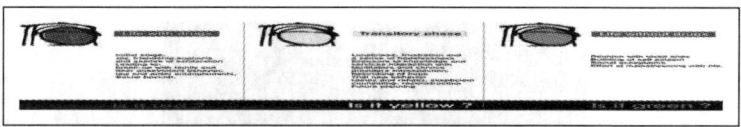

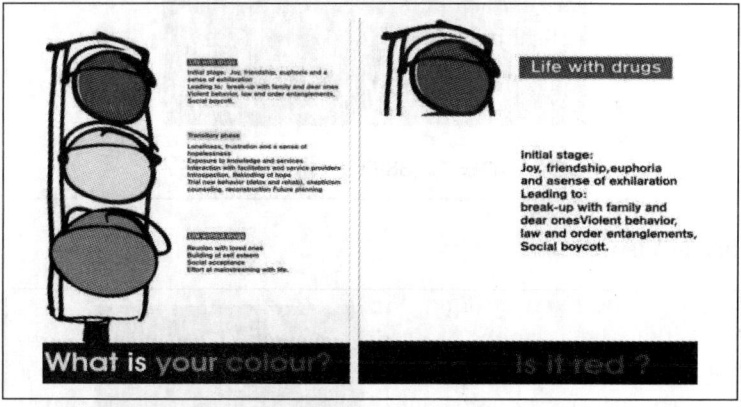

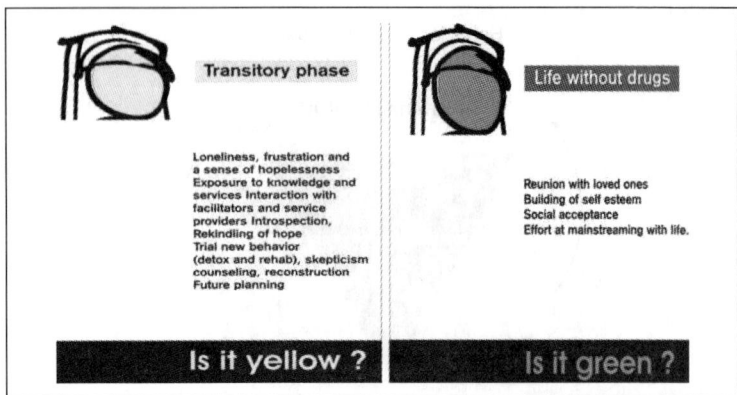

Greeting Card

Front View

Inside View

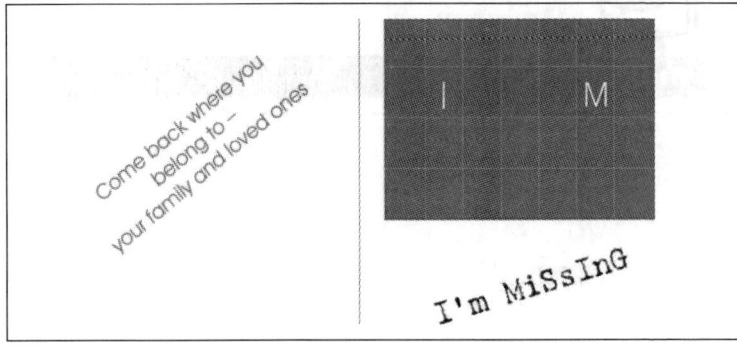

Poster for Drop-in Center

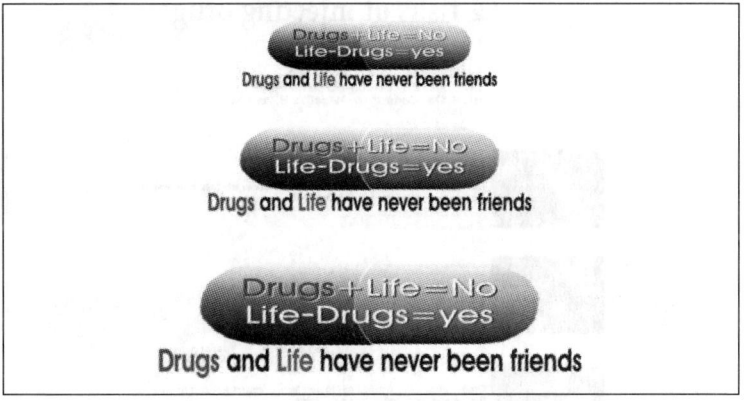

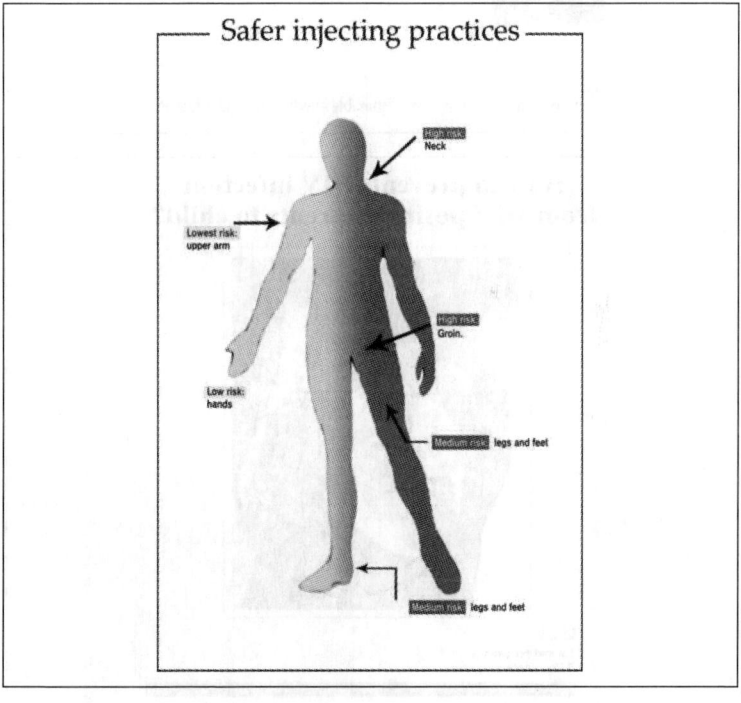

4 risks of injecting drugs

1. Abscesses
2. Accidental overdose
3. Collapsing of veins (thrombosis)
4. Transmission of blood-borne diseases like Hepatitis C, HIV/AIDS, Gonorrhea, Hepatitis B, and Syphilis.

Use appropriate needle; smaller the gauge, lesser the puncture wound, so less the chance for infection to occur.

Don't sharpen the needle on a matchbox, it is dangerous, the burr created can be damaging to your veins.

Drugs when cut/crushed / mixed can have granules which may clog the syringe point and damage the veins.

Best practice:
keep away from drugs, else use disposable injection to avoid infection

---

How to prevent HIV infection from HIV positive parents to child?

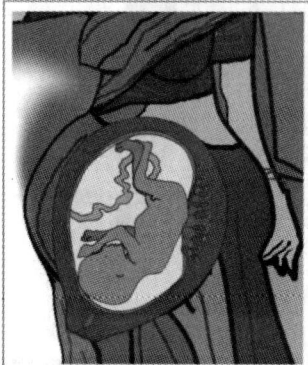

Safest
1. Avoid pregnancy
2. Terminate pregnancy

If you can't terminate for medical or emotional reasons, then observe the following:

• Practice safe sex- use condoms always, as it would help limit more of the virus from traveling to the uterus and fetus.

• Don't take drugs or smoke to avoid deterioration in the placenta and the possibility of blood mixing.

• Immediately go for treatment of sexually transmitted infections to decrease the inflammation in the reproductive tract of would be mother.

• Take supplements of Vitamin A as prescribed by the doctor to ensure decreased risk of low birth weight, pre-term birth, and small size of baby at birth.

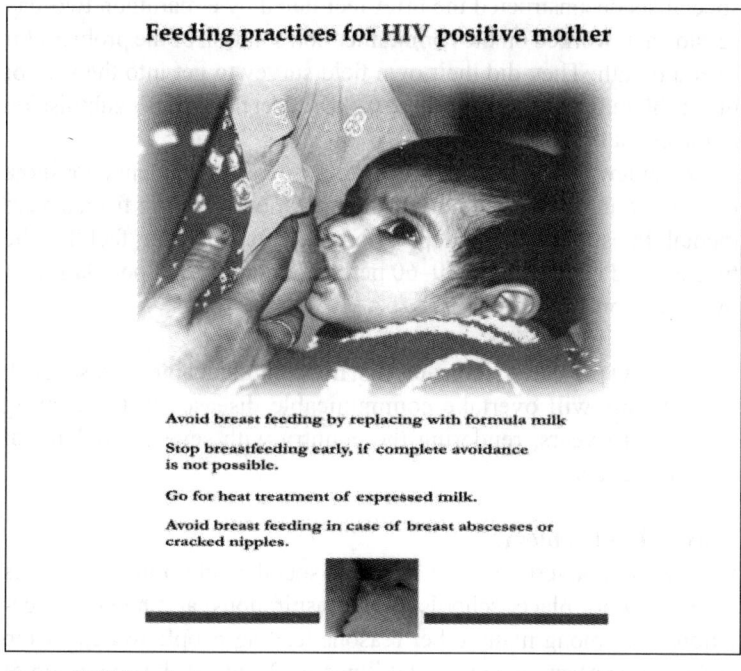

Feeding practices for HIV positive mother

Avoid breast feeding by replacing with formula milk

Stop breastfeeding early, if complete avoidance is not possible.

Go for heat treatment of expressed milk.

Avoid breast feeding in case of breast abscesses or cracked nipples.

Source: SPYM Center.

Case Study 3

IEC Strategy for National Mental Health Program

Based on the two-day workshop conducted by IIMC in collaboration with the Ministry of Health & Family Welfare and WHO on September 20–22, 2004

The brief: To develop guidelines and recommend strategies for production and dissemination of information leading to education and communication of scientific information related to mental health.

The exercise started with a two-day workshop that was attended by some of the best psychiatrics, clinical psychologists, social scientists, policy-makers, and communication specialists, with each group of specialists brainstorming on their perspective of the issue. The communications team comprising of some of the best brains from creative writing, strategists, social marketers, and advocacy and PR specialists deconstructed the brief facilitated by a marathon two-day session and worked on the communication solution of the problem for over a month. They did their own field survey to get into the skin of the problem. The following paragraphs reflect the group's submission to the client organization.

Overview: Mental health problems pose a great challenge for India in view of an estimated one-fourth population suffering from severe mental illness to common depression. Experts, however, feel that the figure could be as high as 50–60 percent among a total population of over a billion.

- WHO projection indicates that noncommunicable diseases such as this will overtake communicable diseases in the coming 10–15 years, rendering the country with severe problems at all levels.

Why Is It a Problem?
Deprivation, poverty, gender inequity, social conditioning, pressures at home, work place, schools, higher aspirations, and higher expectations are among many other reasons leading people to depression and in some cases severe mental illnesses. Youth in the age group of 14–25 are most vulnerable.

- The conditions at mental hospitals are subhuman.
- There is a lack of adequate infrastructure and trained manpower to cope up with the problem at hand.
- The Mental Health Act, 1987 is an anachronism that looks at people with severe mental illness as objects of detention, dangerous, and menace to society.
- There is a strong social stigma against mental illness.

Information, Education, & Communication (IEC) Proposal
The problem

- The triggers that bring on mental health problems will only multiply.
- Therefore, we need to equip caregivers, service providers, and high-risk groups to identify symptoms early

Situation Analysis

- Lack of awareness of symptoms and services
- Hopelessness, helplessness, and stigma
- Apathy

IEC Objectives
Information:

- Available services
- Low cost

Education:

- Symptom identification
- De-stigmatization

Communication:

- General awareness

Stakeholders
Primary:

- General public
- Health service providers

Secondary:

- Planners and policy-makers
- Law enforcement agencies

The Underlying Human Truth:

Nobody wants to suffer or be labeled crazy
"It only hurts when it affects me"

Universal Message:

Early detection is better management

Pneumonic

Smiling brain (three dimensional)
Message

Information:

Within reach

Education:

Myth busters

Communication:

"Mental illness is a medical condition"

Channels

Information:

Medical environment (health service providers, doctors, word-of-mouth, posters, leaflets, and booklets)

Education:

- Press
- Media/PR
- Ground-level activities: Schools, NGOs

Communication:

- Conventional media
- Nonconventional media

IEC Recommendation

- Single visual identity
- Central control on messaging

- Simple, nontechnical language
- No talking down

Impact Assessment

- Continuous documentation
- Periodic research

Why Are We Communicating?

- To create awareness of the issues and services.
- To reduce stigma and distress related to mental health disorders.

Who Are We Communicating With?
Users of a service:

- Family caregivers
- Rights holders (people with mental health disorders)

Providers of the service:

- Care providers (including medical and mental health professionals, traditional healers)
- Potential providers (including corporates)

Influencers:

- NGOs
- Media
- Planners and policy-makers
- Law enforcement agencies
- Teachers

General public
What Do They Currently Believe or Think?
Users of the Service:

- Helpless, vulnerable
- Do not have sufficient information
- Believe the services are inadequate

Providers of the Service:

- Believe there is inadequate manpower and infrastructure
- Inadequate skills among health service providers
- "I am not trained enough for handling these problems" General Practitioner (GP)

Influencers:

- Issues are not important enough

General Public (Potential Users/Unaware):

- "I don't know what it is and I don't know how to handle it."
- Lots of myths leading to fear and stigma

Why Should They Believe Us?

Credible source: Ministry of Health

Evidence base
Where and When Should We Communicate?

1. Mass media (TV/radio/print/magazines/cinema/outdoor/posters/leaflets/booklets)
2. PR (releases, facility visits for media sensitization, events, etc.)
3. Advocacy
4. One-on-one: mailers, SMS
5. Interactive website, the Internet and helplines, etc.

Important: The client, in this case the Ministry of Health and Family Welfare, was counseled that it was imperative to have a common thought across all media and activities for synergy and multiplier impact. Hence, the campaign needed to be centralized to have a complete hold on the central theme which will be reflected in various messages addressed to various constituencies/target audiences keeping in view the regional and cultural diversities and gender sensitivities.

Partnership

- Ministry of Health & Family Welfare (GoI)
- State health directorates
- Specialized hospitals
- Concerned NGOs
- Media institutes
- Media houses (print and electronic)

Recommendations Made to the Sponsoring Body

1. It is proposed to mount a holistic communication program on mental health at the national level in various languages to cater to the linguistic and regional diversities.
2. The communication program has to aim at reaching various target audiences in terms of primary and secondary segmentation, patients, caregivers (families, communities, and authorities), law-enforcing agencies, etc.
3. The target audience (TA) will be segmented on the basis of age, regional, and cultural parameters too.
4. The communication is proposed to be a 360-degree program addressing the issue through mass media, selective media, community intervention, advocacy, event management, and, last but not the least, media sensitization to receive the multiplier impact.
5. The program implementers need to network with various organizations both in the government and NGO sector for synergy.
6. Before the communication program is mounted, there is need to conduct a communication need assessment, prevailing perceptions on a random basis, and a communication audit of the prevailing materials. A national-level agency with a background of similar work is proposed to be commissioned for the purpose.
7. The communication program is proposed to run during the 10th Five Year Plan in the first instance with an inbuilt appraisal mechanism. It is proposed to launch a multilingual program keeping in view the cultural diversities and regional sensitivities.
8. The entire program is proposed to be a single-theme driven communication: *Early Detection Is Better Management*

(Information: to bring home the point that help is within reach; education: aim at busting myths; communication: *Mental Health Is A Medical Condition*).

9. The program is proposed to be multi-message driven keeping in view the TA and the desired response; however, each communication through a medium shall focus on one micro theme and a single message to be effective and avoid confusion.

10. It is proposed that the Ministry of Health & Family Welfare (MoH&FW) will seek proposals for campaign implementation including production of materials, media planning, and buying from among those agencies which have a background in social marketing especially in the areas of health/disability and mental health.

Route 1 Realistic with Real-life Characters

Musaafir Hoon Yaron...
(This one is for you Mr Anu Malik)
In this television ad, the protagonist is someone who is undergoing treatment for mental illness but is also singing in a choir.

Aalaap
(This one is for you Mr A.R. Rehman)
Same as in Musafir...

Jab Koi Baat Bigad Jaaye...
(Talk to a friend)
The TV ad depicted various situations and various age groups of people looking desolate and distressed. Then pictures of happy families, friends emerge and the sound track of popular film song, *Jaab koi baat...* plays.

As Common as Cough and Cold
In this TV ad pictures of people coughing and sneezing are shown and the voice over says that mental illness is a medical condition that needs to be treated as any other ailment including cough and cold.

Route 2 Imagery

Route 2 was an "out of box" solution aimed at creating shock value so that people sit up and realize that routine things that we take for granted or avoid could be the cause for mental distress leading to severe depression.

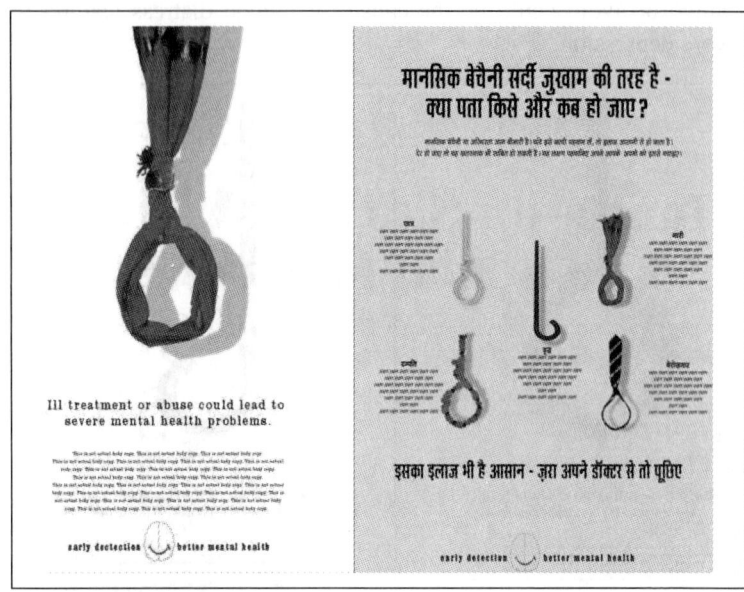

Source: IIMC, New Delhi.

The client ministry, however, did not approve of Route 2 citing negativity in approach as the reason for rejection.

To conclude, any social issue that seeks communication solution needs a thorough understanding of the problem, robust stakeholder segmentation, and an understanding about what is doable and achievable. Once the problem is defined to the core then the team works out the best possible creative, media, and communication strategy to bring about the required change in the existing behavior of the targeted public.

It is imperative that continuous evaluation of the program vis-à-vis the expected behavior change is conducted and mid-course correction undertaken, if required.

Notes and References

1. Paul F. Lazarsfeld and Robert K. Merton, "Mass Communication Popular Taste and Organized Social Actions," 1949. Full chapter at http://www.journalism.wisc.edu/~gdowney/courses/j201/pdf/readings/Lazarsfeld%20P%20et%20al%201948.pdf (accessed on December 8, 2015).
2. See http://inclentrust.org/inclen/page.php?id=308 (accessed on December 10, 2015).

7

Hands-on Skills in Writing and Social Media Use

Introduction

An NGO or program implementation agency often grapples with the problem of tying up various ends that broadly encompass networking, governmental approvals, and raising funds, besides having to constantly undertake the very arduous job of submitting written documents for approvals, advocacy, and publicity. Some of the writing work includes preparing concept notes, writing field reports, annual report, press releases, rejoinders, and backgrounders for media. Larger NGOs and ministries/governmental organizations may also have the task of maintaining their websites. The digital media has thrown open many opportunities on real-time communication with stakeholders including the media. While many organizations, especially the global ones, have now interactive newsrooms, looking at the way the social media is expanding, time is not far when the program implementers in the social sector would also have no choice but to use the new media in their day-to-day functioning. All this requires an avid understanding of the media and a set of concept tools and skills. In this chapter an effort has been made to provide a basic understanding of various kinds of writing and interactive tools followed by templates to facilitate people in charge of communications in the social sector.

Concept Note

A concept note basically aims at initiating a discussion/brainstorming on a future activity. The writer needs to have a clarity of the objective, the reason for undertaking the activity, what is expected from undertaking the activity, how it will be accomplished, and what would be the monitoring parameters.

Let us take an example of say the universal birth registration program of the GOI's goal to attain 100 percent birth registration by the year 2020 to see what the template would be like.

Template

1. **Structure overview/situation analysis** (here define the state of the problem, why it is a problem, that is, what is the percentage of registration in the country as a whole, state-wise data, reasons for low registration based on the data of any baseline surveys, insights on whether the low registration is across states, or whether there are some states where it is low, government documents, etc.). Based on this, draw insights on whether the problems are typical of some states, communities, extraneous reasons, etc.
2. **NGO/program implementer intervention** (here indicate who would be the players in augmenting work/lend its support in ensuring 100 percent birth registration by 2020).
3. **Where would NGO/program implementer be active** (here include the states or say, these would be decided in a meeting with GOI and partners scheduled to be held on X date.).
4. **Strategy** (that is, how it would be achieved. Indicate partnership at grassroots level, community mobilization, use of local media, advocacy, use of celebrities, etc.).
5. **Activity charter, etc.** (here, write about various activities including the time span and who would be responsible for what in a matrix form).
6. **Monitoring** (state how you would monitor the task).

Report Writing

Report Writing Guide

The primary goal of an effective report is to present a record of research work to facilitate decision-making.

The best way for effective report writing is that the author should describe the procedures followed and the results obtained; and then place these results in perspective by relating them to existing knowledge and by interpreting their significance for future study.

The following would help in producing a well-structured, well-written report.

Template

Format

- Title
- Abstract
- Introduction
- Materials and methods
- Results
- Discussion and conclusions, references cited

Style and Content

- Avoid footnotes
- Write in the past tense

Abstract

- This is the most difficult section to write well.
- The abstract should be a concise and exact statement of the problem addressed, the aims and objectives of the study, the procedure followed, the basic findings, and the conclusions drawn.
- The abstract is neither an amplified table of contents nor a shortened version of the report.
- The reader is looking for specific information.

Introduction

- In this section, state the nature of the problem, the aims and objectives of the study, and brief background information.
- Include the justification and relevance of the study.
- State the hypotheses you tested.
- Try to answer the following questions: Why this study?
- What is the existing state of knowledge on this topic?

Materials and Methods

- Include a description of the procedure you used that would enable a reader to duplicate the study (that is, repeatability).
- This will include data collection techniques, the equipment used, the experimental design, and the methods used to record, summarize, and analyze data.
- Minimize descriptions of well-known procedures and use references where appropriate.

Findings

- Summarize the data generated with tables, figures, and descriptive text.
- Do not include raw data.
- Explain and describe your data and the patterns, trends, and relationships observed.
- The written text should deal fully with results, not merely refer to tables and figures.
- Proceed from the most general features of the data to more specific results.
- Reference all tables and figures in the text and number them in the order in which they appear in the text.
- Write so that the figures and tables are not the subject of your sentences (for example, write "Growth rate was higher in the first quarter (Fig. 1)" rather than "Fig. 1 shows higher growth rate in the first quarter").

- Use graphics to display data in preference to tables whenever feasible.
- Use legends and clear, concise, and descriptive titles for tables and figures.
- Ensure all axes of graphs are labeled and that the units are identified in all tables and figures. The results section should be free of interpretation of data.

Discussion and Conclusions

- This section should include an interpretation and evaluation of the results.
- Compare the results with other studies and draw conclusions based on your findings.
- Refer back to the original hypotheses you were testing.
- Draw positive conclusions wherever possible.
- Identify the sources of error and any inadequacies of your techniques.
- Speculate on the broader meanings of the conclusions drawn.
- Address any future study that your research suggests.

References Cited

- List all the references cited in the text.
- Cite references in text by author(s) and date.
- If there are three or more authors of a reference abbreviate by first author surname followed by "et al." (for example, "Gopinath et al. (1995) state that...").
- All references should be listed in full, alphabetically by first author in the References Cited section
- Be consistent with the format; only use references pertinent to your study and your data.

General Comments

- Use and evaluate all the data you report and do not be discouraged if your results differ from published studies or from what you expected.

- Justify all tables and figures by discussing their content and labeling them clearly.
- Be creative in your presentation of data, your analysis, and your interpretation of data: play around with different variations before completing your report.
- Do not force conclusions from your data or fudge data by omitting that which does not support preconceived conclusions.
- Make sure all calculations and analyzes are relevant to the hypotheses you are testing and the overall objectives of the study.
- Justify your ideas and conclusions with data, facts, and background literature, and with sound reasoning.
- Ensure that the different sections of the report are kept discrete, that is, methods in the methods section, results in the results section, and leave discussion and interpretation of those results for the discussion section.
- Plan your writing.
- Organize your thoughts and data, and sketch the report before actually writing.
- This will help maximize your time efficiency and lead to a concise well-structured report. Provide the information to the readers. The review section normally comes at the end of the report. But for long reports, periodic reviews in between can also be done to hold the interest of the reader and help him in connectivity.

The Ending

The ending, as many researches reveal, makes a lasting impression on the reader. The main points of the message and conclusions must be included in the ending.

Yearly Report/Annual Report

An annual report is aimed at providing a balance sheet of expenditure in terms of program intervention and returns in terms of achievements, reasons of shortfall, if any.

The report has to be a cumulative record of the program initiative, various reviews, etc.

Template

- Name of the project under review
- Project goal
- Objectives for the year under reference
- Target area/s
- Year of review
- Project head
- Project partners
- Overview of the project
- Budget allocations
- Detailed activity with expenditure
- Annexure

An Overview of the year under review (here the project head would provide a bird's eye view covering all the above areas, the gains and losses in terms of achievements or shortfall in meeting targets, reasons, corrective measures, and future plan of action. A bit of history about the project, that is, whether it was a continuation of an existing project or a fresh one, and the state of the problem in the area of intervention would add value. It would enhance the value of this section if some graphics and pictures are added. The length of the overview section can be three to five pages. The following pages then would be devoted to detailed activity, area wise.

At the end of the report a few tables, and one master table giving a glimpse of the activities in tabular form, budget/expenditure followed by tables relating to various areas, could go as annexure.

Field Report

NGO representatives and program implementers often have to go for field visits at the beginning of a program or periodically and on return have to submit a report.

Template

- Objectives of visit
- Place/s of visit
- Date/s of visit
- Names of field visitor
- Methodology of fact finding (survey/focus group/participative research/observation)
- Key findings
- Suggestions

In the following paragraphs a prototype of field work has been prepared to facilitate easy understanding.

Mid-term Appraisal of XXXX's Post-tsunami Intervention on Child Care

Introduction

A team of three officers, led by Ms Devika Pradhan, visited Pondicherry and Nagapattinam between April 10 and 12, 2006, with a view to undertake the mid-term appraisal of XXXX's (organization's name) post-tsunami intervention on child care in 20 villages. The two-year project that began in January 2005 is being implemented with the help of XXXX's three local NGO partners, namely, XX, XX, and XX (names of NGOs).

The team that went from Delhi included one member from each NGO partner to facilitate appraisal. The terms of reference of the appraisal broadly covered the following:

(Provide the activity envisaged and periodic targets and achievement against each, reasons for shortfall, if any. The report at the end can attach this chart for a quick glimpse of the progress).

In the following paragraphs, a descriptive analysis of appraisal is provided.

Nagapattinam

Here, the researcher may give a bird's eye view of the demographic profile of the place, the extent of damage brought in by the tsunami, the number of children covered under the plan intervention, age profile, gender divide, etc.

The team visited five child care units on April 11 and had an in-depth discussion with the in-charge of this unit. The key learning also included thorough observation and speaking to a cross section of children and the panchayat head Mrs Anana.

Against a target of providing 50 toilets within six months, that is, between June and December, the team observed a shortfall of 10. The reason ascribed included the theft of material before it could be used for construction. This, however, was not reported by local partners at any time.

Most of the existing toilets were in good condition and kept clean, except at one or two places where the water supply seemed intermittent. The unit in-charge informed that this was a recent phenomenon and was due to break down of a pipe, which was being taken care of.

Key Observations and Suggestions
This was the third field visit of the team in the past about 15 months since the project had been implemented. Most of the areas of concern pointed out to local partners during the last two visits that took place in July 2005 and December 2005 and were taken care of.

Media Writing

The media is seen as a catalyst of change in a developing society. Governments, NGOs, and program implementers need media's active support and partnership to not only reach out to their disparate set of audiences but also to publicize their activities with a "desired" change in mind. It is important that the concerned organization keep the media in the loop constantly by sending press releases, features, and inviting them to press meets and visits to areas of activity. In the following paragraphs we would look at the formats for various media writings and also how to put up an interactive newsroom.

Press Release

For the success of any social program an interface with various kinds of media is imperative. The program implementers need to have proficiency in writing for the media.

What is the right time to issue a press release? Keeping in touch with media needs to be a constant endeavor of the program-implementing agency. A proactive press release posits when the implementing agency is voluntarily sharing information about any aspect which has a news value such as when some targets have been fulfilled, when there is a visit by program head and some decisions have been taken, when a facility has been started for the beneficiaries, etc. A "negative" press release means the implementing agency is volunteering the news that may not be good for the image of the agency but must be shared in public interest, such as when there is some accident at sight, some deaths have occurred due to negligence or otherwise. When organizations share such happenings, it is appreciated and the media does not probe unnecessarily.

Let us look at some basic determinants of news before we talk on the template.

Classic News Determinants

- **Relevance or consequence:** Determine if the information shared was relevant to the readers/watchers of news.
- **Proximity:** It implies that the news is local or has a local connection, if using a local media. If the news is of national and international importance, it would often be taken by the mainstream media.
- **Prominence:** Generally, people attract attention and important people attract more attention. A visit by a minister or an international expert would have news value for the media.
- **Rarity/unusual/bizarre:** People enjoy a break from the routine and so does the media. Small unusual events lighten a page or a program and help the media fill empty space.
- **Human interest:** Readers are interested in other people, even if they are not related. The daily work, triumphs, tragedies, and relationships of people being people have an inherent reader or viewer interest. Media and PR can both contribute in this regard.

Style Considerations

Some media have style books but not all. For those who have to write or supervise media writing, it would help if a regular reading of some important papers and news channels is undertaken to absorb the style. In fact, it is believed that a news release should be written in the style a reporter writes his/her story for the media.

Template for Press Release

From a program implementer's perspective, if the concerned organization, be it the government or an NGO, is willing to share its activities with people then media can be fed with information proactively.

Structure of a News Release

The Five Ws and one H

Who, what, when, where, why, and how
Which W is to be given precedence in the first and second lead is a matter of prudence. There could be clash of interest between the organization and media on this.

Inverted Pyramid Style of Writing Press Release

As explained in the following graphic, the information is to be placed in the press release in order of importance.

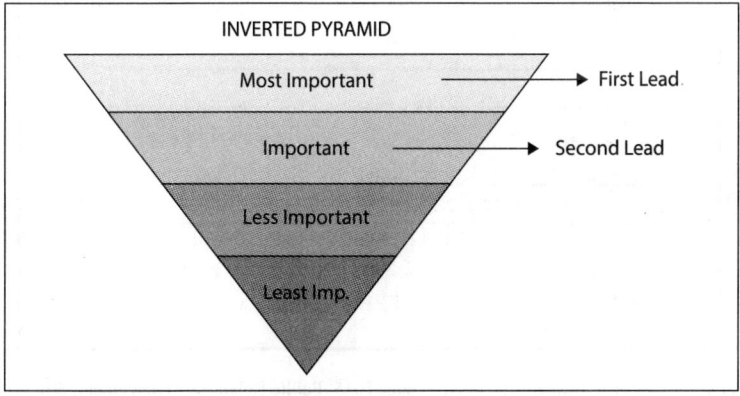

Source: Jaishri Jethwaney and N.N. Sarkar, Public Relations Management, 3rd edition (New Delhi: Sterling Publishers) 2015 p. 161.

Sample of press release page

```
                    Letterhead of the organization

   Press release

   Date...............
                                    For immediate publication/broadcast

                                    On or after ...........................

                               Headline

   First paragraph (first lead)
      .........................................................................................................
      .........................................................................................................
      .........................................................................................................
      .........................................................................................................

   Second paragraph (second lead)
      .........................................................................................................
      .........................................................................................................
      .........................................................................................................

   Less important
      .........................................................................................................
      .........................................................................................................

   Least important
      .........................................................................................................
      .........................................................................................................


   Contact name
   Phone/s/ fax/ e-mail
```

Source: Jaishri Jethwaney and N.N. Sarkar. 2015. Public Relations Management, 3rd edition (New Delhi: Sterling Publishers), p.161.

The Lead

The news lead must meet the basic media requirement of getting the story across in the first sentence or two. Some experts talk of the "20 second rule." If you have 20 seconds to tell a friend about your story, what would you say? Write that down, and you have the first draft of a summary lead.

The Body

Answer the following and you know what the body should contain.

- What is the story about? (a summary lead)
- What is in it for the reader? (provide a reason for further reading)
- Tell me more (give story details)
- What does this mean? (What should the reader do in response to a story?)
- Boilerplate information about the organization. (In the last paragraph every press release must give the basic facts about the organization. It is up to the reporter or news desk to take it or drop it.)

Press Handout

A press handout or release is generally distributed to press persons at a press conference. The handout contains salient points of the issue for which the press conference has been called. A press handout also helps the journalist in quoting the source correctly and ensures the salient points of the press announcement are recorded briefly for ready reference.

Press Note

Information and media persons are interdependent on each other for news. In a press conference or brief, the chief executives provide insights about various issues, which the reporters may be noting down.

A PR officer also notes down his/her comments and turns them into a press note, which may be given exclusively to a journalist on demand shortly after the press conference. This would ensure accuracy in publication of news.

Rejoinders

Rejoinders and denials are not the same. News from a competitor/ adversary may attract a rejoinder. A factually wrong news item may invite a denial from the aggrieved party. It is very important to look at the news item carefully and be sure before responding with a rejoinder. However, there is a need to pause and consider whether issuing a rejoinder might end up blowing the situation out of proportion.

Feature

Features can be written for both mass media and media for internal communication or specialized journals aimed at a certain category of stakeholder.

From the public communication perspective, a feature story is one that does not have topical relevance or urgency but has appeal for readers. The focus is on a special angle of the news, for example, human interest stories, profiles, issues, or general topics. Features can be written on a variety of subjects such as people, case studies, research findings, innovations, special/commemorative occasions, etc.

Internet and Social Media

The Internet has created a seamless world cutting across barriers of time and space. It has created a global community of like-minded people who discuss and deliberate on matters as varied as people, politics, religion, environment, human rights, globalization, markets, brands, and a host of other matters. Social marketers and civil society organizations have discovered a new medium to push their social agenda and mobilize public opinion on issues they feel concerned about. In fact, a new variant of NGOs known as eNGOs has emerged which are doing their work with great élan. Many advocacy groups such as *Change.org* and *Avaaz* have been able to impact policy decisions through online petitions. We shall look at the activities of some of the eNGOs later in the chapter.

In the following paragraphs, some of the Internet tools are discussed which the NGOs and program implementers may like to use from the perspective of communicating with a larger mass of audience, especially as a tool of advocacy.

New media is replete with both pros and cons if it has an instantaneous reach of text, audio and video almost at the speed of thought; on the one hand, it is also an irrevocable fact that it is almost impossible to remove the footprints altogether once these are there on the Internet.

Interactive Newsroom

Media Interface@ Net Age

Legacy media such as television, radio, and press continue to be main-stream, and there is no denying that the Internet continues to draw its ideas in no small measure from it. Journalists working in mainstream media often have their blogs and wish to be followed and interacted with by their readers and program consumers.

The lesson for program implementers is to observe and not necessarily interact with their beat reporters on the Internet. This would lead to the gathering of a lot of insights on day-to-day basis. The latest in the trajectory of media relations is the interactive online newsroom.

What is an Online Newsroom?

An online newsroom is set up in a virtual setting that can be accessed by media persons all the time. A journalist needs a PR source for an update, authentication, sound byte, quote, or an exclusive, etc.

An interactive newsroom is a great way to maintain control of the brand/social issue communication. In crisis times, it is important to keep updating it. Empirical research suggests that in times of crisis, journalists first of all access the concerned company's site.

An online media room has to be constructed after a lot of thinking and strategy. As technology is involved, people in charge of communication in the NGO/government should ensure that the IT department does not create/handle content.

To start with, they need to begin with needs analysis keeping in view their media relations strategy. The navigational design has to be such that it provides valuable information that the visitors may have on their minds.

What Should It Ideally Have?

Key Elements of Interactive Newsroom:

1. Contact information for the organization's communications/PR person and, editorial contact to be clearly listed on the front/ home page with (navigation instruction).
2. Basic facts on the organization, a factsheet, names of key executives, social product/issue and reach/perspectives.
3. Organization's presentations at various forums, speeches, and publicity.
4. Access to financial information, funding sources, expenditure, and figures of the corresponding year.
5. Information is oxygen for journalists so it is important that a lot of background information is created to facilitate the journalist in expanding his/her story.
6. Easy downloadable images of logo, pictures of events with clear labels (quality at least 300 dpi).
7. Archival page with old press releases arranged subject-/year-/ date-wise.
8. Press reports/coverage (the organization has to be careful if it wishes to add this page. By just uploading favorable coverage and not negative one may create credibility gap).
9. Register journalists for password enabled information. Send weekly updates in the newsroom through e-mail alerts to journalists on the beat.

Journalists can be offered to have personal folders in the newsroom with a password protected area to store information that they may have researched and wish to archive on a company's site for future use. The new rules of media relations in the web age have now changed. Experts believe that to be successful in new media age they need to keep the following in view:

1. Nontargeted pitches are spam.
2. News releases sent to reporters in subject areas they do not cover are also spam.
3. Communications professionals need to pitch bloggers because being connected will have them noticed by mainstream media.
4. Personal relations with reporters despite online interactive newsroom are a must.[1]

In Adverse Times

If in crisis, an interactive newsroom can become an organization's life support system in explaining itself, disseminating information quickly, reaching out to its various stakeholders through the media as well as the website and, most importantly, facilitating media to have a continuous flow of information, graphics, and video clippings.

Some Dos

1. Constantly update information.
2. Add sound bytes of those who matter. The communication must not only be read but also seen as authentic and reasonable.
3. Videos of the happening/accident site.
4. Videos of acts of human kindness/beyond the call of duty.

Keep e-press kits ready for the scribes on specific targeted news releases, images, statements, and related content.

Some Don'ts

1. When in crisis do not argue in the organization's supposed interest; explain its perspective.
2. Be empathetic in words, body language, and intent.

3. The viral nature of communication can make it worse, so have patience as soon as the crisis breaks. People would like to know what you are doing to mitigate the crisis, especially if human life is involved.
4. The organization may not have been directly responsible for the crisis but issuing denials when the suffering of the people is apparent would boomerang.
5. Share your concern, the plan of action with facts, figures, and graphics/videos for credibility.
6. Look for sound bytes from people who trust you. It will make a difference.[2]

Blogging

The number of people joining the social media seems to change every few minutes! When we look at the data from 2010 to 2014 with projections until 2016, it is estimated that there will be around 2.13 billion social network users around the globe, up from 1.4 billion in 2012.

It is estimated that one billion pages are added every day on the worldwide web. Not all that is uploaded may make sense, but the Web indeed has provided a democratic platform to a large number of people to express themselves, give vent to their innermost feelings, question those in authority, be critical of policies and products that they are not happy about and make the governments, organizations, and their friends know about it.

The new media has thrown open immense opportunities for the social sector to reach out to people and bring about the necessary change. NGOs, in order to be catalysts of change, must use the social media, especially blogging, to express themselves. A blog is successful if does well on traffic and reputation. It is however important to decide how often an NGO should blog. According to World Bank, in the context of blogging, NGOs must "strive for scale if they want to fulfill their role as enablers and incubators in striving for development."[3]

Barring some blogs run by large reputed organizations in the social sector, it is believed that a lot of NGOs do not really do well on traffic and reputation.[4]

How to Succeed on the Blog Space?

There are some ground rules to follow to draw traffic and interest in a particular blog.

- **Vision:** The vision needs to be simple to understand and must look realistic to achieve.
- **Content:** A blogger, whether as an individual or an organization must reflect scholarship on the subject? Organizational blogs often have expert communications persons creating the content. It is important to have domain experts' input too on the blog. The organization needs to have a sustainability strategy during quiet times.[5]
- **Storytelling Expertise:** Social media experts believe that organizations, including NGOs, must build on storytellers from among the noncommunications staff.
- **Witness Bearing:** A blog when reflects the lives of the affected people in their words through words and visual medium is always more powerful and credible. With one billion users, 300 hours of videos are uploaded every minute on YouTube. YouTube is localized in 75 countries and is available in 61 languages.[6] Social sector organizations can befittingly use the power of visual media by uploading stories that reach millions of people.

Social Media

Where to Be Seen on the Net

The profile of the target audience, an NGO, or the area the program implementer is trying to reach out to would determine where it should be more visible on the digital media. Facebook, Twitter, Instagram, Pinterest, Flickr, LinkedIn, Google+, apps, podcasts, videos, WhatsApp, messaging, etc. are some of the popular digital media that tens of thousands people across all ages, especially the youth and professionals, are hooked on to. All these can be befittingly used by social sector organizations and program implementers. Let us look at some of the social media that can be used by program implementers and social sector organizations:

Facebook

As soon as one opens one's Facebook page, it is not uncommon to find brands and issues being talked about and sometimes endorsed by friends. Many a time friends tag videos, research site links, advocacy organizations' links to reflect that they endorse that cause/brand, subtly exhorting others to take a call on that. For instance, *The Times of India*'s *Tum chalo toh Hindustan chaley!* (When you walk forward; India walks with you) was one of the talked about advocacy ads on Facebook for long. The ad started with a traffic jam as a huge tree fell due to incessant rains and blocked the road. Suddenly, a young school kid came to push the tree to clear the road block. Seeing him struggle, other kids and pedestrians joined him and managed to remove the log to clear the traffic. With a musical score from the famous trio Shankar, Ehsaan, and Loy, the ad subtly conveyed that if you take the initiative, others are bound to lend a helping hand to make things move.[7] *The Hindu*'s "Behave yourself India. The youth are watching" was another video that went viral on the social media. In the ad, students were seen enacting a mock parliament in college. As the debate started, the classroom turned into a fight zone with pandemonium and mayhem all around. As the teacher watched with surprise, *Vaishnav jan to* played in the background.[8]

Twitter

Twitter is fast becoming the instant communication tool for political bigwigs including presidents, prime ministers, ministers, corporate honchos, and celebrities from the world of sports and entertainment. The success of this medium rests on the premise that one is there constantly, responds, and tweets and re-tweets. The number of followers determines the popularity of the twitter account holder. Both the above ads *Watch yourself India. The Youth are watching* and *Tum chalo toh Hindustan Chale* were tagged by many twitter users. For advocacy, twitter can be an important social media tool.

Given below is an outline of an interesting movement in the USA that became huge and all pervasive due to the use of social media.

#*Giving Tuesday* was launched in September 2012 and two and a half months later after Thanksgiving, Americans in all the 50 states came together to inaugurate a new "Opening day" for the giving season.

Social media, as analyzed in a case study in the Harvard Business Review (HBR), helped the organizers get there; 2,600 partners including multinationals and NGOs actively took part in the movement. The White House endorsed it along with billionaire philanthropist Bill Gates. It generated 800 media features and mentions in news channels such as CNN and CBS News and newspapers such as *The Washington Post*. The hash tag *#Giving Tuesday* trended as the number one story on Twitter. The outcome of media hype was the opening of many online donation platforms. The organizer, who truly was the catalyst and incubator for *#GivingTuesday*, was the 92nd Street Y, a 139-year-old Jewish cultural and community center that reaches out to serve people of all backgrounds (founded in 1874 as a Young Men's Hebrew Association).

The organizers had envisioned that #Giving Tuesday became as well known as the *Black Friday* or *Cyber Monday* in terms of positioning. *#GivingTuesday* began with a simple question: On the heels of Black Friday and *Cyber Monday*, could we trigger a new day of giving after two days of getting?[9]

The HBR case study ascribes the following reasons on why *#Giving Tuesday* became so successful:

1. **Think movement, not initiative:** The movement started from the 92nd Street, NYC; UN Foundation worked with it closely; it brought a battery of leaders from the Stanford University and gradually many communities got into the ring.
2. **Think upload, not download:** It focused on people's desire to upload, with an idea of being social ambassadors to spread the word about the movement and also engage with their organizations.
3. **Think current, not currency:** *#Giving Tuesday* was not something one could "own" but as something with a flow of its own, the movement "bubbled up, flowed and ebbed and at the right moment surged."
4. **Think tools, not rules:** The core function of the *#Giving Tuesday* team was to empower, to provide the right resources to support the community and champions in its efforts.[10]

One of the interesting insights of the campaign was various spokespersons appearing from across various communities in the morning shows and using the "talking points" of the movement as their own and that was the biggest triumph of the program.[11]

Nearer to home, we can talk about the Anti-Corruption Movement spearheaded by Gandhian Anna Hazare in 2012 that saw a frenzied social media space exhorting friends and communities to reach out to the place where Hazare was fasting in Delhi, the capital city of India. Thousands of people, especially the youth, missed their colleges and jobs and rushed to the venue to lend support. It was an unprecedented show of solidarity by the citizens of Delhi. Many celebrities from varying fields from various states came to Delhi to express their oneness with the movement and the crusader. Some columnists commented that it was reminiscent of the freedom struggle against the British. Corporate giant Hero kickstarted its brand campaign on the same day: *Ham mein hai hero* (there is a leader within us) and one saw owners of Hero motorcycle exhorting their friends on the social media to ride their "Hero" and reach the venue. Hundreds of bikers could be seen going together to the site of action.

Email

E-mail may be old in comparison to other tools, but its value and impact cannot be underestimated. Many empirical studies suggest that a personal email has better chance of being seen than social media platform. The reasons are not far to seek. An e-mail has a designated target audience; people have the habit of checking their mail boxes many times in a day. With Internet facilities on smart phones, an alert on phone is instantly received as soon as a message arrives in the mail box. Getting support from friends is easier for a cause via a personal mail, than when they look at the message on a social networking space.

Videos

YouTube uploads user created video material worth 300 hours every minute; that speaks volumes of videos on a variety of subjects and emotions available at the click of the button. With most smart phones enabled to take high-definition video, which could be instantly edited on the phone itself, the next obvious stage for a lot of people is to post it on social networking sites. Social marketers and advocacy organizations can befittingly use the medium to advocate the issues spearheaded by them.

There are many examples to cite here, but the long drawn Narmada Bhachao Andolan (Save Narmada) saw the protagonists using video uploading strategy to advocate the movement's stand and the perspective of the displaced families. When the supreme Court's verdict went against the movement's charter on the height of the dam, one saw a weeping Medha Patekar, the chief protagonist in the video. In the same movement, Booker award winning author turned activist Arundhati Roy was also seen anchoring a film to give the perspective on the issue and the alleged contempt of court on her part.

Online media if used strategically can be of great value to social issues and movements.

Lha Charitable Trust (LHT), a Tibetan organization located in Dharmshala, Himachal Pradesh as per its website, "plays a crucial role in facilitating the transition of Tibetan refugees from their homeland to the Indian community by providing long-term rehabilitation and education resources." According to analysts, the NGO uses every kind of conceivable digital platform to fulfill its program goals. The LHA is able to draw funds from all over the world in pursuance of its activities through its online magazine *Contact*. The NGO runs a Tibetan language website to reach out to the diaspora to share community information.[12]

In Rajasthan, Annakshetra, an NGO runs programs such as "We can end hunger." They have a 24×7 helpline and website through which it connects with organizations that have excess food and those who are in need of food. Their online presence has seen people and organizations connecting with them for food. On its website, the NGO claims that it has been able to serve a million meals to the poor people.

In Mumbai, Sounds of Silence claims to be "India's first technology-based NGO" connecting through the digital tools with the deaf and the mute.

To quota digital media expert and activist Osama Manzar,

The eNGO challenge platform, which aggregates best practices of NGOs using digital tools for good, is actually showing a world where the impact of digital media, e-commerce, e-learning, crowd sourcing, mobiles and apps can be seen making a more equitable society where dependency on government and business is lesser and citizen participation is higher.[13]

To conclude, communication is the lifeline of social cause movements and campaigns. While there are professionals and communications agencies that can be engaged by large NGOs and civil society organizations, a working knowledge of how various media function, basic writing skills, and an insight into the digital media functioning would go a long way in facilitating the job of a social sector worker.

Notes and References

1. Jaishri Jethwaney and N. N. Sarkar, *Public Relations Management*, 2nd ed. (New Delhi: Sterling Publishers, 2010), 286–287.
2. Jethwaney and Sarkar, *Public Relations Management*, 223–225.
3. http://blogs.worldbank.org/publicsphere/redefining-roles-ngos (accessed on December 30, 2015).
4. Duncan Green, strategic adviser for Oxfam GB and author of *From Poverty to Power*, http://oxfamblogs.org/fp2p/ngos-and-blogging-on-development-why-do-we-find-it-so-hard/ (accessed on December 10, 2015).
5. Roger Burks, http://www.bloggingforpeoplewhoshould.com/category/blogging-for-ngos/ (accessed on December 10, 2015).
6. https://www.youtube.com/yt/press/statistics.html (accessed on December 11, 2015).
7. https://www.facebook.com/pages/Tum-Chalo-to-Hindustan-Chale/111733655549136
8. https://www.youtube.com/watch?v=r4_0rDE8Jqo (accessed on February 17, 2016).
9. HBR Guide to Networking (HBR Guide Series), https://hbr.org/2013/03/creating-social-change-with-so (accessed on December 11, 2015).
10. https://hbr.org/2013/03/creating-social-change-with-so (accessed on December 11, 2015).
11. Ibid.
12. Osama Manzar, "The Digital Voices of NGOs," *Mint* (August 26, 2015): 26.
13. http://www.livemint.com/Opinion/hNf6wRlshy6h4w6sR7xjuM/The-digital-voices-of-NGOS.html (accessed on December 13, 2015).

Index

About the Author

Jaishri Jethwaney is Professor and Program Director (Advertising and Public Relations) at the Indian Institute of Mass Communication (IIMC), New Delhi. She has more than 34 years of experience in brand management and corporate communications as well as in academia. She has conducted short courses on corporate communication, health communication, and advertising. Dr Jethwaney has also worked as a Project Director for UNESCO on the project "Reporting HIV and AIDS: A Media Tool Kit." Her published works include *Corporate Communication: Principles & Practices* (2010), *Advertising Management* (with Shruti Jain) (2nd edition, 2012), and *Public Relations Management* (with N.N. Sarkar) (3rd edition, 2015).

Play your cards right

A1 Here are *some* of the words you might have come up with: probable, certain, never, once in a blue moon, no chance, unlikely.
You should be able to suggest a few more.

Impossible   Certain

A2 Here are some suggestions – your answers may be better!
(a) fairly likely (it depends on where you live and on the time of year)   (b) impossible
(c) very likely   (d) no chance

A3 This is for you to decide!

A4 This is for you to decide!

A5 You are more likely to pick a red card.

A6 See the answers to A7 (b) and (c).

A7 (a) 4 chances out of 5 or $\frac{4}{5}$.
(b) 5 chances out of 5 or $\frac{5}{5}$ (certain).
(c) No chances out of 5 (impossible or no chance).

A8 $\frac{2}{5}$ is the same as 0·4 and $\frac{3}{5}$ is the same as 0·6.

B1 Check through your list carefully.
If you and your partner disagree about the lists, discuss them with your teacher.

B2 If you think of a probability scale from 0% (impossible or no chance) to 100% (certain or a probability of 1), then a point which is exactly half-way between the two is 50%.

B3 Re-check this through for yourselves.

B4 Re-check this througn for yourselves.

C1 (a) There is 1 chance out of 4 that ? will be less than 5, so the probability that ? will be less than 5 is $\frac{1}{4}$.
(b) There is no chance that ? will be equal to 5, so the probability that ? will be equal to 5 is zero!

C2 (a) 1 chance out of 5 or $\frac{1}{5}$
(b) 4 chances out of 5 or $\frac{4}{5}$
(c) $\frac{1}{5} + \frac{4}{5} = 1$

C3 There are two ways of doing this.

The first is to remember that one of the cards left is less than six. So the probability that the next card is less than six is 1 chance out of 4, or $\frac{1}{4}$.

Secondly, if the probability of the next card being greater than six is $\frac{3}{4}$, then the probability that the next card is less than six is $1 - \frac{3}{4}$, which is $\frac{1}{4}$.

D1 Remember that $\frac{4}{5}$ is the same as $4 \div 5 = 0·8$ and $\frac{7}{8}$ is the same as $7 \div 8 = 0·875$. So $\frac{7}{8}$ is larger than $\frac{4}{5}$.

D2 Look carefully at Mark's working. He has done the division the wrong way round. $\frac{5}{8}$ is $5 \div 8 = 0·625$. Mark worked this out as $8 \div 5 = 1·6$!

D3 $\frac{3}{10} = 0·3$ and $\frac{7}{25} = 7 \div 25 = 0·28$. This means that getting a 6 is slightly more likely.

E1 The probability of Fajal winning by getting a 3 or 7 with a 10-sided dice is $\frac{2}{10} = 0·2$.

E2 Audrey has 3 out of 10 chances of winning. This gives a probability of $\frac{3}{10}$. As a decimal this is 0·3.

E3 (a) $\frac{1}{10} = 0·1$
(b) With an 8-sided dice there are four chances of an even number (2, 4, 6 or 8).
This gives a probability of $\frac{4}{8}$ or $\frac{1}{2}$.
This is equal to 0·5.
(c) There is 1 chance out of 4 of getting a 2 with a 4-sided dice. So the probability of getting a 2 with a 4-sided dice is $\frac{1}{4}$ or 0·25.
(d) There are 7 numbers which are less than 8 on a 10-sided dice. These are 1, 2, 3, 4, 5, 6 and 7. This means that the probability of a score of less than 8 from a 10-sided dice is $\frac{7}{10}$. This is 0·7 as a decimal.

E4 Put in order of probability:
(a) has a probability of 0·1
(c) has a probability of 0·25
(b) has a probability of 0·5
(d) has a probability of 0·7

Games of chance

A1 Most of us would agree that snakes and ladders, bingo, and ludo are games of chance. The others all need skill but involve some luck. For example, in trivial pursuit you need to know the answers but where your counter lands depends on luck. Chess is a game of pure skill, but your opponent may make a mistake!

A2 Each player in a fair game should win, **on average,** roughly the same number of times.
The game which John and Jasmine are playing is probably fair.
The game which Susan and Sajit are playing is probably not fair.
The game which Suki and Shirley are playing might be fair, it's hard to be sure.

B1 Show your results to your teacher.

B2 How did you record your results?
Were they easy to understand?

B3 Here are the results of some games.
They will not be the same as yours.
It would be strange if they were! Why?

Differences

<u>Odd</u>   ЖНТ ЖНТ ЖНТ ЖНТ ЖНТ ЖНТ III

<u>Even</u>   IIHT ЖНТ ЖНТ ЖНТ ЖНТ ЖНТ ЖНТ II

Multiplying

<u>Odd</u>   ЖНТ III

<u>Even</u>   ЖНТ ЖНТ ЖНТ ЖНТ ЖНТ ЖНТ ЖНТ ЖНТ II

'Differences' seems to be the fair game.
Each player wins the same number of games on average.
It looks as if 'Multiplying' is not fair.

C1 (a) 16   (b) 8
    (c) Even and odd come up equally, so the game is fair.

C2 (a) 16   (b) 4
    (c) There are fewer chances for getting 'odd' than for getting 'even'.
There are only 4 chances for 'odd' but 12 for 'even'.

C3 Being 'even' gives you more chances of winning.

C4 Anna is more likely to win 'Differences'. In 'Differences', both 'odd' and 'even' have an equal chance of winning, but in 'Multiplying', 'even' is more likely to win.

C5 (a) Playing with a 4-sided or a 6-sided dice does not make any difference. If you are not sure, draw up a table like the ones on pages six and seven. For 'Multiplying', being 'even' would be better. It does not matter for 'Differences'.
    (b) How have you displayed your results?
Is it easy to check for repeats or missing numbers?

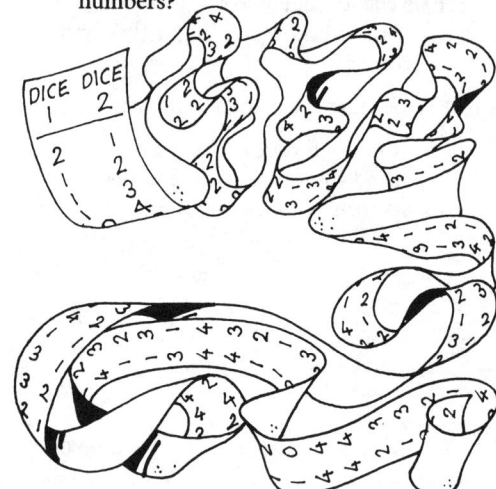

D1 Liz's method is probably the better one.
You can easily see if any numbers are missing.

D2 If any of your methods are different from those on page ten, show them to your teacher.

D3 If you are not sure about your lists, show them to your teacher.

D4 40 (10 × 4 = 40)
(For two 6-sided dice it would be 6 × 6 = 36)

D5 (b) There are 4 ways to get a total of 8.

D6 The least likely scores are 2 and 14.
Look at your table. You will see that there is only
1 way to get each of these scores.

D7 Play your game with a friend.

E First a little revision.

> The probability of something (an event) is
> worked out by using the formula:
>
> $$\frac{number\ of\ ways\ you\ can\ get\ the\ result}{total\ number\ of\ possible\ outcomes}$$
>
> or *by dividing the number of ways you can get the
> result by the total number of outcomes.*

E1 (a) There are 2 ways that Ken can get a total of
3. (1 and 2, 2 and 1)
(b) If you use the probability formula the answer
is $\frac{2}{16}$ or $\frac{1}{8}$.

E2 Here are all the different totals and the number
of different ways you can get them.

Total	Number of ways
2	1
3	2
4	3
5	4
6	3
7	2
8	1

The total which comes up the most is 5
(four times). This is the best score to choose.

E3 (a) The probability of getting a total of 5 is $\frac{4}{16}$.
This is the same as $\frac{1}{4}$.
On average, about a quarter of the 32 throws
will give a total of 5.
In other words, about 8 of the throws will
give a total of 5.
(b) Ken would expect about $\frac{2}{16}$ or $\frac{1}{8}$ of his throws
to give a total of 3.
About 4 of his 32 throws should give a total
of 3.
(c) Here are roughly the number of throws for
each total. Remember, these are only the
numbers you can expect **on average**.

Total	Probability	Number of times in 32 throws (on average)
2	$\frac{1}{16}$	2
3	$\frac{2}{16}$	4
4	$\frac{3}{16}$	6
5	$\frac{4}{16}$	8
6	$\frac{3}{16}$	6
7	$\frac{2}{16}$	4
8	$\frac{1}{16}$	2

E4 It would be very suspicious if your answers were
exactly the same as in the table in E3. Ask your
teacher if you are not quite sure why this is so.

F1 (a) The probability of throwing a 1 is $\frac{1}{4}$.
(b) Hint: there are 3 ways of not getting a
1 (2, 3 or a 4).
So the probability of not getting a 1 is $\frac{3}{4}$.
(c) $\frac{1}{4} + \frac{3}{4} = 1$

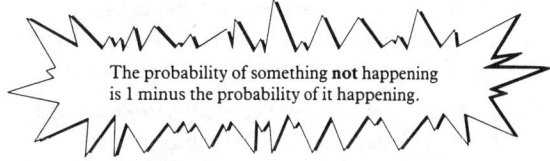

The probability of something **not** happening
is 1 minus the probability of it happening.

F2 (a) $\frac{1}{10}$ (b) $\frac{9}{10}$
(c) $1 - \frac{1}{10} = \frac{9}{10}$

F3 $\frac{995}{1000}$

F4 $1 - 0 \cdot 4 = 0 \cdot 6$

F5 $100\% - 40\% = 60\%$

F6 The probability of getting a 2 and a head is $\frac{1}{8}$.
There are 2 ways of getting a 2 or 3 **and** a head
(2, head and 3, head).
There are 8 possible outcomes (look at the grid),
so the probability is $\frac{2}{8}$ or $\frac{1}{4}$. You could tell straight
away that Alex was wrong, because according to
her answer the probability of getting a 2 or 3 **and**
a head is 1, in other words certain! Alan has
forgotten that there are 2 ways to get a 2 or 3 **and**
a head.

Experimental probability

Late	ⅢⅡ ⅢⅡ ⅢⅡ ∥	17
On time	ⅢⅡ ⅢⅡ ⅢⅡ ⅢⅡ ⅢⅡ ⅢⅡ	30
	Total	47

A1 Make a survey to find the most popular car colour.
A guess would then be more sensible.

A2 From Jason's results the best guess is a red car.
You can't be certain, but this is better than just guessing at random.

A3 8 out of 20 cars were blue.
This is the same as $\frac{8}{20}$ or $8 \div 20 \, (= 0\cdot4)$.
So the experimental probability that the next car that Nadine sees will be blue is 0·4.

A4 3 out of 5 or $3 \div 5$ which is 0·6.

A5 Wayne must have thought that 3 out of 5 was
$5 \div 3 = 1\cdot666\,666\,66$.
Check this on a calculator yourselves.
Wayne should have realised that he was wrong, because a probability can never be more than 1.
(You can't be more certain than certain!)

A6 He did not have enough results to work out a sensible experimental probability.
How many results do **you** think would be enough?

B1 Show your results to your teacher.

B2 You will find that the probability depends on the length of the match.

B3 This depends on your own results.
It is possible to work it out using the probability formula.
An answer of about 0·1 is reasonable.

B4 Your own results.

Snap!

B5 Your own results.

C1 Do a survey over several weeks, like this:

C2 Throw a 6-sided dice many times.
If the dice was fair, you would expect each of the numbers 1 to 6 to come up **roughly** the same number of times.

C3 The only way you can do this is to play the game yourself.
Keep a record of trebles and non-trebles.
It may look something like this:

Treble	ⅢⅡ ∥	7
Not a treble	ⅢⅡ ⅢⅡ ⅢⅡ ⅢⅡ ⅢⅡ ⅢⅡ	30
	Total	37

C4 Check the dates of birth in some class registers.
You will be surprised how likely it is that two people have the same birthday.

D1 (a) Rajid threw the two dice 39 times (you can work this out from the graph).
He got a total of 5 ten times (10 out of 39).
So the experimental probability of getting a total of 5 was $10 \div 39 = 0\cdot2564\ldots$

(b) There are 16 different outcomes, but there is only one way of getting a 2.

The probability of something (an event) is worked out by using the formula

$$\frac{number\ of\ ways\ you\ can\ get\ the\ result}{total\ number\ of\ possible\ outcomes}$$

or *by dividing the number of ways you can get the result by the total number of outcomes.*

So the probability of getting a score of 2 is
$1 \div 16 = 0\cdot0625$.
This is quite a small probability.

(c) As it's such a small probability it did not show up in Rajid's experiment.

D2 (a) Your own results.
(b) It's probably not a fair dice because all the numbers do not come up roughly the same number of times.
(c) and (d) Your own results.

All change

A1 You could get a rough idea by looking at the daily temperatures in a newspaper.

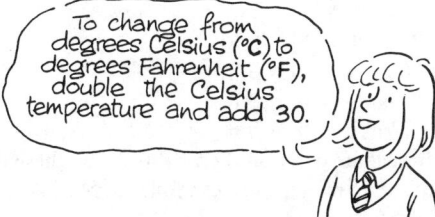

A2

	°F	°C
Avignon	110	40
London	90	30

So Avignon was the warmer.

A3 (a) Rob used the correct rule but in the wrong order. He added 30 and then doubled the result. He should have doubled the original value and then added 30 to the result.
Correct answer:
$$34 \times 2 = 68$$
$$68 + 30 = 98°F$$

(b) He got the order wrong again!
Correct answer:
$$34 - 30 = 4$$
$$4 \div 2 = 2°C$$

(c) Not only did Rob miss out the units, he used the wrong rule!
Correct answer:
$$50 \times 2 = 100$$
$$100 + 30 = 130°F, \text{ a very}$$
$$\text{hot day!}$$

A4

	°F	°C
Birmingham	75	24
Nice	86	30
London	90	32
Avignon	104	40

Your answers may be a degree or so out.
Just in case you got them completely wrong:
Each division on the °F scale is worth 2° and each division on the °C scale is worth 1°.

B1 Your graph should look something like this:

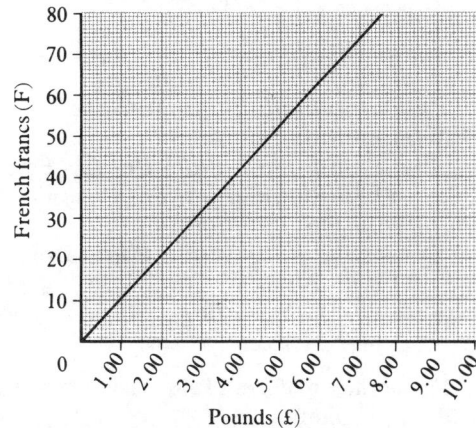

B2 It's more accurate to use 105 F and £10. You can be sure of drawing an accurate straight line.

B3

	Francs	Pounds	Rounded
Cola	12 F	£1·14	£1·15
Cafe au lait	5 F	£0·48	50p
Model	60 F	£5·71	£5·70
Chocolates	39 F	£3·71	£3·70
Wine	35 F	£3·33	£3·35

Your answers may differ by about 2p because the graph is hard to read. It might be more sensible to round your answers.

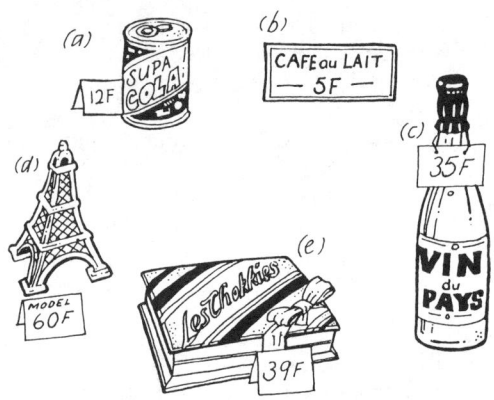

B4 A rough rule to convert French francs (F) into English pounds (£) is to divide the number of French francs by 10.

For B3 this would give you these rough answers:

	Francs (F)	Pounds (£)
Cola	12	1·20
Cafe au lait	5	0·50 (=50p)
Model	60	6·00
Chocolates	39	3·90
Wine	35	3·50

C1 There are several routes from Boulogne to Avignon. Here are just three:
(a) Boulogne – Arras – Paris – Orleans – Bourges – Clermont-Ferrand – Lyon – Orange – Avignon
(b) Boulogne – Arras – Paris – Dijon – Lyon – Orange – Avignon
(c) Boulogne – Arras – Reims – Dijon – Lyon – Orange – Avignon

C2 For the three routes in C1 (you may have different routes):
(a) $100 + 175 + 100 + 200 + 180 + 150 + 180 + 25 = 1110\,\text{km}.$
(b) $100 + 175 + 300 + 175 + 180 + 25 = 955\,\text{km}.$
(c) $100 + 150 + 250 + 175 + 180 + 25 = 880\,\text{km}.$

C3 For the three routes in C1 only:
(a) $1 + 1\frac{3}{4} + 1 + 2 + 1\frac{3}{4} + 1\frac{1}{2} + 1\frac{3}{4} + \frac{1}{4}$
$= 8 + \frac{3}{4} + \frac{3}{4} + \frac{1}{2} + \frac{3}{4} + \frac{1}{4}$
$= 8 + 1\frac{1}{2} + \frac{1}{2} + 1$
$= 11 \text{ hours.}$
(b) $1 + 1\frac{3}{4} + 3 + 1\frac{3}{4} + 1\frac{3}{4} + \frac{1}{4}$
$= 7 + 1\frac{1}{2} + \frac{3}{4} + \frac{1}{4}$
$= 8\frac{1}{2} + 1$
$= 9\frac{1}{2} \text{ hours.}$

(c) $1 + 1\frac{1}{2} + 2\frac{1}{2} + 1\frac{3}{4} + 1\frac{3}{4} + \frac{1}{4}$
$= 6 + \frac{1}{2} + \frac{1}{2} + \frac{3}{4} + \frac{3}{4} + \frac{1}{4}$
$= 8\frac{3}{4} \text{ hours.}$

C4 Somewhere near to Dijon or Bourges would be a reasonable half-way place to stop for the night.

D1

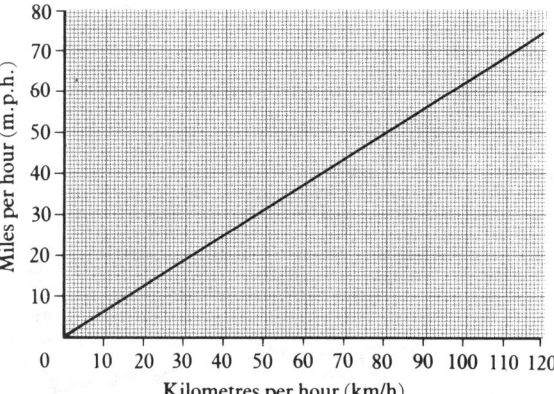

D2 $120\,\text{km/h} = 75\,\text{m.p.h.}$
$90\,\text{km/h} = 56\,\text{m.p.h.}$
$60\,\text{km/h} = 38\,\text{m.p.h.}$
$45\,\text{km/h} = 28\,\text{m.p.h.}$
In real life you would probably round these to the nearest 5 m.p.h. (For example 75, 55, 40, 30 m.p.h.).

D3 $120\,\text{km/h}$ is about $75\,\text{m.p.h.}$
$90\,\text{km/h}$ is about $56\,\text{m.p.h.}$
$60\,\text{km/h}$ is about $38\,\text{m.p.h.}$
$45\,\text{km/h}$ is about $28\,\text{m.p.h.}$

D4 Remember each small division represents 5 km/h.
(a) $125 \times 5 = 625$
$625 \div 8 = 78·125\,\text{m.p.h.}$ (about 80 m.p.h.)
(b) $75 \times 5 = 375$
$375 \div 8 = 46·875\,\text{m.p.h.}$ (about 45 m.p.h.)

E1 (a) I'm a size 12 dress size.
What's this in Continental sizes?   A size 42
(b) Ann and I both wear size 6 shoes.
What size is this in France?   A size $39\frac{1}{2}$
(c) The car takes 10 gallons when full.
How many litres will this be?   About 45 litres
(d) I don't really want to drive more than about 100 miles without a rest.
How many kilometres is this?   About 160 km
(e) According to the manual the tyre pressure needs to be 24 lb per sq. in.

What is this in kg per sq. cm?

1·75kg per sq. cm
or between 1·7 and 1·8kg
per sq. cm

E2 50 000 French francs is about £5000!
For these questions, look in the newspapers!

Go with the flow

Making squash   **Snap**

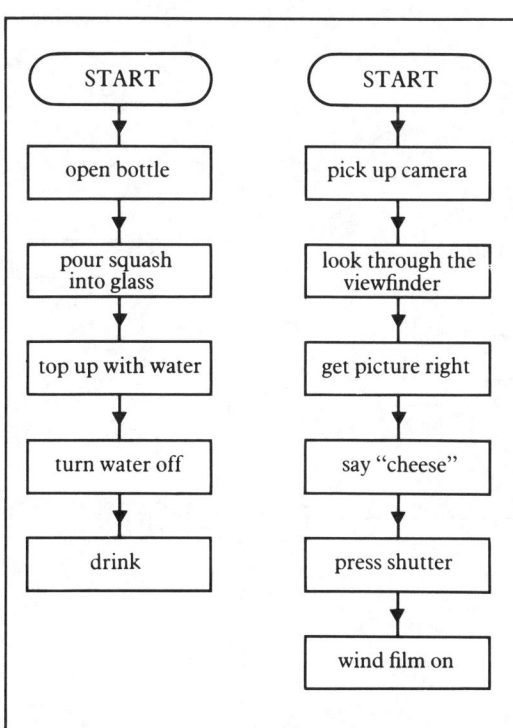

(b) The Friesian is the only cow that is black and white.

C2 Highland cattle have long horns so they must go in the grey box.

C3

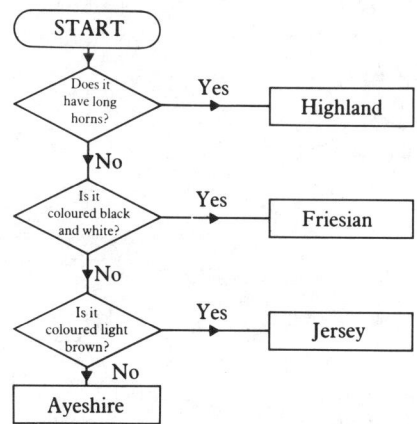

Name of dog	Border Collie	Dalmation	Spaniel	West Highland terrier
Ears	Floppy	Floppy	Floppy	Upright
Tail	Long	Long	Short	Short
Hair	Long	Short	long	Long

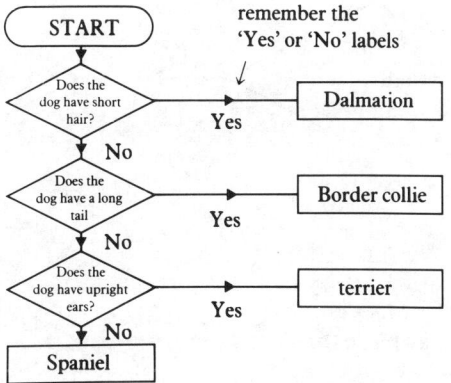

A2 Did your flow chart work?

B1 A triangle

   B rhombus or diamond or square

   D rectangle

B2 C trapezium

C1 (a) The only cow with long hair is the Highland.

There are other answers to this question.
If yours is different, try it out.

7

D1 (a) Kiro   (b) Addend   (c) Snatcher
      (d) Bracketer   (e) Sea flyer   (f) Thwait

D2   A . . . Rugby   B . . . Table tennis
      C . . . Rounders   D . . . Soccer
      E . . . Tennis   F . . . Archery
      G . . . Golf

D3 (a) Schooner   (b) Ketch   (c) Sloop
      (d) Ketch   (e) Yawl   (f) Cutter
      (g) Sloop   (h) Schooner   (i) Yawl

D4 There are several different ways of doing this question. Here is one:

The best way of testing your flowchart is to try it out for all the birds it is sorting.

E1 (a) Robot Walkman was told to look for cars, but was not told about lorries.
      (b) It was not told that it could ignore parked cars.
      (c) It was not told to stop when it got to the other side.
      (d) It was not told to watch out for road works and to walk around them.

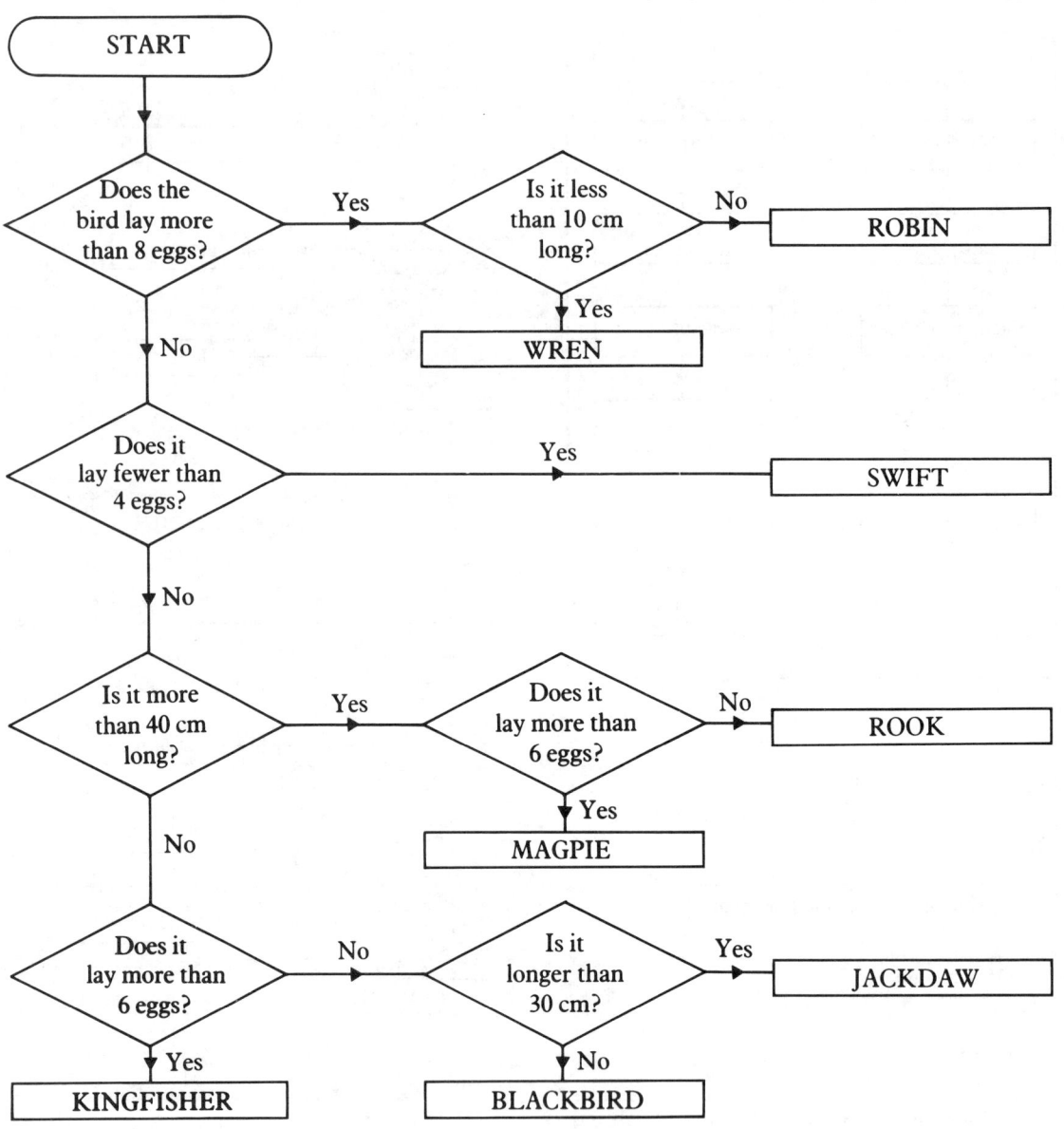

8

Range and mean

A1 This is up to your group.

A2 The mean for Sharon's group was 28 ÷ 4 = 7 kg.
The mean for Jason's group was 36 ÷ 6 = 6 kg.
Did you remember to count Sharon and Jason in with their group?

A3 (a) 8L collected 36 bottles.
(b) The mean number of bottles collected by 8L was 36 ÷ 20 = 1·8 bottles.
A mean does not always have to be a whole number.
(c) 8N collected a total of 60 bottles.
This gives a mean of 60 ÷ 24 = 2·5 bottles.
(Remember that even if someone does not collect any bottles, that person is still counted when the mean is calculated!)
(d) 8N should win because they collected the largest mean number of bottles.
(e) 8L collected a total of 40 cans.
This is a mean (or average) of 40 ÷ 20 = 2 cans.
8N collected a total of 50 cans.
This is an average of 50 ÷ 24 = 2·083 333 cans.
This is greater than the mean of 2 cans from 8L.
8N should win.
(f) What do you think?

A4 Probably the best way to answer these questions is to calculate the mean load pulled by a member of each team.

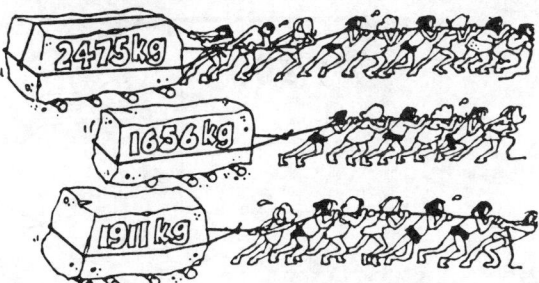

Team	Mean load pulled
2475 kg	2475 ÷ 9 = 227 kg
1656 kg	1656 ÷ 6 = 276 kg
1911 kg	1911 ÷ 7 = 273 kg

(a) Team B, pulling 1656 kg, is probably working the hardest.
(b) Team C, pulling 1911 kg, probably has the easiest job.

B1 Check your answers with those on page eight of the booklet.

B2 (a) Five children are taller than Lorna.
(b) Four children are shorter than Jill.
(c) Six children are between 1430 mm and 1530 mm tall.

B3 What do you think?

B4 There may be more than one correct answer to some of these.

(a) Lorna   middle
(b) Eric   short
(c) Rukshana   short
(d) Karen   tall
(e) Harry   middle
(f) Gary   middle

B5 Four out of sixteen in the class have heights of 1350 mm or less. In other words, $\frac{4}{16}$ or $\frac{1}{4}$ of the class have heights of 1350 mm or less.

B6 Ask your teacher about your answers to this question.

C1 The girls' heights range from 1640 mm to 1330 mm, a range of 310 mm.
The boys' heights range from 1610 mm to 1270 mm, a range of 340 mm.
So the boys' heights are more spread out.

C2 The range of the girls' heights is 310 mm.

C3 (a) The boys' weights range from 45 kg to 33 kg, a range of 12 kg.
(b) The girls' weights range from 48 kg to 31 kg, a range of 17 kg.
(c) The girls' weights are more spread out.

C4 The mean weight of the girls is 360 ÷ 9 = 40 kg.
The mean weight of the boys is 273 ÷ 7 = 39 kg.
The girls are heavier than the boys.

D1 (a) The main road journey times are from 58 minutes to 31 minutes.
This is a range of 58 − 31 = 27 minutes.

(b) The country lane journey times are from 50 minutes to 39 minutes.
This is a range of 50 − 39 = 11 minutes.

D2 (a) The main road journey took longer than 50 minutes four times.
(b) The main road journey took less than 40 minutes five times.

D3 She needs the most reliable route. Which one is this?

D4 Show your results to your teacher.

E1 You will probably need these figures:

Holiday resort		
	Highest	Lowest
Ilfrapool	70	23
Blackcombe	53	35

Hours of sunshine	
Range (hours)	Mean (hours)
47	48
18	43·5

Blackcombe has the smaller mean number of hours of sunshine, but it has the smaller range. So Blackcombe is probably the better bet for a suntan. It is more reliable. What do you think?

E2 Here are some figures for Tina and Pauline.

Runner	Slowest time(s)	Fastest time(s)
Pauline	82	78
Tina	84	75

Range(s)	Mean(s)
4	80
9	80·5

Pauline seems to be the fastest runner, but is she as consistent as Tina?
Who would you choose?

E3 (a) Have you ever seen 0·1p or 0·01p coins? Of course not!
(b) £1·38 would be a more sensible figure. Can you see why?

E4 It can sometimes help to display results in a table.

Shoe size	Tally	Frequency
3	I	1
4	IIII	4
5	IIII	4
6	II	2
7	LHT LHT I	11
8	II	2

She would be wise to re-order the most popular size, 7, not the mean (average) size.

E5 (a) In a year, an average of 500 mm of rain falls on Sacramento.
(b) The average (or mean) monthly rainfall is 500 ÷ 12 = 41·666 mm.
This is 42 mm to the nearest mm.
(c) There will always be times when it rains more than the average (mean). Can you think of any other reasons?

Zoo time

A1 Here are a few, you may be able to think of some better ones of your own.

(a) What do the visitors think about keeping some of the larger animals in cages?

(b) How many children visit the zoo?

(c) How many handicapped people visit the zoo?

(d) How many wheel-chair ramps need to be built, and where?

(e) How many children visit Pets' Corner?

Day	Number of visitors
Sunday	4315
Monday	1279
Tuesday	2351
Wednesday	504
Thursday	1965
Friday	2853
Saturday	4290

A2 There were most visitors on Sunday, when there were 4315 visitors.

A3 There were 17 557 visitors during the week.

A4 Half of 17 557 is 8778·5 (check this with your calculator).
You can't have half (0·5) of a child!
The half is only approximate. A reasonable answer would be around 8780 children.

A5 Wednesday was probably half-day closing because there were only 504 visitors that day.

A6 You probably won't agree; it's quite hard to keep track of the tallies the way Stuart has drawn them.

A7 Your own method.

A8 Twenty-three people had lunch in the restaurant on Monday.

A9 There were the most customers on Thursday, when there were 44.

A10 Some people may join the queue to buy things for several other people. The man in the cartoon is buying for several other people.

A11 Probably not for the reasons given in A10. But if Stuart thought hard and made a few guesses, he might get some useful information from the receipts. For example, if four teas were shown on a receipt, this would probably be the order for four people.

B1 Probably between 17°C and 22°C, depending on the season.

B2 and **B3** The answers are in this table:

Size of clutch	Tally	Frequency
4	ⅢⅠ	5
5	Ⅰ	1
6	ⅢⅠ	4
7	Ⅰ	1
8	ⅢⅠ ⅢⅠ	9
9	ⅢⅠ	5
10	ⅢⅠ ⅢⅠ	10
11	ⅠⅠ	2
12	ⅢⅠ Ⅲ	8
13	Ⅰ	1
14	ⅢⅠ	4

B4 The total of the frequency column is 50. This is the same as the total number of clutches. This makes a useful check to make sure you haven't missed any out.

B5 Stuart has made some serious mistakes! It's probably easiest to draw up a fresh frequency table.

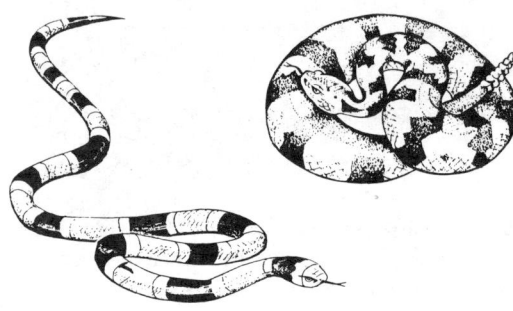

Clutch size	Tally	Frequency
1	⊔⊔⊤	5
2					3
3	⊔⊔⊤		6
4					3
5					3
	Total	20

Stuart should have noticed that the total of his frequency column did not give 20!
He does not seem to know that ⊔⊔⊤ means 5. You may have some other ideas where he went wrong; show them to your teacher.

B6 Debbie's stick graph should look like this.

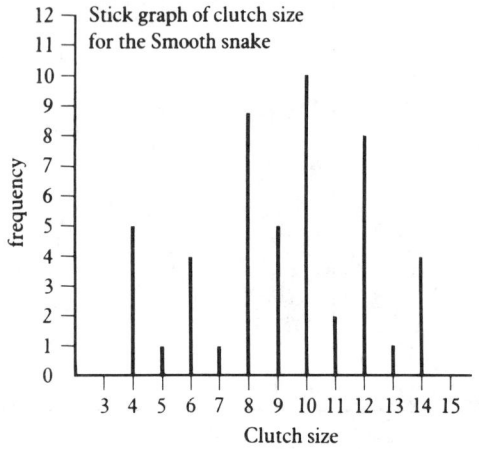

B7 Show your answers to your teacher.
Some points you might have noticed are:
(a) On average the clutch size for the Leopard Snake is larger than the clutch size for the Green Whip Snake. The Ladder Snake clutch sizes are larger still.

(b) The Ladder Snake clutch sizes have a wider spread than the other two.

B8 Discuss these with your teacher.

B9 Here is Debbie's completed table.

Clutch size	Tally	Frequency
10 to 19	||||	4
20 to 29	⊔⊔⊤ ||	7
30 to 39	⊔⊔⊤ ||||	9
40 to 49	⊔⊔⊤ ||||	9
50 to 59	⊔⊔⊤		6
	Total	35

Check the original figures.

B10 (Hint: 10–14 is just a short way of writing 10 to 14)

Clutch size	Tally	Frequency
10–14	|||	3
15–19			1
20–24	⊔⊔⊤	5
25–29	||	2
30–34	⊔⊔⊤ |||	8
35–39			1
40–44	⊔⊔⊤ ||	8
45–49			1
50–54	⊔⊔⊤		6
55–59		0
	Total	35

B11 An interval of twenty would not give as much information.
Look at this table.

Clutch size	Tally	Frequency
10–29	⊔⊔⊤ ⊔⊔⊤		11
30–49	⊔⊔⊤ ⊔⊔⊤ ⊔⊔⊤ |||	18
50–69	⊔⊔⊤		6
	Total	35

Check to make sure that all the intervals in the table are twenty!

B12 Show your answers to your teacher.

C1 The clutch size 20–24 occurs the most often (13 times).

C2 There were a total of 13 + 8 = 21 clutches in the interval 20 to 29.

C3 Show your answers to your teacher.

D1 and **D2** Here is one way to group the data.

Number of cars	Tally	Frequency
0–49	IIII II	7
50–99		0
100–149	I	1
150–199		0
200–249	IIII II	7
250–299	II	2
300–349	IIII	5
350–399	III	3
400–499	IIII II	7
450–499	III	3
500–549	IIII IIII IIII	14
	Total	49

Check to make sure that the intervals are equal. Why would the intervals 0–50, 51–100, 101–150, 151–200, etc. be unsuitable?

D3 (a) You can see from the figures that 500 is the largest number of cars seen in the car park. It looks as if 500 is the maximum number of cars that the car park will hold.
(b) Wednesday is probably half-day closing.
(c) The figures suggest that the car park is full on more than ten days. It would therefore seem sensible to extend the car park.
(d) Which two weeks had the most visitors?
(e) Which week had the least number of visitors?

D4 What do you think?

Trains

A1 (a) Richard is probably wrong. It just seems as if trains are always late.
(b) The only way to check whether Richard is right to collect some information by doing a survey.
(c) This one is up to you!

A2 About 7% of the trains were late in the morning.

A3 About 33 to 34% of the trains were late in the evening.

A4 It probably depends on how important the journey is. Being 5 minutes late to meet a friend is probably all right. Would it be all right if you were 5 minutes late for a lesson?

A5 300 × 500 = 150 000 passengers.

A6 150 000 ÷ 4 = 37 500 cars.

A7 37 500 × 5 = 187 500 metres.
This is 187 500 ÷ 1000 km, which is 187·5 km, a lot of road!

Minutes late	Tally	Frequency
1–5		23
5–10		17
10–15		4
15–20		7
20–25		3
25–30		2
30–35		0
	Total	56

13

A8 Ela has made several mistakes:
  (i) trains which were 5, 10, 15 etc. minutes late would be counted twice;
  (ii) the frequency column total should be the same as the total number of trains late.
  Don't forget to show your answers to your teacher.

B1 (a) Fourteen trains were 5–9 minutes late.
  (b) Five trains were 20 or more minutes late.

B2 This one is up to the two of you.

B3 One way to check for equal intervals is to use a number line.
  You may have some better ideas of your own. Ask your teacher if you are not sure about your own method.

B4

Minutes Late	Tally	Frequency
0 or more but less than 5	ᵁᴴIII	8
5 or more but less than 10	IIII	4
10 or more but less than 15	III	3
15 or more but less than 20	III	3
20 or more but less than 15	I	1
	Total	19

The total of the frequency column is 19.
This is correct because there are 19 train times.

B5 It is probably not worth the trouble.

C1 > means greater than, for example, $6 > 4$.
  ≥ means greater than or equal to, for example, $3 \geq 2$.
  These are all true: for time = 10 minutes
  time > 9 minutes, time ≥ 10
  time ≥ 8 minutes, 18 ≥ time.
  Think carefully about the last one.

C2 (a) 5 minutes.
  (b) In other words, time < 3 minutes.
    This is true for all of these:
    2 minutes 30 s, 1 minute 45 s, 1 minute 40 s, 30 s.
  (c) The time is less than or equal to 5 minutes.
    This is true for all of these:
    2 minute 30 s, 4 minutes 15 s, 3 minutes, 30 s, 5 minutes, 1 minute 45 s, 1 minute 40 s.
  (d) 30 s is less than or equal to the time, or the time is greater than or equal to 30 s.
    This is true for all the times.

C3 One way of saying 12 ≤ time < 22 is that 12 minutes is less than or equal to the time **and** the time is less than 22 minutes.
  This is another way:
  the time is greater than or equal to 12 minutes but less than 22 minutes.
  Show your own answers to your teacher.

D Show the results of your investigations to your teacher.

E1 (a) On the way from Norwich to Peterborough, the train could stop at March, Ely and Thetford.
  (b) If you were at Preston and wanted to go to Sheffield, you could catch the Peterborough train.

E2 It is about 70 miles from Preston to Carlisle.

E3 Look for yourselves.

E4 Look for yourselves.

E5 The London Underground map and some airline maps are good examples of network maps. You may have found some more; show them to your teacher.

E6 Manchester to Leeds and back is 80 miles.

E7 $2 \times 40 + 2 \times 194 + 2 \times 35 = 538$ miles.
  Don't forget to add in the return journey!

E8 Here is one network; there are lots of others.

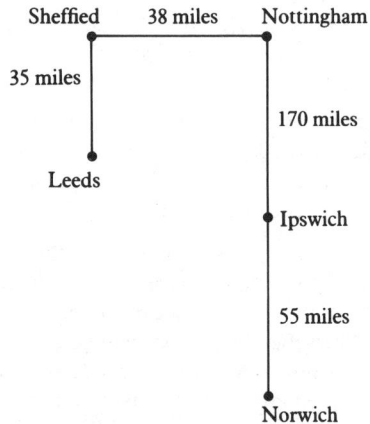

F1 This one is up to you.
  Most people would say A.

F2 Graph B seems to show a more rapid improvement.

F3 Of course it does not mean this.
  Points between the weeks do not mean anything.

F4 Show these to your friends and to your teacher.

Rubbish

A1 Your own answers.

A2 Your own answers.

A4 Check your pie chart using a pie chart scale and the table.

A5 Here is Jennifer's completed table.

Biodegradable	Recyclable	Non-recyclable
Food waste 5235 g	Metal 1326 g Glass 3094 g Paper 5303 g	Plastic 878 g
Total 5235 g	9723 g	878 g

The total weight of rubbish was 15 836 g.

A6

Biodegradable	Recyclable	Non-recyclable
33%	61%	6%

See your teacher if you got any of these wrong.

A7 Only the plastic rubbish could not be put to another use.
This was 898 g out of a total of 15 836 g.
This was about 6%.
94% of the rubbish could be put to another use.

A8 276 g out of the 1326 g of metal rubbish was aluminium.
21% of the metal rubbish was aluminium.
Check your pie chart by using a pie chart scale.

B1 Each star represents 10 kg, so $25 \times 10 = 250$ kg of paper was thrown out by this average household.

B2 Ten stars, in other words $10 \times 10 = 100$ kg of glass.

B3 If one star represents 10 kg, then half a star represents 5 kg.

B4 Show your own pictogram to your teacher.

B5 Show your own pictogram to your teacher.

B6 Show your own pictogram to your teacher.

C1 This is for you to do together.

C2 This is for you to do together.

C3 (a) Four thousand million in figures is 4 000 000 000.
(b) It will depend on your calculator!

C4 (a) Jennifer's family threw out $1078 + 2105 = 3183$ g of newspapers and magazines a week.
(b) 3183 g is 3 kg to the nearest kg.
(c) There are 52 weeks in a year. So in a year they would throw out $52 \times 3 = 156$ kg.

C5 Check through your working together.

C6 The 23 books will weigh $23 \times 150 = 3450$ g.
This is about 3 kg.

C7 For 30 pupils the total weight of exercise books will be about $30 \times 3 = 90$ kg.

C8 600 kg of paper can be produced from one tree.
The number of trees needed to make 90 kg of paper will be $90 \div 600 = 0 \cdot 15$, which is a small fraction of a single tree. If you got an answer of

6·66666 trees, see if you can work out together where you went wrong; if you can't, see your teacher.

C9 This depends on the size of your school.

C10 This depends on the size of your school.

D1 14 million tabloids are sold on a Sunday.

D2 A total of 17 million newspapers are sold on a Sunday.

D3 84 million tabloids are sold in a full week (14 million plus 70 million).

D4 A total of 101 million newspapers are sold in a full week!

E1 If you count only plastics (878 g) and paper cartons and wrappers (529 g), only about 9% of the rubbish is packaging. But if you count tins, cans, jars and the washing powder box, it is much greater than this. Some packaging is needed, but some firms use far too much.

E2 Show your results to your teacher.

F Show your display to your teacher. Ask if you can display it on the wall.

Using statistics

A1 What do you think?

A2 (a) You can't really know what sort of dice they used, or even if they were the same sort of dice.
(b) They seem to, but check again.
(c) They threw the two dice 100 times.
(d) Their experimental probability calculation is correct.
(e) They don't mention what they did if both dice showed the same number.

A3 They used two 4-sided dice. When the two dice showed the same number, this was taken to be the smaller number.

A4 You could have used a frequency chart.

A5 The number 1 is the smaller number seven times.

A6 Here is Beatty's completed table.

Smaller number	Frequency
1	7
2	5
3	3
4	1
Total	16

Think about this one!

A7 Remember, the probability of something (an event) is worked out using the formula:

$$\frac{number\ of\ ways\ you\ can\ get\ the\ result}{total\ number\ of\ possible\ outcomes}$$

The probability that the smaller number is 1 is $\frac{7}{16}$ or 0·4375.

A8 It would be suspicious if these two were *exactly* the same! Why?

A9 How clear was your report to others? A good report should make sense to someone who does not know what you have been doing.

B1 This is for your group to decide.

B2 This is for your group to decide.

B3 This is for your group to decide.

B4 This is for your group to decide.

C1 Dice A is probably not fair because it kept giving the numbers 1, 2, 3, 4, 5 and 6 in order. Dice B is probably not fair because the number 6 did not come up at all. Dice C may or may not be fair, since 3 and 4 both came up five times and 1 only came up once. You would need more throws to be sure.

C2 Show your report to your teacher.

D1 (a) There were 3 520 000 0–4 year olds in 1982. Remember that the figures in the table are given in thousands.

(b) In 1985, there were 56 618 000 people and of these 27 574 000 were males, so there were 56 618 000 − 27 574 000 = 29 044 000 females.

(c) The number of pedestrians under 10, killed or seriously injured in 1987 was 819 + 2335 = 3154.

D2 In 1978, there were 4 243 000 5–10 year olds and 4 686 000 10–14 year olds. To find the approximate number of 15 and 16 year olds, work out how many of the 4 469 000 15–19 year olds are likely to have been 15 or 16.
This is two out of five years, so the number of 15 and 16 year olds was about $\frac{2}{5} \times 4\,469\,000 = 1\,787\,600$.
So the number of school places needed was about 4 243 000 + 4 686 000 + 1 787 600 = 10 716 600.

D3 The number of females (in thousands) is given in the following table.

Year	Number of females (thousands)
1978	28 848
1979	28 867
1980	28 919
1981	28 943
1982	28 920
1983	28 930
1984	28 973
1985	29 044
1986	29 116
1987	29 193

Over the period as a whole, the number of females increased, but there was a drop in 1982.

D4 The 5–9 year olds have the most accidents, 28 816 in this period.

D5 The total number of pedestrian accidents is given in this table.

Year	Number of accidents
1978	21 233
1979	20 328
1980	18 915
1981	18 364
1982	18 864
1983	18 668
1984	19 297
1985	19 239
1986	18 872
1987	17 950

On the whole, pedestrian accidents are decreasing. Possible reasons for this are that cars travel more on motorways where there are no pedestrians and that some city centres ban all car traffic. You may have some other reasons.

D6 Show your article to your teacher.

E Show your report to your teacher.

Holidays

If you find several mistakes in your answers, ask your teacher whether you can have another turn on the computer so that you can see where you went wrong.

A1 There are flights to Ibiza from Luton and Manchester airports.

A2 She will be away 14 nights.

A3 Holiday advertisers usually state how many nights the holiday is for. Mr Rees wants a two-week holiday. He will be looking for a 13 or 14-night holiday. He could chose from holidays in Ibiza or Rimini.

B1 Marathon is in Greece.

B2 The holiday in Morocco departs from Gatwick. It costs £308 for an adult and £216 for a child.

B3 There are two holidays which leave Norwich Airport. They both leave on a Thursday.

B4 The Rio Park is a two star (2★) hotel. There are two holidays at this hotel.

B5 There are two holidays in Sliema. The 4★ hotel in Sliema is called the Preluna.

C1 You probably found it imposible to key in East Midlands. If you use *includes* then 'East Mid' will be all right, or you could even key in just 'East'. There are three 14-night holidays. These are:

Resort	Cost for an adult
Costa Brava	£426
Kos	£477
Zakynthos	£427

C2 If you *sort* on number of nights, holidays with the same number of nights will be grouped together. Using **sort** saves having to go through the whole list of Holidays from East Midlands airport.

C3 There are several ways of doing this question. One way is to search for Italy on the field **country**. The holidays in Italy could then be sorted for the resort Lido di Jesolo. These would be grouped together. Another way would be to search on the field **resort** for Lido di Jesolo. There may be other ways! There are four holidays to Lido di Jesolo.

C4 The way you do this question probably depends on how you did C3. There are four holidays to Italy which depart from Manchester airport.

Two of these are to Rimini. The others are to Lido di Jesolo and Sardinia.

C5 Of all the holidays departing on a Wednesday:
(a) five of them depart from Manchester airport;
(b) three are bed and breakfast (B and B).

C6 This one is for you!

D1 (a) 12% of the holidays depart on a Tuesday.
(b) What do you think? Why?
(c) If Saturday and Sunday are counted as the weekend, 25% of all departures are at the weekend.

D2 Most of the holidays (Nimbus 43%, BBC 41%!) are in Spain.

D3 The most popular range of prices for holidays for adults is £350–£399.

D4 The average (or mean) price of a holiday for an adult is £374·20. (£374 Nimbus)

D5 This one is up to you.

E The cheapest holiday for an adult is a 7-night holiday in Ibiza, Spain. It costs £204.

There are nine 5★ hotels in the datafile.

There are no 14-night holidays to Italy which depart from East Midlands airport. There is a bed and breakfast holiday available in Rimini, which departs from Manchester.

The most expensive holiday for adults costs £689. It is in Crete and is for 14 nights.

Kids like us

If you find several mistakes in your answers, ask your teacher whether you can have another turn on the computer so that you can see where you went wrong.

A1 The tallest person is Zoe Fields, who is 170 cm tall. Four people are taller than Salik. All these people have the same shoe size as Sarah: Salik, Stuart, Paul, Claire, Jamie and Helen. The ten tallest people are

Zoe	170 cm
Michaela	163 cm
Wayne	160 cm
Paul	157 cm
Salik	152 cm
Stuart	152 cm
Jamie	152 cm
Helen	151 cm
Jamie Andrews	150 cm
Jane	149 cm

A2 There are no right answers here. It depends on your group. Most people find putting in order of height the hardest.

B1 They have collected 88 records. This number is shown on the screen in the top right-hand corner.

B2 Here is Sarah's record:

SCHOOL	:	RUTLAND
FIRST NAME	:	SARAH
LAST NAME	:	HAWES
SEX	:	F
HANDEDNESS	:	R
SHOE SIZE	:	5
HEIGHT	:	140 cm
REACH	:	142 cm
HANDSPAN	:	18 cm

B3 This is Salik's record:

SCHOOL	:	RUTLAND
FIRST NAME	:	SALIK
LAST NAME	:	HEGALJAI
SEX	:	M
HANDEDNESS	:	R
SHOE SIZE	:	5
HEIGHT	:	152 cm
REACH	:	147 cm
HANDSPAN	:	20 cm

B4 Nineteen other people had the same shoe size as Sarah. These are: Salik, Stuart, Paul, Claire, Jamie, Helen, Christopher, Lyndsey Utley, Samantha, Lindsay, James, Sara, Lindsey, Lynsey, Christopher, Kirsty, Louise, Lyndsey Darling, Lee.

B5 39 people were taller than Salik. Eighteen were male and twenty-one were female. To find these figures you would need to *narrow down* the search and use '*and sex includes*' m or f. Then either subtract your answer from 39 or start a fresh search.

B6 There are five Janes. They have last names Smith, Mellor, Bright, Rollings and Curry.

B7 Here is Jane Smith's record:

SCHOOL	:	RUTLAND
FIRST NAME	:	JANE
LAST NAME	:	SMITH
SEX	:	F
HANDEDNESS	:	R
SHOE SIZE	:	3
HEIGHT	:	149 cm
REACH	:	148 cm
HANDSPAN	:	19 cm

B8 Twenty-three people were taller than Sarah and had a smaller shoe size than her.
(Remember you need to search the field **height** for greater than 140 cm and then narrow down the search using the field **shoe size** less than 5. All this information is displayed on the screen.)
They were:

Jane Smith,	Stephanie Heywood,
Alison Vaines,	Teresa McGinn,
Malcom Brennan,	David Davies,
Jane Mellor,	Lee Osgathorpe,
Ryan Gledhill,	Jane Bright,
Maria Smith,	Jane Curry,
Suzanne Bennett,	Claire Golby,
Ian Cutts,	Mark Cooper,
Jonathan Lang,	Tara Reddington,

Wayne Frostick,   Kelly Ellis,
Michael Bissell,   Dale Mallison,
Jacqueline Chesworth.

C1 There are 42 girls. The following table shows the number of pairs of skates that will be required in each size.

Skate size	Number of pairs
1	2
1·5	1
2	1
2·5	3
3	5
3·5	1
4	3
4·5	1
5	12
5·5	3
6	3
6·5	2
7	4
7·5	1

C2 The following table shows the number of pairs of each size that will be required by the boys.

Skate size	Number of pairs
1	1
2	1
2·5	2
3	3
4	8
4·5	1
5	8
5·5	3
6	7
6·5	3
7	5
7·5	1
8	1
9	1
10	1

C3 How could you check to see whether your printed list was correct?

C4 The following cannot go on the super looper: Claire, Daniel, David, Emma, Gary, Rosemarie and Steven.

C5 Questions such as 'Who is the tallest?', 'Who is the shortest?', 'Who are the ten tallest people?' are probably easier to answer if you have sorted, or put in order, the heights.

D1 This is the data for your group.
Be careful about the units and remember that the computer cannot understand '$\frac{1}{2}$' in a shoe size, so you must use the decimal form (0·5).

D2 This depends on your data.
Check that it seems sensible.

D3 This depends on your data.
Check that it seems sensible.

D4 This depends on your data.
Check that it seems sensible.

D5 This depends on your data.
Check that it seems sensible.

E1 Show your result to your teacher.

E2 Show your result to your teacher.

E3 Your scatter graph should look like this one:

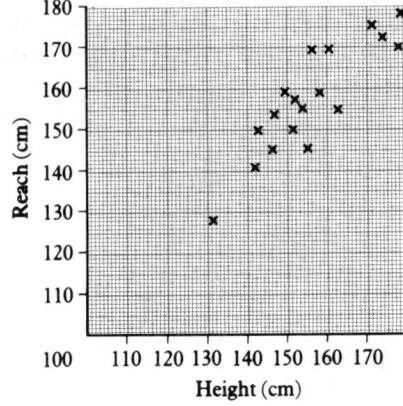

E4 There is a fairly high correlation between height and reach for these students.

F1 Your scatter graph should look something like this:

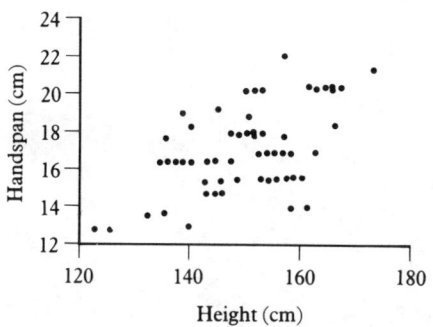

F2 Your scatter graph should look something like this

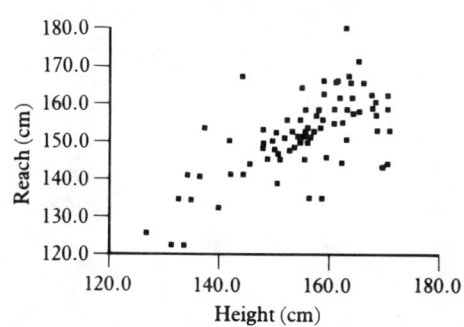

F3 What do you think?

G1 About 88% are right-handed and 12% are left-handed. In other words, there are about seven times more right-handed people than left-handed people.

G2 What did you find out?

G3 There are a large number of tall pupils at Luttleby. You may have some better reasons of your own!

G4 Show your answers to your teacher.

G5 Here are the histograms. What do you notice?

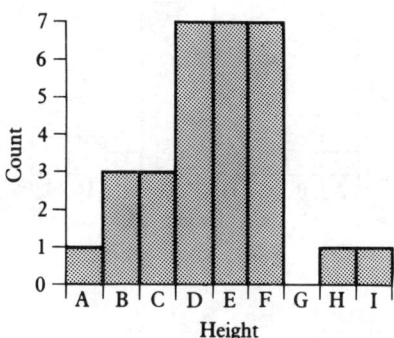

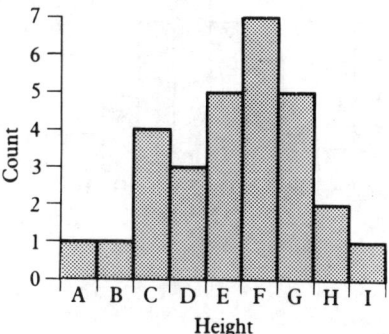

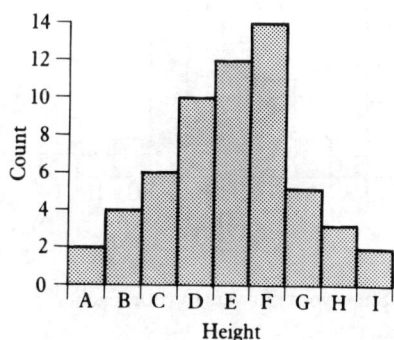

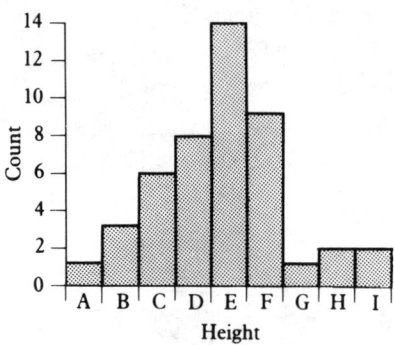

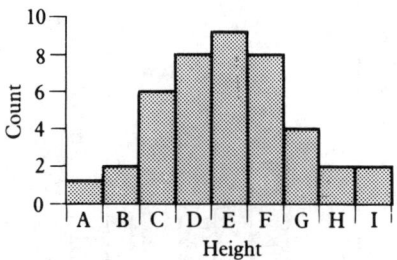

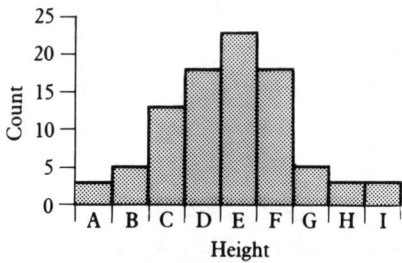

G6 Show your answers to your teacher.